W7-BOO-067

D0020320

PEOPLE STYLES AT WORK...AND BEYOND

Making Bad Relationships Good and Good Relationships Better

SECOND EDITION

Robert Bolton
Dorothy Grover Bolton

AMERICAN MANAGEMENT ASSOCIATION

New York • Atlanta • Brussels • Chicago • Mexico City • San Francisco
Shanghai • Tokyo • Toronto • Washington, D.C.

Special discounts on bulk quantities of AMACOM books are available to corporations, professional associations, and other organizations. For details, contact Special Sales Department, AMACOM, a division of American Management Association, 1601 Broadway, New York, NY 10019.
Tel: 800-250-5308. Fax: 518-891-2372.
E-mail: specialsls@amanet.org
Website: www.amacombooks.org/go/specialsales
To view all AMACOM titles go to: www.amacombooks.org

This publication is designed to provide accurate and authoritative information in regard to the subject matter covered. It is sold with the understanding that the publisher is not engaged in rendering legal, accounting, or other professional service. If legal advice or other expert assistance is required, the services of a competent professional person should be sought.

Library of Congress Cataloging-in-Publication Data

Bolton, Robert.
  People styles at work—and beyond : making bad relationships good and good relationships better / Robert Bolton and Dorothy Grover Bolton.—2nd ed.
     p. cm.
  Includes bibliographical references and index.
  ISBN-13: 978-0-8144-1342-5 (pbk.)
  ISBN-10: 0-8144-1342-0 (pbk.)
  1. Psychology, Industrial.   2. Interpersonal relations.   3. Interpersonal communication.
I. Bolton, Dorothy Grover.   II. Title.

  HF5548.8.B634   2009
  650.1'3—dc22

                                                                        2009004049

© 2009 Ridge Associates, Inc.
All rights reserved.
Printed in the United States of America.

This publication may not be reproduced, stored in a retrieval system, or transmitted in whole or in part, in any form or by any means, electronic, mechanical, photocopying, recording, or otherwise, without the prior written permission of AMACOM, a division of American Management Association, 1601 Broadway, New York, NY 10019.

Printing number

10   9

PEOPLE STYLES AT WORK . . . AND BEYOND

SECOND EDITION

Other Books by the Boltons

Praise for the previous edition of *People Styles at Work:*

"We love it! Extremely well done and as useful as they get."
—*Soundview Executive Book Summaries*

Praise for *Social Style Management Style: Developing Productive Work Relationships:*

"Easy to read but well-researched and annotated . . . . The generally fine writing sets this book apart from so many attempts to communicate a difficult subject to a lay audience."
—*Training* magazine

We dedicate this book to:

Bill Gabor

Bob Gabor

Hallie Hawkins

Jim Bolton

Betsy Bolton

Doug Bolton

Kristin Bolton

the sons/stepsons and

daughters/stepdaughters

of our blended family.

CONTENTS

Introduction   1

PART ONE
Understanding Yourself and Others

1 No Wonder We Have People Problems   7

2 People Are More Predictable than You Might Think   16

3 What's Your Style?   24

4 Two Keys to Understanding People   28

5 See Yourself as Others See You   38

6 The Driving Style and the Expressive Style   43

7 The Amiable Style and the Analytical Style   54

8 Make the Most of Your Gifts   63

9 Backup Styles: Extreme, Inappropriate, and Inflexible Behavior   72

10 Coping with Backup Behavior   82

PART TWO
Style Flex: A Key to Improved Relationships

11 The Style Flex Solution to People Differences   91

12 Four Steps to Better Relationships   99

13 How to Identify Someone's Style   107

14 Flexing in Special Situations   117

15 Three Keys to Good Relationships   127

PART THREE

People Styles and Family Relationships

16 The Art of Loving Someone Very Different from Yourself   137

17 Style-Based Parenting   147

APPENDICES

I   For *Amiables* Only: How to Flex to Each Style   155

II   For *Drivers* Only: How to Flex to Each Style   169

III For *Expressives* Only: How to Flex to Each Style   187

IV   For *Analyticals* Only: How to Flex to Each Style   202

Bibliography   219

Index   225

PEOPLE STYLES AT WORK . . . AND BEYOND

SECOND EDITION

INTRODUCTION

BOTH AT WORK and at home, success and happiness depend on relating to others across a chasm of significant differences. If you could figure out how to bridge the gap between yourself and others, you could make your life—and theirs—much easier, happier, and more productive. How to do that is what this book is about.

> The differences between people are a major source of friction. For example, our friend Michelle does everything in a rush. She walks fast, talks fast, decides fast. And she completes projects in a flurry. As luck would have it, she's often teamed with John, who is very deliberate. John walks slowly, talks slowly, decides slowly. Although these differences may not seem like a big deal, if they're not managed well they're likely to erode Michelle's and John's working relationship. You've undoubtedly seen how differences like these can undermine cooperation, hamper performance, and add considerable stress to people's lives.

This book shows how you can manage those kinds of differences in ways that enhance your relationships, increase your productivity, and add richness and spice to your life. It's about making people differences work *for*, rather than against, you.

There are three parts to the book:

- Part One: Understanding Yourself and Others

- Part Two: Style Flex: A Key to Improved Relationships

- Part Three: People Styles and Family Relationships

Part One: Understanding Yourself and Others provides a pragmatic way of understanding the differences between people. Rather than delve into esoteric psychological theory, it provides a straightforward, practical explanation of what you need to know to relate more effectively to others.

Chapter 1 notes some of the differences between the four people styles and how those differences can lead to people problems. Chapter 2 describes the *people styles model* and explains how it can help you relate more effectively to people very different from yourself. Chapter 3 helps you capture data for identifying your own style. The two dimensions of behavior that are key to understanding yourself and others are highlighted in Chapter 4. With this background, Chapter 5 guides you through an assessment that shows how you come across to other people. The four people styles are described in Chapters 6 and 7. Chapter 8 depicts each style's tendency toward certain strengths and weaknesses. Chapter 9 describes backup styles—the four dysfunctional and relationship-straining ways in which people of each style react to excessive stress. In Chapter 10, you'll learn how to cope productively both with your own and with other people's stressed-out behavior.

Part Two: Style Flex: A Key to Improved Relationships shows how to create more productive interactions by applying the knowledge of yourself and others gained in Part One. Chapter 11 introduces you to *style flex,* a way of creating common ground with people very different from yourself. Style flex is the intriguing ability to be true to yourself while relating to someone else on that person's wavelength. The four steps involved in flexing to another person's style are presented in Chapter 12. In Chapter 13, you learn how to identify another person's style. Chapter 14 describes how to use style flex in several special situations. The final chapter of Part Two describes basic flex—three personal qualities that undergird style flex.

Parts One and Two are equally applicable to personal and work relationships. However, the people styles model has some unique and beneficial applications to personal relationships. So *Part Three: People Styles and Family Relationships* discusses applications of the people styles model to two of these types of personal relationships. Chapter 16, "The Art of Loving Someone Very Different from Yourself," shows how to forge an even better relationship with your domestic partner. In Chapter 17, you'll find style-based parenting guidelines that will help you have more enjoyable relationships with your kids while helping them increase their self-esteem and develop their unique strengths.

There are four appendices—one for each of the four styles. The appendix for your style presents specific guidelines on how to flex to persons of each of the four styles.

Many of the concepts in this book will come not as news but as reminders. We're often told that this way of organizing interpersonal data helps people sharpen insights they've already gained from their life experience. This familiarity makes it easier for readers to implement the relationship-enhancing methods found in these pages.

We hope the concepts and methods presented in this book will enrich your life and relationships as much as they've enhanced ours.

PART ONE

Understanding Yourself
and Others

"I could save myself a lot of wear and tear with people if I just
learned to understand them."

—RALPH ELLISON

CHAPTER 1

No Wonder We Have People Problems

AS LONG AS YOU LIVE, you'll have at least some unwelcome and unproductive friction with others. There are difficulties to be worked through in the best of relationships. In more troubled ones, people problems undermine productivity, erode friendships, and stress families.

Of all the problems we face, people problems are often the toughest to solve. Difficult as task problems may be, most of us would choose them over people problems. Besides, when a task problem is especially difficult, one or more painful people problems are often at the heart of it.

People problems tend to take the greatest toll on us personally. They produce significant emotional wear and tear. They disturb our sleep. Too often, people problems drag on endlessly and continue to deteriorate over time.

PEOPLE ARE DIFFERENT FROM EACH OTHER IN FUNDAMENTAL WAYS

It's no wonder that everyone has people problems. Psychological researchers discovered that 75 percent of the population is significantly different from each of us. Three of four people important to your success and happiness:

- Think differently
- Decide differently
- Use time differently
- Handle emotions differently
- Manage stress differently
- Communicate differently
- Deal with conflict differently

Not necessarily worse. Not necessarily better. But different. Behaviorally speaking, you are in a minority. Everyone is.

PEOPLE DIFFERENCES TRIGGER PEOPLE PROBLEMS

Social psychologists have found that people with significantly different behavioral patterns:

- Have a harder time establishing rapport
- Are less likely to be persuasive with one another
- Miscommunicate more often
- Tend to rub each other the wrong way—just by being themselves

These facts help explain why it's quite a stretch for you to work effectively with a number of your colleagues. The more you think about it, the more understandable it is that there are so many people problems at work and elsewhere. Obviously, differences between people aren't the only sources of interpersonal tension. They are, however, a major factor in much misunderstanding and conflict. Spencer learned this the hard way.

Spencer had had an excellent working relationship with Jan White, his manager for over three years. Then Jan was transferred. Spencer didn't hit it off nearly as well with Bill Freed, his new manager. It wasn't that

Bill was unreasonable; he was well-liked by most employees. Spencer was puzzled. Why wasn't he able to work as effectively with Bill as he had with Jan?

Spencer was a conscientious manager who believed that detailed information is essential to good decision making. He made sure his employees filled him in on the nitty-gritty of their work. That's how he stayed on top of what was happening in his department. Because Spencer appreciated detailed communication, he diligently filled Bill in on all the fine points of each of his projects.

Before long, Spencer noted that in their weekly meetings Bill would often tense up. When Spencer reported on a project, Bill often fiddled with his pencil. Soon, he'd pace about the room, appearing impatient and distracted. Clearly, Bill was frustrated by something Spencer was doing. But what?

At times, Bill said, "Just give me the big picture on this one. I trust that you've done your usual thorough job on it." Spencer, though, was uncomfortable providing what he thought would be a less than adequate briefing. So he continued giving exhaustive reports on all the minute particulars of his work. After all, that's what he would have wanted if he were in Bill's shoes.

The problem, of course, was that Spencer wasn't in Bill's shoes. Bill was. And Bill's working style was very different from Spencer's. Even when Spencer saw that his way of communicating was disconcerting to Bill, he clung rigidly to his habitual way of interacting. Because neither person adapted to the other, their working relationship continued to deteriorate.

PEOPLE DIFFERENCES GENERATE STRESS ON THE HOME FRONT

It's not just at work that people's different behavioral patterns complicate their interactions. In ongoing intimate relationships, people are generally attracted to those who are significantly different from themselves. Screenwriter Nora Ephron said, "You fall in love with someone, and part of what you love about him are the differences between you; and then you get married and the differences drive you crazy."

Don and Charlene met at a party thrown by a mutual friend and started dating the following week. He was attracted by Charlene's light and carefree manner. Her spontaneity was a welcome antidote to his thorough but plodding approach. Her enthusiasm and humor lifted Don out of his customary seriousness and he found her captivating.

Charlene was equally enamored of Don. Don had an inner strength that made Charlene feel safe and secure. His logical approach and attention to detail saved the day on numerous occasions. Don didn't talk much, but when he did, it was clear to Charlene that he'd thought things through. There was a quiet earnestness about this man that she liked.

Eight-and-a-half months after their first date, they married. Both held full-time jobs so they split the housekeeping chores. Don, who did the shopping, turned out to be compulsive about purchasing specific brands and storing them in a highly organized way. It was bad enough that he stored the spices in alphabetical order; he insisted that Charlene do the same. Her spirit wilted in the face of what seemed to be bureaucratic procedures in her own home, when it was bad enough to have to cope with them at work. Also, Charlene thrived on an active and bustling charge through life. Don, however, was committed to a quiet lifestyle. Charlene could bear the peace and quiet for just so long. Then it began to feel oppressive. Many of Don's qualities that once seemed attractive were now perceived as negatives.

Don also became disillusioned with marriage to the outgoing Charlene. He resonated to the word-picture the minister painted during the wedding: "May the home you are establishing be a haven to rest and a place of peace." His life with Charlene, however, had turned into a whirlwind of activity. She seemed to always be on the go—and wanting him to be part of the whirlwind. Then, too, Don often described himself as a "neatnic." Charlene, by contrast, didn't seem to understand the concept of closets and drawers—she left piles of dishes in the kitchen sink and a trail of discarded clothes throughout the house.

Behavioral differences in intimate relationships can be more grating than they are in work relationships. It's one thing to tolerate bothersome behaviors that only occur occasionally. But it's quite a different matter to live with annoyances that are in your face every day. Less than a year after their wedding, both Charlene and Don were wondering whether their marriage had been a mistake.

If you are in a long-term couple relationship there's a statistical likelihood that the two of you are from a somewhat similar socioeconomic background. However, there's a 95 percent probability that, like Don and Charlene, your partner's behavioral style is significantly different from yours. We base this estimate on more than three decades of self-reports by people in our workshops, as well as on our observations of couples we've met. As you read further, you'll gain the kinds of insights and learn the interpersonal methods that helped Charlene and Don build a supportive and loving relationship.

We're not suggesting that it's more desirable to link up romantically with a person whose behavioral style is similar to yours. When both partners have a similar style, it does not bode particularly well or ill for the relationship. Same-style couples simply face a different set of challenges. We'll show how two people of the same style can relate more successfully both at work and in couple relationships.

YOU CAN ONLY RELATE TO ANOTHER PERSON'S UNIQUENESS IN LIMITED WAYS

We are not only different from one another—each of us is unique, bewilderingly so. It's common knowledge that each person's fingerprints are distinct from those of every other person. Experts can also distinguish your voice from all other voices. These are surface indicators of an amazing fact: At birth, you were endowed with an individuality of personhood that can never be duplicated. So was everyone else. "It is never possible to completely understand any other human being," wrote anthropologist Edward T. Hall, "the complexity is too great."

The experiences of the people you've met in this chapter demonstrate that it doesn't work to go through life merely doing your own thing with whomever you meet. "Different strokes for different folks" is a much better guideline. However, when trying to give different strokes to different folks, you confront a major difficulty: the number of differences between people is overwhelming. It's humanly impossible to fully adapt to everyone's idiosyncrasies.

THE TYPES APPROACH TO GETTING IN SYNC WITH OTHERS

Many theorists and practitioners such as Hippocrates (460–377 BC), "the father of medicine," and Carl Jung (1875–1961), one of the towering figures of psychology, realized the limitations inherent in trying to relate solely to each person's uniqueness. So they devised methods of building relationships across the chasm of human differences. The common thread of those methods was the fact that *in significant ways, each of us is more like some people than others.* In other words they found that, to some degree at least, *people come in types.*

The early descriptions of people types left much to be desired. There's no point burdening you with information about all the typologies that have been developed through the centuries. Most were minimally useful and some were decidedly harmful.

In the early 1960s, Dr. David Merrill, an industrial psychologist, developed a typology that focused on the *behavioral* differences between people. The *people styles model* (also referred to as a behavioral styles model) that is the subject of this book is an offshoot of Merrill's approach. We incorporated enhancements for improving relationships and augmenting self-development. So it's primarily the greater number of applications and the specificity of the how-tos that distinguish the people styles model from Merrill's approach.

You'll learn about the people styles model and methods in coming chapters. For now, it's enough to say this:

- There are four people styles, none of which is better or worse than any of the other styles.

- Although each person is unique, people of the same style are similar in important ways.

- Each style has potential strengths and weaknesses that aren't shared by the other styles.

- No style is more or less likely to be a predictor of success or failure.

- The behavioral patterns of each style tend to trigger tension in people of the other styles.

- Getting in sync with the style-based behaviors of the person you are with helps reduce interpersonal tension, thereby fostering well-functioning and productive relationships.

"ISN'T THAT JUST ANOTHER WAY OF STEREOTYPING PEOPLE?"

At this point in a presentation of the people styles model, someone is likely to say, "Isn't that just another way of stereotyping people?" By

Figure 1-1
Different styles can produce the same favorable results.

SOURCE: Robert Bolton and Dorothy Grover Bolton, *Social Style/Management Style* (New York: Amacom, 1984), p. 23.

stereotyping, the questioner usually means "derogatorily caricaturing people" (see Figure 1-1).

We have to admit that some people pervert this model into a means of caricaturing the people they relate to. Their descriptions of people of other styles consist mainly of simplistic put-downs.

However, that's a flagrant distortion of this way of understanding people. An antijudgmental orientation is built into the very foundation of this model. As mentioned earlier, the people styles approach holds that there are no better or worse styles—just different ones. It affirms that every style is a good place to be. It emphasizes the importance of style acceptance and celebrates the fundamental worth of each style, while cautioning against blowing out of proportion the weaknesses of any style.

After this type of explanation, the person who asked the question is apt to say, "OK, the model isn't a way of stereotyping folks. *But it is a way of categorizing people, isn't it?*" The assumption behind this question is that it's wrong to categorize people.

The people styles model *is* a way of categorizing people. Experts on the workings of the mind found that we can't avoid categorizing people or anything else that we want to understand and communicate about. We can categorize well or we can categorize poorly. But we can't not categorize. We place people in categories whenever we use words like *customer, supplier, team leader, trainee, friend, neighbor, wife, son,* and so on.

Without the economies of categorization, our mental processes would quickly become overloaded. Categorization provides a cognitive shortcut that reduces the infinite differences among people to usable proportions. It's an ability that's essential to our survival.

As essential as categorizing is to our ability to think, communicate, and act effectively, it's a process that needs to be used with particular care, especially when applied to people. To categorize effectively, one needs to use a top-notch set of categories. Our experience suggests that the categories of the people styles model provide a first-rate aid to understanding people and improving relationships. And, once you have a high-quality set of categories, you need to use them skillfully. Even the best of models can be used glibly or even destructively. Throughout these pages, we'll point out dangers to avoid and sound practices to use in applying this approach to understanding the differences between people.

MAKE PEOPLE DIFFERENCES WORK FOR RATHER THAN AGAINST YOU

Problems can be opportunities in disguise. Although it may be challenging to work with someone very different from yourself, you can make those differences work *for* rather than against you and your co-workers. Ditto for relating to the people who are closest to you.

You can gain a competitive advantage from mastering an ability that's in high demand and short supply. When you learn to work productively with all types of people, especially in this era of diversity, you'll be far more valuable to your employer.

There's another way that people differences can be made to work for you and others. No one is outstanding at everything. Different types of people have different kinds of abilities. You can benefit from recognizing that *people differ in valuable ways* and supplement your own abilities with the strengths of people who are very different from yourself. As you become expert at identifying and collaborating with those whose skills complement yours, you'll become a stronger and more versatile contributor. That's what Spencer finally did.

After a particularly stressful interaction with Bill, Spencer realized that he needed to come up with a different way of relating to his manager. Spencer remembered having heard that people have different working styles and that to function well with another person, it's helpful to understand that person's style and how it's different from your own. Then you need to figure out how to bridge the interpersonal gap so you are in sync with the other person's way of working. Since there was no place for the relationship to go but up, Spencer decided to give this strategy a try. He eliminated much of the detail from his reports and stepped up the pace of his conversations with Bill. Spencer was surprised to find that these and a few other well-targeted changes in his interactions with his manager significantly decreased their interpersonal tension and helped them forge a better working relationship.

Within a year, Spencer's collaboration with Bill had become even more productive than it had been with Jan. As he put it, "Jan and I got a lot done, but we were too similar. Bill often has a different perspective on things than I have. He's more people-oriented and much faster-paced. That complements my task-focused, detail-oriented approach. Now that we've learned to augment each other, we're great at selling proposals to top management and gaining cooperation from other divisions. When my technical and administrative skills are linked to Bill's networking ability, we're some team."

You don't have to wait until friction develops to make changes that will produce a more satisfying and productive relationship. When you know what to observe in a person's behavior, you can generally predict how that person would like to be treated in future interactions. The next chapter describes how the prediction process works.

CHAPTER 2

People Are More Predictable than You Might Think

EVER BEEN BAFFLED by a person's reaction to something you've said or done? Join the club. Perhaps you've acted with the very best of intentions only to learn that what you did irritated the other person. It's discouraging to be ambushed by negative reactions that you don't think you deserve.

Such experiences lead many to throw up their hands in despair at ever being able to understand other people. It's a widespread opinion that you can't predict how other human beings will react. Lewis Thomas, the noted physician and essayist, wrote in exasperation, "Our behavior toward each other is the strangest, most unpredictable, and almost entirely unaccountable of all the phenomena with which we are obliged to live."

Although people sometimes act in erratic and inconsistent ways, human behavior isn't nearly as random as is commonly believed. Behavioral scientists tell us that, in many ways, people are surprisingly predictable. Think of opinion polling. On Election Day morning in 1980, Hamilton Jordan, who managed President Jimmy Carter's reelection campaign, was given the results of a last-minute poll that foretold a lopsided loss for the president. "What a funny feeling," Jordan thought. "Not a single person in the country has voted, and we already know we've been defeated." The outcome was just what the poll predicted—Reagan won by a landslide.

Another of the many studies of human predictability comes from psychologist Arnold Mandell. Through long and careful observation of

National Football League players, he was able to predict a great deal about the behavior of the athletes by simply observing their lockers. When Mandell saw a neat locker, he would predict, usually correctly, that the player was on the offensive team, liked structure and discipline, enjoyed the repetitious practice of well-designed plays, and was rather conservative. When he saw a messy locker, Mandell was generally successful in assuming that the player was on the defensive team, disliked structure, was apt to challenge rules and regulations, and would be more difficult to manage than his counterparts on the offensive team.

THE PERVASIVENESS OF PREDICTION

Predictions play a major role in our lives. They influence our actions. Tiffany exercises regularly because she predicts that, as a result, she'll feel better and will be healthier. Our predictions even affect many of our most mundane and insignificant acts. You turn on a faucet because you expect (predict) that water will be released. You turn a doorknob and pull because you predict that this action will open the door.

Predictions are a key factor in our decision making. When you decide to invest in a given stock, make a major career shift, or purchase a new car, your choice is usually based on your prediction that the option selected will, on the whole, be more satisfying than others you considered.

A GOOD MODEL HELPS YOU MAKE BETTER PREDICTIONS

Opinion polls generally make surprisingly accurate forecasts because they are based on reliable demographic models. Arnold Mandell was able to predict with considerable accuracy because he developed a model that was useful for anticipating certain types of behaviors in the population he was studying.

Since good models enhance the accuracy of predictions, it makes sense to create a model that forecasts how different types of people in the overall population like to be treated. The people styles model was developed to do just that. We think you'll be amazed at the usefulness of this model as you learn to employ it to create better relationships with a wide variety of people.

Since people styles is a model, you'll be more adept at using this way of improving your relationships if you have a basic understanding of the nature, uses, and limitations of models. Models are tools for the mind. They are designed to improve understanding and performance by reducing complexity to a manageable level. Here, in a nutshell, is how models function:

- Models identify and concentrate attention on the few really significant factors in a situation.

- They enable you to interpret what you observe. They help you organize your observations so you can find new and rich meaning from data that previously would not have had much, if any, significance for you.

- Models provide a reasonably accurate picture of reality despite all the data they eliminate from consideration.

- They enable you to predict the probable outcome of a course of action, with the result that you are able to perform model-related functions better and faster.

The major complaint with models is that they're too simplistic. As we've seen, models are, by definition, a simplification of reality. So the issue is, does a particular model *over*simplify—is it so barebones that it is inadequate for achieving its intended purpose? Based on our experience, as well as on feedback that we've received from participants in our workshops and readers of our previous books on people styles, this model passes that test with flying colors. When properly applied, the people styles model enhances the user's ability to create and maintain more harmonious and productive relationships with all sorts of people. It also fosters greater self-understanding and improved self-management.

THE PEOPLE STYLES MODEL

Let's begin with a description of the nature and benefits of this model. *A people style is a cluster of habitual assertive and responsive behaviors that have a pervasive and enduring influence on one's actions.* The population in our culture is evenly divided between four people styles. There's no linkage between one's style and success or failure. The people styles model fosters increased self-awareness and self-acceptance, as well as greater understanding and acceptance of others. Let's examine some of the key words and phrases in this description.

Behaviors

As indicated in Chapter 1, this approach to understanding people is distinguished from many others in that it focuses on behavior rather than personality. *Behavior is what a person does.* When using this model, you concentrate on what you see with your own eyes and hear with your own ears. How fast does the person walk? How much does he gesture? How loudly does he speak? How much inflection does he use? How much facial animation does he show? As you'll soon see, that kind of data is sufficient for understanding how to improve your relationships with all sorts of people. By contrast, one's *personality* includes inner characteristics like beliefs, thoughts, motives, values, attitudes, feelings, etc. as well as behaviors.

A number of psychological typologies focus mainly on a person's inner qualities. Our bias is that a strictly behavioral model is preferable to a psychological model that has you speculate about the inner world of other people. The late Peter Drucker, possibly the world's most respected organizational consultant, said this:

> An employer has no business with a man's personality. Employment is
> a specific contract calling for a specific performance, and nothing else.
> Any attempt by an employer to go beyond this is usurpation. It is an
> immoral as well as illegal intrusion of privacy.

You don't need to probe the inner sanctum of your co-workers, friends, or loved ones to improve your relationship with them. All you need to do is better understand the behavior that's there for you and everyone else to see. Then respond appropriately.

Habitualness

One's style is determined by *habitual* rather than occasional behaviors. It's about the things a person does over and over again, day after day, for the umpteenth time. Habitual actions are called "second nature" because we rely on them almost instinctively—like hitting the brakes when the car in front of us suddenly slows down. Because behaviors associated with our style are so habitual, they feel natural. We feel at home with them. That's why our style is often referred to as our *comfort zone.*

Obviously, people aren't robots doing exactly the same behavior again and again. Rather, they do the same *type* of behavior repeatedly. Skeptical? Many people are. But think about it. Don't your friends and acquaintances have habitual behavioral tendencies? As you read the following statements, mentally fill in each blank with the name of a person who matches the description that follows the blank:

_____   is typically late for appointments and meetings.

_____   tends to be very thorough.

_____   keeps touching base with people.

_____   has a story for nearly every occasion.

_____   is a no-nonsense, "just do it" kind of person.

Behavioral tendencies like these tend to remain fairly consistent from one situation to another. This high degree of behavioral consistency makes it possible to predict how people are likely to behave in the future.

Clusters of Behaviors

Some of our habitual behaviors are linked to other often-recurring behaviors to form clusters. These clusters of interrelated behaviors are key to understanding ourselves and others. Learned Hand, the renowned federal judge, stated, "A man's life, like a piece of tapestry, is made up of many strands which, interwoven, make a pattern. To separate a single one and look at it alone not only destroys the whole, but gives the strand itself a false value."

An understanding of behavioral clusters enables us to predict many of the ways that another person would like to be treated. When you note a person using some behaviors that are associated with a particular cluster, you may speculate that certain other behaviors linked to that cluster are part of that person's mode of operation. Like Mandell, you can predict behavioral characteristics that you haven't observed based on others that you have observed. Future chapters will spell out how this prediction process works.

Psychologist Albert Mehrabian said, "There is something about each person, a pervasive style that applies to almost everything he does. . . . Probably it is not just one isolated behavior here or there that gives an impression but rather a composite of behaviors that are indicative of a certain style. One question, therefore, is 'What are these clusters?'"

Assertive and Responsive Behaviors

Behavioral scientists and leadership researchers found that assertiveness and responsiveness are two clusters of behavior that are especially important in determining a person's style. In fact, by concentrating on just these two clusters of behavior, you can improve your understanding of and relationship with nearly everyone you meet. That's a crucial finding, because once you start paying close attention to a person's behavior, you'll note that there's an enormous amount of it. In fact, in any given conversation far more behavior is taking place than it's humanly possible to observe.

It is difficult to believe that by focusing on only two clusters of behavior, you can learn enough about yourself and others to greatly enhance your relationships. But, we'll show you how to do it and, when you give this approach a try, we're confident you'll find that it works. Chapter 4 describes these two influential keys to better understanding yourself as well as other people.

Pervasive and Enduring Influence

These clusters of assertive and responsive behaviors are pervasive—they're present in much of what a person does. So they're fundamental to your interactions with others.

In his book *Human Nature and Its Remaking*, philosopher William Ernest Hocking emphasized the fact that of all creatures, human beings have the greatest capability to modify themselves. He said, "To everyone who asserts as dogma that 'Human nature never changes,' it is fair to reply, 'It is human nature to change itself.'"

The other side of the coin is that there are also some large patterns of continuity in people's lives. For example, research indicates that the two dimensions of people styles—one's typical level of *assertiveness* and *responsiveness (emotiveness)*—are remarkably constant throughout one's life. Psychologists Paul Costa Jr. and Robert McCrae of the National Institute on Aging reviewed large-scale, long-term studies in which researchers followed subjects throughout the many stages of adult life. A major finding was that "the assertive nineteen-year-old is the assertive forty-year-old is the assertive eighty-year-old." Researchers also found that across a person's lifetime his degree of emotiveness is very stable.

This may seem like a theoretical issue but it has practical consequences. Since you can't change your dominant style, you'd be wise to accept and celebrate it. And because other people can't change their dominant style, you'll interact more effectively with them when you respect and get in sync with their natural style.

PEOPLE STYLES IN A NUTSHELL

We will describe each of the people styles in subsequent chapters. Just remember:

- There are four people styles, none of which is better or worse than any of the other styles.
- The population is evenly divided among the styles.
- We are all four-style people—that is, each of us has some degree of access to the characteristic behavioral tendencies of all four of the styles.
- Each of us, however, has a dominant style—a set of behaviors that we're more adept at, especially comfortable with, and use frequently.

The people styles model is based on research conducted with residents of the United States. That population is equally divided among the four styles. The feedback we get from users in other cultures is that the people styles model is useful in their culture (our previous books on people styles have been translated into 10 languages). However, we're told that the population of many countries is divided *unequally* among the four people styles.

THE IMPORTANCE OF PROBABILITIES

When we say that people are fairly predictable, we're not suggesting that you'll be able to foretell someone's every move. Nor do we claim that you can know for sure how a person will react. *When you are dealing with people, there are no certainties—but there are significant probabilities.* By probable, we mean "more likely than not." Thus, when we discuss predictions about people, we avoid words like *whenever, always,* or *never.* Instead, we rely on *usually, frequently, tends to,* and so forth. In the following pages, we sometimes omit these qualifiers for the sake of readability, but do understand that we're talking about probabilities rather than certainties.

Some people are unimpressed with predictions that are only probabilities. They want something more definite. However, when it comes to anticipating how a given person will react, you can never be absolutely sure.

We're comfortable with this degree of uncertainty. Without spontaneity in our relationships, much of the joy of living would be forfeited.

We think you'll enjoy the improvements you can make in relationships when you are guided by strong probabilities. As the *New Yorker*'s James Thurber noted, "A pinch of probability is worth a pound of perhaps."

In the next chapter you'll find an inventory that will help you identify your own style. Then, in Chapter 4, we'll describe assertiveness and responsiveness and will show how these two clusters of behavior determine one's style.

CHAPTER 3

What's Your Style?

"Who am I and what, if anything, can I do about it?"
—ALDOUS HUXLEY

AFTER REVIEWING the history of philosophy, Aldous Huxley concluded that this is the most important question one can ask. The more accurate a person's self-perception, the more likely she will make the most of her strengths and avoid being brought low by her limitations. Moreover, a high degree of self-awareness contributes to establishing and maintaining good relationships with others. And, it's a requirement for effective leadership. As the sixteenth-century philosopher Machiavelli noted in his treatise on leadership, "To lead or attempt to lead without first having a knowledge of self is foolhardy and is sure to bring disaster and defeat."

Most people find that understanding their people style—how *other people* perceive them—adds an important dimension to their self-awareness. So the focus of this chapter is a self-assessment inventory that can help you identify your people style.

GUIDELINES FOR COMPLETING THE PEOPLE STYLES SELF-ASSESSMENT INVENTORY

Your people style is based on *other people's* perceptions of you—*not* on how *you* see yourself. Therefore, in filling out the inventory, read each item from the standpoint of the way you think *other people* see you. It may help to think of three people you work with and try to view yourself through their eyes as you take the inventory.

There are no good or bad styles; there are only differences among people. Success or failure is unrelated to any style. So, there are no good or bad choices on the inventory—no right or wrong answers.

Of course, each of us has a picture of how we'd like to be seen by others. And because we're human, there's always some disparity between our daily actions and the way we hope others perceive us. Discipline yourself to be as objective as possible. Select those items that, to the best of your knowledge, reflect the way *other people* experience you.

This inventory consists of eighteen pairs of statements. Choose the statement in each pair that you think most accurately expresses how other people see you. Sometimes you may think neither statement reflects how you come across to others. Nevertheless, choose the statement you think more closely describes how others view your behavior. On some items, you may think some people would see you as described by one statement while other people might think of you as portrayed by the other state-ment. For those items, select the statement that represents how a majority might view you—even a small majority of 51 percent. Force yourself to make a choice between each of the paired statements.

Each inventory item has a word in it that suggests a comparison: *more, less, fewer, softer, slower,* and so forth. You may wonder, "More than what?" "Slower than what?" In each case, think in terms of "more than" or "slower than" *half of the population.*

Indicate your choice by drawing an X in the box to the left of the statement in each pair that best describes how you think others see you. In the following example, if you think "'less use of hands when talking" is a more accurate statement of how you come across than "more use of hands when talking," mark an X in the box in front of the first statement.

❑   Less use of hands when talking

    ❑   More use of hands when talking

THE PEOPLE STYLES SELF-ASSESSMENT INVENTORY

Select *one* statement from each of the pairs. Be sure to put the X in the correct box.

1. ❑ More likely to lean back when stating opinions

　　❑ More likely to be erect or lean forward when stating opinions

2. 　　❑ Less use of hands when talking

　　　❑ More use of hands when talking

3. ❑ Demonstrates less energy

　　❑ Demonstrates more energy

4. 　　❑ More controlled body movement

　　　❑ More flowing body movement

5. ❑ Less forceful gestures

　　❑ More forceful gestures

6. 　　❑ Less facial expressiveness

　　　❑ More facial expressiveness

7. ❑ Softer voice

　　❑ Louder voice

8. 　　❑ Appears more serious

　　　❑ Appears more fun-loving

9. ❑ More likely to ask questions

　　❑ More likely to make statements

10. 　　❑ Less inflection in voice

　　　❑ More inflection in voice

11. ❑ Less apt to exert pressure for action

　　❑ More apt to exert pressure for action

12. 　　❑ Less apt to show feelings

　　　❑ More apt to show feelings

13. ❑ More tentative when expressing opinions

    ❑ Less tentative when expressing opinions

14.   ❑ More task-oriented conversations

      ❑ More people-oriented conversations

15. ❑ Slower to resolve problem situations

   ❑ Quicker to resolve problem situations

16.   ❑ More oriented toward facts and logic

    ❑ More oriented toward feelings and opinions

17. ❑ Slower-paced

  ❑ Faster-paced

18.   ❑ Less likely to use small-talk or tell anecdotes

    ❑ More likely to use small-talk and tell anecdotes

— — — — **Total Scores**

INTERPRETING THE INVENTORY

Although it's best to *complete* the inventory before you've learned much about the people styles model, it's best to *interpret* the results of the inventory after you know more about the model. So we'll wait for several pages before describing how to calculate your style from the inventory. Your style is based on the two clusters of behavior that are described in the next chapter.

CHAPTER 4

Two Keys to Understanding People

IN THE LONG SWEEP of history, there's been no dearth of methods for fostering self-awareness and greater understanding of others. Most of the systems, however, didn't facilitate accurate prediction, and many were too complex for use by the average person.

Part of the genius of the people styles approach is that it offers a surprisingly accurate guide to understanding all sorts of people by focusing on just two clusters of behavior. All you have to do is determine whether a person is in the more assertive half of the population or in the less assertive half. Then do the same for the person's level of responsiveness. It doesn't seem possible, but that's all the data you need in order to identify that person's style. And once you know the person's style, you'll be able to predict much that will help you relate better and work more effectively with him or her. This chapter describes these two crucial clusters of behavior.

ASSERTIVENESS

In the people styles model, *a person's level of assertiveness is the degree to which his behavior is typically seen by others as being forceful or directive.* The gradations of behavior along the assertiveness continuum are indicated by a gradual darkening of the continuum, as you look from left to right in Figure 4-1. Research on success in management and sales positions found that there's no better or worse place to be on the assertion continuum.

At this point, we're only concerned about whether a person's behavior tends to be more assertive or less assertive than that of half of the population. Thus, a line divides the continuum into two equal parts. People whose characteristic behavior is more assertive than half of the population are sometimes referred to as "right-of-the-line" because that's where they're located on the continuum. People whose behavior places them in the less assertive half of the continuum get their needs met by using a less forceful and less directive manner than half of the population. We sometimes speak of them as "left-of-the-line."

Figure 4-1
The assertiveness continuum.

left-of-the-line   right-of-the-line

People often equate a high level of assertiveness with aggressiveness. Although that's the case with some people who are more assertive than average, it's not typical of most of them.

Regarding the other half of the continuum, people sometimes assume that lower levels of assertiveness indicate submissiveness. Not so. While some less assertive people are submissive, most of these folks simply use less forceful ways to achieve their goals.

When we say that someone is less assertive or more assertive, we don't mean that he or she is always that way. Some behaviors of a less assertive person may be directive. Some behaviors of a more assertive person may be low key. Most of a person's behaviors, however, will fall within a somewhat limited area of the assertion continuum. People often think they move about the continuum rather freely. But we're creatures of habit, and that's rarely the case.

Participants in our people styles workshops sometimes wonder how less assertive people can be successful. Bear in mind that in the people styles model, assertiveness refers to a person's *behavior*—that which can be seen and heard—rather than to inner qualities. Many less-assertive people have a strong inner drive, despite the fact that what people see—

their behavior—would not generally be perceived as forceful or directive. They achieve success in a manner that's softer and quieter than that of their behaviorally more assertive colleagues.

Perhaps you recall from Chapter 3 that in determining someone's style, we use comparative words such as more, less, louder, softer, and so forth. When estimating a person's level of assertiveness, we do the same thing: we try to determine whether that person exhibits more or less of certain patterns of behavior than half of the population.

To help you picture what more assertive and less assertive behaviors are like, let's look at some characteristics of a typical person on each half of the assertiveness continuum.

Characteristic Behaviors of More-Assertive People

Compared to less assertive people, those who are more assertive:

- Gesture more vigorously

- Have more intense eye contact

- Move more rapidly

- Exude more energy

- Are more erect or forward leaning, especially when making a point

- Speak more rapidly

- Speak louder

- Speak more often

- Address problems more quickly

- Decide more quickly

- Exhibit more risk-oriented behavior

- Are more confrontational

- Are more direct and forceful when expressing opinions, making requests, and giving directions

- Exert more pressure for making a decision or for taking action

- Demonstrate anger more quickly

Right-of-the-line people have most but not necessarily all of these characteristics.

Characteristic Behaviors of Less-Assertive People

Compared to more assertive people, those who are less assertive do the following:

- Gesture less vigorously
- Have less intense eye contact
- Move more slowly
- Demonstrate less energy
- Lean back a bit when making a point
- Speak less rapidly
- Speak more softly
- Speak less often
- Are slower to address problems
- Take more time to arrive at decisions
- Exhibit less risk-oriented behavior
- Are less confrontational
- Are less direct and less forceful when expressing opinions, making requests, and giving directions
- Exert less pressure for making a decision or taking action
- Demonstrate anger less quickly

People who are left-of-the-line have most but not necessarily all of these characteristics.

RESPONSIVENESS

Responsiveness is the other dimension of behavior in the people styles model. *A person's level of responsiveness is the degree to which she is seen by others as showing her own emotions and demonstrating awareness of the feelings of others.* The gradations of behavior along the responsiveness continuum are indicated by a gradual darkening of the continuum as you look from the top to the bottom of Figure 4-2.

At present we're only concerned about whether a person's behavior tends to be more responsive or less responsive than that of half of the population. The responsiveness continuum in Figure 4-2 is cut in half by a line to distinguish between people who are less emotive than half of the population and those who are more emotive than half of the population. Individuals who tend to be emotionally reserved are said to be "above the line." Those who are more emotionally disclosing and more aware of the feelings of others are referred to as "below the line."

When we say that someone is emotionally responsive, we don't mean that he always "lets it all hang out." There will be times when this type of person will mute his expression of feelings. However, he's usually more demonstrative than above-the-liners. Likewise, people who tend to be emotionally restrained may sometimes be quite demonstrative. J. P. Morgan, the famous banker, was aloof at work and in public. At times, though, as when he read *A Christmas Carol* to his family, the normally unexpressive financier would get all choked up. So when we say someone is emotionally reserved or that another person is emotionally demonstrative, we don't mean that all of their behavior is restricted to that segment of the continuum. However, most of their behavior occurs within a rather narrow stretch of the continuum.

It's often believed that people who are emotionally reserved simply lack feelings. However, above-the-line people sometimes experience strong feelings but tend to hold them in. Take Joe DiMaggio, the legendary baseball player. Interviewer Warner Wolf said to him, "Joe, you had a reputation for being an unemotional player, as though you never felt the pressure. . . ." DiMaggio responded, "They said I had a poker face, but I knew what was going on inside. All those years, my stomach was churning. Outside, I didn't show emotion. But inside I was plenty emotional."

Researchers found that no position on the responsiveness continuum is a predictor of a person's success or failure.

To help you picture what more and less-responsive behaviors are like, let's look at some characteristics of a typical person on each half of the continuum.

Characteristic Behaviors of More-Responsive People

Compared to the less-responsive half of the population, more-responsive people:

- Express feelings more openly

- Appear more friendly

- Are more facially expressive

- Gesture more freely

- Have more vocal inflection

- Are more comfortable with small talk

- Use more anecdotes and stories

- Express more concern about the impact that decisions and policies may have on people

Figure 4-2
The responsiveness continuum.

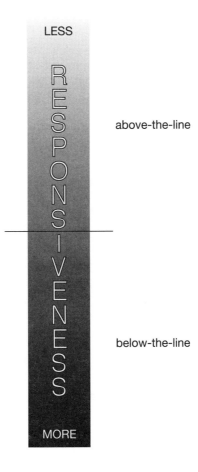

- Prefer working with others to working alone

- Dress more casually

- Are less structured in their use of time

More-responsive people have most, but not necessarily all, of these characteristics.

Characteristic Behaviors of Less-Responsive People

Compared to the more-responsive half of the population, less-responsive people:

- Are less disclosing of feelings

- Appear more reserved

- Have less facial expressiveness

- Gesture less often

- Have less vocal inflection

- Are less interested in and less adept at "small talk"

- Use facts and logic more than anecdotes

- Are more task-oriented

- Are more comfortable working alone

- Dress more formally

- Are more structured in their use of time

People who are less responsive than half the population have most but not necessarily all of these characteristics.

THE FOUR PEOPLE STYLES

The assertiveness continuum and the responsiveness continuum form the axes of the people styles grid, as shown in Figure 4-3. The four quadrants represent the four people styles. No style is inherently better or worse than any other. Each style has potential strengths and potential limitations. Some people of each style are successful and some are not. Each style has its good and bad examples.

Figure 4-3
The people style grid.

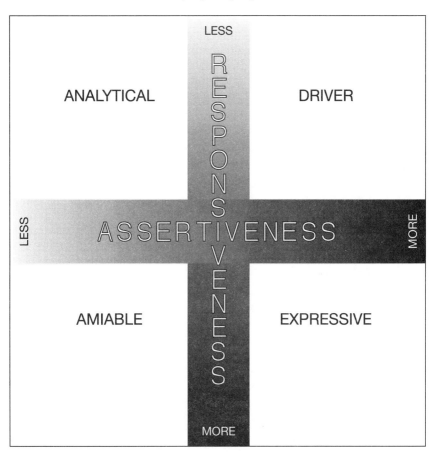

- *Analytical* is the name given to the style in the upper-left portion of the people styles grid. Analyticals combine greater-than-average emotional restraint with lower-than-average assertiveness.

- The *Driving* style is found in the upper-right section of the grid. Drivers combine greater-than-average emotional restraint with a higher-than-average level of assertiveness.

- The *Amiable* style is located in the lower-left quadrant. Amiables integrate higher-than-average emotional responsiveness with less assertiveness than half of the population.

- *Expressives* are positioned in the lower-right area of the grid. They blend a higher-than-average level of assertiveness with a higher-than-average level of emotional expressiveness.

The people styles model assumes that, like everyone else, you have *a dominant style.* That is, you usually prefer to relate and work in ways that are characteristic of one of the four styles. Early in life, one style emerged as your favorite, and you now rely primarily on that style. Because that style has become habitual, it's easiest for you to function with those patterns of behavior. This is your "comfort zone."

Although you have a dominant style, it's also true that you are a four-style person. While one style predominates in each person, behaviorally we're all a bit of a mixed bag. However strong our dominant style, we can all find traces or even large amounts of the other styles in our behavior. Like a right-handed person who relies on her left hand some of the time, each person uses some behaviors associated with the other styles.

WHATEVER YOUR STYLE, IT'S A GOOD ONE

Dr. Merrill, whose research highlighted the importance of assertiveness and responsiveness, initially assumed that certain combinations of these clusters of behavior would be associated with success in the workplace. He conducted research on managers and salespeople to determine the relationship between a person's likelihood of success and her location on the styles grid. Much to his surprise, there was no connection. As Merrill and his colleague Roger Reid noted:

> When our research was completed . . . we had evidence to challenge the notion that the most successful persons in business are more assertive. In addition, responsiveness or lack of it did not appear to be consistently related to success. Successful, well-regarded career persons were found along all ranges of the assertiveness and responsiveness scales— just as were less successful individuals.

So, whatever your style turns out to be, it's a good one.

The effective organization is made up of and values all four types of people. Peter Drucker, the noted management consultant, was fond of saying that top-management requires four kinds of human beings: the "thought person" [Analytical], the "action person" [Driver], the "people person" [Amiable], and the "front person" [Expressive]. Drucker adds that you won't find all the strengths of all four types in any one manager.

Want to know your style? Chapter 5 shows how to calculate your style using the information generated by completing the People Styles Inventory in Chapter 3, pages 26–27.

CHAPTER 5

See Yourself as Others See You

TO ASCERTAIN YOUR STYLE, turn to the People Styles Self-Assessment Inventory that you filled out in Chapter 3 (pages 26–27). The inventory is not a test. There is no better or worse combination of scores. As you recall, each style has tendencies to important strengths, and each has propensities to some weaknesses.

In each column, count the number of boxes you checked and record the totals in the appropriate "Total Scores" spaces.

Here's what the totals mean. In the column farthest to the left, you tallied the *less assertive* (*left*-of-the-line) behaviors that characterize you. The column next to it is where you tallied behaviors that are more assertive (*right*-of-the-line). Place a checkmark in the box that represents the *higher* of these two scores:

❏ *less assertive* (*left*-of-the-line)   ❏ *more assertive* (*right*-of-the-line)

On that same page, the column farthest to the right is where you tallied the *more emotionally responsive* (*below*-the-line) behaviors that characterize you. The column just to the left of it is where you tallied the *less emotionally responsive* (*above*-the-line) behaviors. Check the box below which represents the *higher* of these two scores:

❏ *less responsive* (*above*-the-line)   ❏ *more responsive* (*below*-the-line)

If your highest scores are:

Less assertive and less responsive: You think others perceive you as an *Analytical.*

More assertive and less responsive: You think others perceive you as a *Driver.*

Less assertive and more responsive: You think others perceive you as an *Amiable.*

More assertive and more responsive: You think others perceive you as an *Expressive.*

In Figure 5-1, place an X in the quadrant of the grid that represents this self-assessment of your people style. As we've emphasized before, there's no better or worse combination of scores. No style is superior or inferior to any other style.

STYLE NAMES: A NECESSARY EVIL

In order to communicate easily about the four styles, each style must have a label—a name. But names or labels never do justice to the reality they identify. In that sense, all labels are libels. One of the problems with style names is that some people focus on what the name implies to them rather than on the full spectrum of behaviors that characterize that style. For example, the label "Driver" suggests only a part of that style's richness of behavior. By focusing on the label "Driver," some may think of the person as overpowering. Some Drivers are that way, but many are not. Like people of other styles, many Drivers are participative and empowering. As you read the descriptions of the styles in the following two chapters you'll see that each style is far richer than its name suggests.

THE CHALLENGE OF SEEING YOURSELF AS OTHERS SEE YOU

In *Poor Richard's Almanack,* Benjamin Franklin wrote, "There are three things extremely hard: steel, a diamond, and to know one's self." Jennifer

Figure 5-1
A people styles grid for self-assessment.

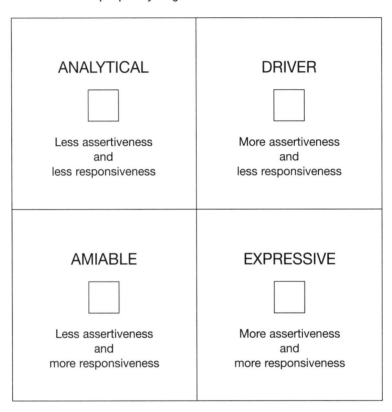

Darden began to realize the wisdom of that statement during an executive counseling session. When preparing for the session, Jennifer used the People Styles Self-Assessment Inventory, which indicated that she saw herself as an Analytical. She also asked five colleagues to complete the inventory on their perception of her and to mail it to the executive coach. Her co-workers saw her as an Expressive. The two styles are opposites in many ways:

Analytical	*Expressive*
Reserved	Gregarious
Formal	Informal
Quiet	Loud
Less assertive	More assertive

As you can imagine, Jennifer's misperception of how others saw her had serious interpersonal consequences. When there were difficulties with other people, Jennifer often misread the dynamics of the situation and therefore was ineffective in trying to resolve it.

Over two centuries ago, Scottish poet Robert Burns noted both the difficulty and the importance of knowing how we come across to others:

> O would some Power the gift to give us,
> To see ourselves as others see us!
> It would free us from many a blunder
> And foolish notion.

A WORKING HYPOTHESIS

Although few are as mistaken about their style as Jennifer was, about half of the people doing a People Style Self-Assessment don't identify their style correctly. That's why it makes sense to treat this self-assessment as a working hypothesis. Ask yourself these questions to help you improve your understanding of how you come across to others:

- Do most other people perceive you as more assertive or less assertive than half of the population? Review the lists of characteristic behaviors of more-assertive people and those of less-assertive people (Chapter 4, pages 30–31).

- Do most other people perceive you as more-responsive or less-responsive than half of the population? Review the lists of characteristic behaviors of more- and less-responsive people (Chapter 4, pages 32–34). In what quadrant of the people styles grid would the assessment of both questions place you?

- Chapters 6 and 7 portray each of the four styles in some detail. As you read those chapters, ask yourself which of the style portraits is most like you.

- Chapter 8 discusses the different ways that people of the various styles tend to react to excess stress. What does this information suggest about your style?

Since your people style is how you are perceived by others, it's useful to get feedback from some other folks.

Want to gain further understanding of yourself as well as of your manager, co-workers, customers, suppliers, family members, and friends? They're all described in Chapters 6 and 7.

CHAPTER 6

The Driving Style and the Expressive Style

WE'VE SEEN THAT the characteristics of each person's style are determined by the degree of assertiveness and responsiveness associated with that style. But how do these combinations of assertiveness and responsiveness play out in daily life? This chapter provides a description of Drivers and Expressives—the two styles that are characterized by higher-than-average levels of assertiveness. You'll learn about the other two styles in the next chapter.

THE DRIVER STYLE

The Driver style is located in the upper-right area of the people styles grid (see Figure 6-1). Drivers blend a higher-than-average degree of assertiveness with less-than-average responsiveness.

Drivers are fast-paced. They speak rapidly, walk swiftly, decide quickly, and work efficiently. When they delegate, they're apt to want the assignment completed "yesterday." They sometimes get impatient if you are not speaking, deciding, and producing at the fast clip they expect.

These are get-it-done people. When a group of Drivers in a people styles workshop is asked to come up with a motto for the Driver style, they often decide on, "Damn the torpedoes, full steam ahead." The rush

43

Figure 6-1
Drivers show more-than-average assertiveness and
less-than-average responsiveness.

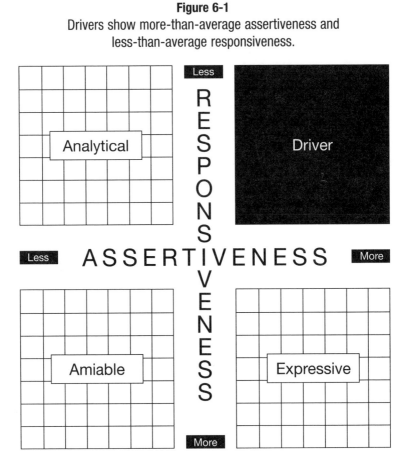

to get on with it may or may not produce a desirable outcome. But the Driver feels relieved that at least *something* is being done about the situation.

Decisiveness is a salient characteristic of Drivers. They don't agonize over decisions like some people do. Drivers assume that indecision *is* a decision, and inevitably a bad one. Furthermore, these people are not compulsive about the quality of their decisions. Their desire for closure can be so strong that they sometimes make snap decisions with minimal information gathering—even when the issues are significant. Rather than try to make the best decision each time, rather than secure guarantees that her decisions will work, a Driver friend says, "If six out of ten of my decisions pan out, I'm ahead of the game." When a decision turns out poorly, the Driver often takes it philosophically: "You win some, you lose some." This fast-paced approach to decision making can seem irresponsible to left-of-the-line people.

Drivers are more likely to change their minds than are people who are less assertive. Because people of this style tend to be very definite in their opinions, others are often surprised by abrupt changes in their thinking and sudden shifts in their plans. It's not unlike a Driver to do a reversal that leaves everybody astounded. President Richard Nixon, a Driver, was one of communism's most implacable foes. He surprised the world by suddenly doing an about-face as he established diplomatic relations with Communist China.

Drivers are often puzzled by others' strong reactions to their reversals of position. In the Driver's mind, if something isn't working as planned, or if the situation has changed, or if a new opportunity is spotted, one's response must change. Those changes are often beneficial. But Drivers are so fast-paced and action-oriented that they sometimes improvise a hasty and ill-conceived change of course that merely sets the stage for a new set of problems.

People of this style typically excel at time management. Books and workshops on this topic consist of a smorgasbord of methods designed to enhance efficiency. When we studied the time-management practices of three hundred managers, we found that the way the Drivers worked was by far the closest match to the usual cluster of time management techniques.

These go-getters are the most results-focused of the styles. They like situations in which they can achieve immediate, tangible results. Drivers love to set high but realistic objectives and then make steady and efficient progress toward achieving them. Being highly independent, Drivers work best at tasks that they themselves have chosen. And, when doing those tasks, they want to set their own goals rather than have someone else do it for them.

People of this style pride themselves on their bottom-line orientation. They're often more focused on the outcome than on the quality of the means used to achieve that outcome. Although this type of expediency often works, it can backfire if the Driver becomes overly cavalier about the means employed.

Much of the Drivers' body language telegraphs their purposefulness. Their posture is erect. They seem to lean into everything they do. They walk and move faster than most people. Their gestures can be very forceful. The Driver's facial expression tends to be more serious than that of the below-the-line styles and more intense than that of the Analytical.

When stating a point of view, the Driver's voice is louder than most people's and eye contact is direct—sometimes to the listener's discomfort.

Of the three time frames—past, present, and future—Drivers are "now" people who concentrate on the present moment. They follow Thomas Carlyle's dictum, "Our business is not to see what lies at a distance, but to do what lies clearly at hand." People of this style can be so preoccupied with the immediate situation that they are unaware of valuable lessons from the past. They also may not recognize the contribution that continuity can make to an organization's performance. An excessive focus on the present sometimes makes Drivers oblivious to potential unintended but highly negative consequences of their current actions.

When communicating, Drivers get to the point quickly and are succinct. And they prefer spoken to written communication.

Drivers are less emotionally expressive than most people. Their facial expression and other body language seldom gives as strong clues about their feelings as you'll find with Amiables and Expressives. And when they speak, they focus more on facts than on feelings. In their relationships with others they don't convey as much warmth as below-the-liners.

Drivers are tell-oriented. Their speech is fast-paced, their comments are direct and to the point, and they include less detail and redundancy than most people.

You'll rarely hear these forthright people "beat around the bush." They make strong statements, saying flat-out what they mean. And they can be quite blunt about it. (Typically, they also expect you to be candid with them.) When a Driver combines straight-from-the-shoulder content with rapid delivery, a louder than average volume, a leaning-in posture, forceful gestures, and intense eye contact, it's not difficult to see why less assertive people are sometimes intimidated by this style of communication.

Drivers tend to be more task-oriented than people-oriented. In their push to get the job done, they show less-than-average concern for personal relationships or for the feelings of others. Drivers may train themselves to engage in a bit of "small talk," but it's seldom their forte. Once conversational preliminaries are dispensed with, many Drivers keep the focus on *their* task-based agenda. Analyticals and Amiables, who are slower-paced and less assertive, may chafe at the Driver's single-minded concentration on her own set of concerns. Although Drivers often accomplish a tremendous amount in a short time, if others feel bulldozed or depersonalized by the process, there's a danger that the progress may be more illusory than real. Other people's lack of buy-in or outright resistance may delay or undermine the outcome. Some Drivers need to learn that task accomplishment is seldom compromised by paying attention to the feelings of others or taking the time to build good relationships.

When we say the Driver is task-oriented rather than people-oriented, we don't mean to imply that Drivers have a basic lack of concern for others. Over the years, we've witnessed the trauma of downsizing in one corporation after another and have seen a number of Drivers make a greater effort to give tangible assistance to those affected than some of their colleagues who, on the surface, appeared more person-centered.

However, the Drivers' exceptionally strong focus on task sometimes makes them oblivious to other people's needs and interests. And when they do become aware of someone's plight, they probably won't verbalize their concern as sensitively as a below-the-line person might. Also, their body language may not reveal the level of compassion that Drivers actually feel. In place of the empathic words and body language that others might use, Drivers tend to express their concern by the "language of action." Unfortunately, other people (including a Driver's friends and family members) may not notice the level of caring that Drivers often believe should be perceived from their actions.

Drivers are generally so busy doing and talking that they don't do nearly enough listening. An important growth step for most people of this style is to spend more time listening to other people's issues, concerns, ideas, and feelings. When there's a difference of opinion, Drivers need to demonstrate greater interest in understanding the other person's side of things than they typically do. This increased receptivity to and respect for the input of others is especially important when relating to members of their family, as well as to those in the workplace who are lower on the pecking order. When Drivers listen better, they will strengthen their relationships while gaining important, performance-enhancing information.

No one is completely true to type. The average Driver will have most of the characteristics described here but not all of them. So when working with a Driver, be alert to the typical characteristics of this style but also look for behaviors that may be unique to this person.

As with each of the styles, there are pluses and minuses to the Driver's way of doing things. When people do this style poorly, it's a nonproductive way of working. However, Drivers who use their style effectively are on a well-traveled pathway to success.

Since about 25 percent of the people you interact with are Drivers, you'll be dealing with these folks every day. In Part Two of this book as well as in the appendix for your style, you'll learn how to improve your relationships with these practical realists.

THE EXPRESSIVE STYLE

This style is located in the lower-right portion of the people styles grid (see Figure 6-2). People in this quadrant integrate a high level of assertiveness with a high level of emotional expressiveness.

Figure 6-2
Expressives show more than average assertiveness
and more than average responsiveness.

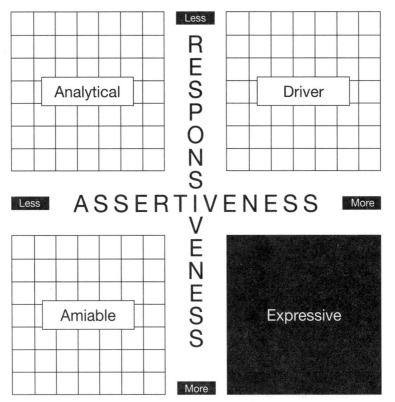

Drivers and Expressives have some characteristics in common because people of both styles demonstrate more than average assertiveness. There are also similarities between Expressives and Amiables—styles that are more people-oriented and more tuned in to emotions than the above-the-line styles. There are many characteristics, however, that are distinctive to the Expressive.

This is the most flamboyant of the styles. Expressives like bright colors, bold statements, and eye-catching projects. Their mode of operation often has a theatrical flourish to it. Expressives love the limelight. They work best when they receive lots of positive feedback.

This spirited style bristles with energy. Expressives seem to have pep enough for any two people. Their vim and vigor is evident in nearly everything they do. Their high energy, when combined with other aspects of their high assertiveness, can make them seem overwhelming at times.

Expressives want to be where the action is. They gravitate toward exciting, fast-moving activities. They like to be continually on the go. Jobs that confine a person to a desk for most of the day are not for these restless people.

Expressives tend to be visionaries. They push people to look beyond the merely mundane and practical in order to undertake bold and imaginative goals. They love blue-skying sessions, where one's imagination can soar without concern for pragmatic constraints. They delight in envisioning "castles in the air"—lofty undertakings designed to create a bigger, better, and brighter future for the department or organization—and, of course, themselves.

Thoreau once said that it's fine to build castles in the air—but you need to follow through and build foundations under them. Follow-through is where Expressives tend to be especially weak. They're quickly bored with the many humdrum details that are often essential to achieving their goals. So, while you and others are hard at work building a foundation under a castle in the air that an Expressive sold you on, he'll probably be off somewhere else—dreaming of other castles to build.

Expressives are impulsive. They're likely to change directions on the spur of the moment. People of this style have a tendency to act first and think later. Many Expressives use the same image to describe this aspect of their style: "First I dive into a pool and then I look to see if there's any water in it." As a result of this tendency, Expressives have to work their way out of more than their share of problems of their own making. After observing an Expressive friend trying to recover from yet another crisis that seemed unnecessary, an Analytical asked why she didn't plan ahead to avoid the needless hassles. "Ultimately," said the Expressive, "*my* way takes *less* time. You Analyticals plan for eventualities that never happen. And planning is such a drag. Besides, I like the excitement of improvising myself out of these jams. It's far more interesting than all that planning."

Time management is a major challenge for Expressives. These easily diverted people pay less attention to clock and calendar time than the other styles do. They're often late to meetings or may miss them altogether. And they're frequently behind schedule with projects. Some habitually miss deadlines. Others become adept at catching up at the last minute. People of other styles are often annoyed by the Expressive's free and easy approach to time.

The Expressive is the most outgoing of the styles. These extroverts relate easily and seemingly effortlessly to strangers and have a large circle of acquaintances. When Expressives have a choice of doing something alone or with other people, they prefer to link up with others. They invite people for lunch, to play tennis after work, to go cycling on the weekend. When they travel out of town, they make the effort to look up old acquaintances in the area they're visiting. These high-contact people spend a great deal of time on the phone. They are naturals at networking and have innumerable contacts who can help them achieve their goals. People of this style lend credibility to the saying, "Who you know is more important than what you know."

Feelings play a greater-than-average role in the Expressive's life. More than other styles, the Expressive is on an emotional roller coaster. And, since these folks tend to "let it all hang out" and "wear their heart on their sleeve" you'll undoubtedly be very aware of the emotions that they're experiencing. People sometimes find it difficult to deal with the Expressive's emotional ups and downs. Yet, in their frequent up times, the Expressive's enthusiasm is contagious, which contributes to their exceptional ability to motivate others.

Emotions play a dominant role in the Expressive's decision-making process. They rely less on facts and more on hunches, opinions, and intuition than do people of the other styles. As an Expressive explained to others in a workshop, "When we Expressives make a decision, it's basically a gut call."

When required to sit through meetings, an Expressive's restless energy is evident. If there's a discussion that interests her, she'll probably be a highly active and animated participant. When bored at meetings, instead of being unobtrusively tuned out, the Expressive may be engaged in a side conversation or be unmistakably disengaged.

Expressives are definitely *tell*-oriented. And they're the most verbally fluent of the styles. They speak rapidly, and their words seem to flow effortlessly. These loquacious people tend to have strong opinions and often launch into long-winded explanations of their thoughts. Sometimes they can be fascinating; at other times just wearisome.

You don't have to strain to hear what these hale and hearty people are saying. Many of them crank up the volume when they speak. In a restaurant, it may be easier to hear the Expressive four tables away than to hear your left-of-the-line dinner partner who is sitting directly across from you.

When Expressives speak, their whole body joins in. Their gestures are animated, their facial expressions are highly communicative, and their varied inflection heightens the listener's interest and enjoyment. When this caliber of delivery is combined with the Expressive's verbal fluency, it's easy to see why people of this style can be exceptionally persuasive.

Expressives often speak before giving thought to what they say. As a number of Expressives told us, "I speak to find out what I'm thinking." Digressions are par for the course for this style. When an Expressive is holding the floor, he may skip from topic to topic in ways that defy logic.

Storytelling is part and parcel of the Expressive's approach to communicating. He often builds rapport by describing a humorous incident that happened recently. And, if a little embellishment will improve the story, so be it. When making a point, he's more likely to cite an example than present a string of facts. He probably won't quote any statistics—unless, of course, the numbers are very dramatic.

As you listen to their conversations you'll soon note that these gregarious folks are more people-oriented than task-oriented. It's not that they are disinterested in getting the assignment completed; it's just that their manner of doing it has more of a focus on people. For example, if you meet with an Expressive about a specific issue, don't expect her to get to the point right away. If she takes the lead, as will often happen, the initial part of the interaction is likely to be about almost anything other than the reason for the conversation. People who are more task-oriented often consider this extended rapport building a waste of time and may get tense waiting for the Expressive to get down to business. The Expressive thinks this *is* business: "After all, what is business if it's not people talking to each other?"

The Expressive will likely be up-front about saying what he does or doesn't like. This is a tell-it-like-it-is style. The Expressive's willingness to raise hard issues can be crucial to healthy relationships and heightened productivity. Sometimes, however, his frank opinions are expressed tactlessly and he can be insensitive to the hurt his words triggered in the other person.

Expressives are long on talking and short on listening. They advocate more than they inquire, and many are apt to interrupt others and monopolize the conversation. To repeatedly be on the listening end of an Expressive's one-way conversations gets old in a hurry. People of this style do well to make a concerted effort to listen—to understand where other people are coming from.

When you want to communicate with an Expressive, do it verbally if you can, and face-to-face if that's possible. If the message is important, it's worth the extra time and effort. Some Expressives are so averse to doing paperwork that they often leave memos and reports unread. They'll probably glance at a short e-mail, though.

This is the most playful and fun loving of the styles. They delight in a good time themselves, and get a charge out of stimulating it in others. They engage in friendly banter, tell jokes, think up pranks, and laugh heartily. A person noted for throwing great parties explained that one key to a lively gathering is to be sure a number of Expressives are invited. The world would certainly be a drearier place without these upbeat people.

Expressives look for ways to make work more enjoyable. They're apt to suggest that a meeting take place at a restaurant rather than the office. They typically kid around for a few minutes before plunging into the topic at hand. They'll often find a humorous slant on something in an otherwise serious discussion. One Expressive CEO we know gave each new employee a Mickey Mouse wristwatch. "If work ever stops being fun," he'd say, "turn in your watch and find a job you enjoy." This very competitive executive assumed that if people have fun at work, it's not only more fulfilling for them but they'll be more productive, too.

No one is completely true to type. The average Expressive will have most of the characteristics described here but not all of them. So when working with an Expressive, be alert to the typical characteristics of this style but also look for behaviors that may be unique to this person.

As with each of the styles, there are pluses and minuses to the Expressive's way of doing things. When people do this style poorly, it's a nonproductive way of working. However, Expressives who use their style effectively are on a well-traveled pathway to success.

Since about 25 percent of the people you interact with are Expressives, you'll be dealing with these folks every day. In Part Two of this book, as well as in the Appendix for your style, you'll learn how to improve your relationships with these energetic and imaginative competitors who encourage colleagues to dream bigger and aim higher.

CHAPTER 7

The Amiable Style and the Analytical Style

IN THIS CHAPTER, we discuss the two less assertive pathways to success—the approaches taken by Amiables and Analyticals.

THE AMIABLE STYLE

The Amiable style is located in the lower-left quadrant of the people styles grid (see Figure 7-1). The Amiable gets things done in a manner that's less assertive than average, combined with more-than-average responsiveness.

As you read these descriptions, you will note some similarities between Amiables and Analyticals, since these two styles share a similar level of assertiveness. You will also see occasional likenesses between Amiables and Expressives.

Amiables are very people-oriented. Their friendly, easygoing manner lends warmth and harmony to their interactions with others. And their relationships with others are often more personal than is characteristic of the other styles. This style's quiet friendliness can be a major asset in working with others.

Amiables undergird their friendliness with empathy. They're concerned about what other people think and want. They're often more interested in hearing your concerns than in expressing their own. Amiables are especially sensitive to other people's feelings. They're more likely than people of other

Figure 7-1

Amiables show less-than-average assertiveness and
more-than-average responsiveness.

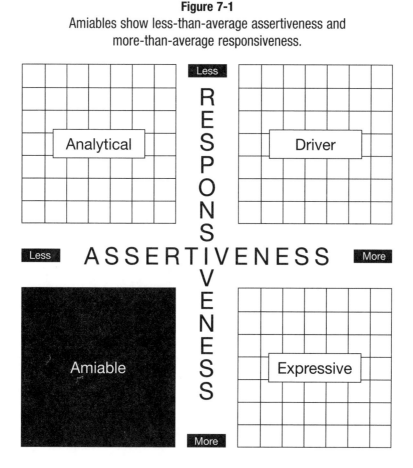

styles to be able to vicariously put themselves in another person's shoes. Their compassion shows on their faces and in their eyes, as well as in their words. It's no wonder that people often confide in them.

Although people of some styles prefer to work independently, the Amiable normally likes to work with others, especially in small groups or one on one. He doesn't seek the spotlight and seldom gets into ego clashes with others. Amiables are less likely than the more assertive styles to seek power for themselves. Many are skilled at encouraging others to expand on their ideas and are adept at seeing value in other people's contributions. As a result of their openness to the opinions of others, they are sometimes able to salvage a person's worthwhile ideas that other team members were quick to discount. People of this style are often effective at integrating conflicting opinions into a synthesis that all parties can genuinely support.

Amiables' effectiveness as team players is often enhanced by their generosity with their time. If a co-worker asks for advice or help, Amiables are more likely than others to drop whatever they're doing in order to help out. They often volunteer to do unglamorous, out-of-the-limelight activities for the team. Because of their dedicated backstage work, they are the unsung heroes of many a team effort. While this unselfishness is often constructive, Amiables may overdo it to such an extent as to default on completing their own commitments in a timely manner.

In conversation, Amiables tend to use less "air time" than the more assertive styles. Also, they're usually slower in forming an opinion than Drivers or Expressives. So when an issue surfaces during a conversation or meeting, the Amiable's input may come late in the session, or perhaps not at all.

As you'd expect from what's been said so far, Amiables speak more about people and feelings than the above-the-line styles. Amiables are gracious with small talk. They're apt to ask you how your trip went last week or how your child fared in a recent competition. Their focus on people and feelings continues when the discussion turns to work issues. As part of a management team, Amiables are often more able than other styles to speak realistically about the human consequences of a decision under consideration. This consistent attention to the human component of work can enhance morale and make the process of change far less disruptive than it might be without the Amiable's influence.

The Amiable's body language is relaxed and low key. People of this style walk more slowly than more-assertive styles and have a more relaxed posture. They often lean back in their chair, even when making a request or stating an opinion. The Amiable's voice is warm and the volume is low. Amiables speak more slowly than people whose style is more assertive. They rely on gestures when communicating, and their movements tend to be fluid and graceful, though not dramatic. They're comfortable with eye contact and are facially expressive.

Many Amiables are reluctant to "tell it like it is" for fear of alienating the other person. When opinions are divided about a course of action, Amiables are more likely than the average person to withhold their point of view—even when they think they're right and important issues are at stake. Some dislike conflict so much that they occasionally say what they think the other person wants to hear rather than what they really believe. When Amiables don't overcome this reticence to take a stand, they may lose credibility with people who doubt that they can be counted on when the chips are down.

When Amiables make a request or state an opinion, they're inclined to phrase it indirectly. They often state their point of view by asking a question. Rather than declaring, "Let's move ahead with Campaign X," an Amiable might ask, "Do you think Campaign X is the way to go?" Or he may quote others who share the same opinion: "A lot of people are saying that Campaign X is the way to go." This nonconfrontational manner of speaking is sometimes effective, but if the ask-oriented tendency becomes too pronounced, people are likely to complain, "I don't know where Ken is coming from. I wish he'd take a clear-cut stand on things."

People of this style reveal personal things about themselves that make people feel as though they know them better than they know most other acquaintances. Amiables, however, are generally guarded about expressing "negative" feelings like anger. When seething inwardly, they often present a calm exterior.

For some Amiables, the desire to maintain pleasant relationships translates into an unwillingness to confront a subordinate's or co-worker's performance problems. They may water down corrective feedback or avoid giving it altogether. Sometimes they're more critical than they let on, complaining to a third party about matters that would do more good if stated directly to the person whose performance is below par. Some people of this style are squeamish about using authority, and when they finally apply it, they may use it inconsistently.

High-performing Amiables overcome the tendency to conceal their true opinions yet continue to maintain their concern for the other person and the desire not to harm the relationship. Their tact enables them to say hard things without harming the other person's ego. Their diplomatic timing and phrasing often enables difficult messages to get through to people who would be closed to the same idea when expressed more bluntly by others.

When people work or live together, there's bound to be conflict. Because Amiables treasure harmonious relationships, they are natural peacemakers and are often found pouring oil on troubled water. Their efforts at conciliation often make continued collaboration possible.

The Amiable tends to perform best in a stable, clearly structured situation. This style is not as enamored of goal setting and planning as the above-the-line types. Some Amiables prefer to have the organization define their role and set their goals—as long as the demands aren't unreasonable. Once their role is clarified and the direction is set, they work steadily in the performance of their responsibilities. As a rule, people of this style are industrious, service-oriented workers. Because of their easygoing, friendly, unpretentious ways, other people may not realize how much work they turn out.

Some people are better at creating products, strategies, organizations, and so on, while others are better at maintaining them. Amiables shine as maintainers. They tend to value what has already been created and find satisfaction in working to preserve it. Also, to a greater degree than most people, Amiables are comfortable doing routine procedures and following processes established by others.

The Amiable takes a cautious approach to decision making, looking for guarantees to lower the risks involved. They may delay making decisions, especially when the risks are fairly high or when it's a controversial call and others may be upset by the outcome. They often employ a collaborative style of decision making and change management that generally lowers resistance and facilitates a smoother and more effective transition to the new mode of operation. And when it's their responsibility to make the final call, Amiables generally touch base with those who are affected before they arrive at their decision.

Amiables are slower to anger than most people. They do have a limit, though. If you persist too long in treating them in ways they don't like, they'll eventually become angry and can be slow to forgive or forget.

Of course, no one is completely true to type. The typical Amiable will have most of the characteristics described here but not all of them. So when working with an Amiable, be alert to the characteristics of this style but also look for behaviors that may be unique to this person.

As with each of the styles, there are pluses and minuses to the Amiable's way of doing things. When people do this style poorly, it's a nonproductive way of working. However, Amiables who use their style effectively are on a well-traveled pathway to success.

Since about 25 percent of the people you interact with are Amiables, you'll be dealing with these folks every day. In Part Two of this book and in the Appendix for your style, you'll learn how to make the most of your relationships with these reliable collaborators who are such key contributors to high-performing teams. By the way, Dot, a co-author of this book, is an Amiable.

THE ANALYTICAL STYLE

The style in the upper-left portion of the grid is called Analytical. People in this quadrant combine considerable emotional restraint with less than average assertiveness (see Figure 7-2).

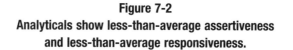

Figure 7-2
Analyticals show less-than-average assertiveness
and less-than-average responsiveness.

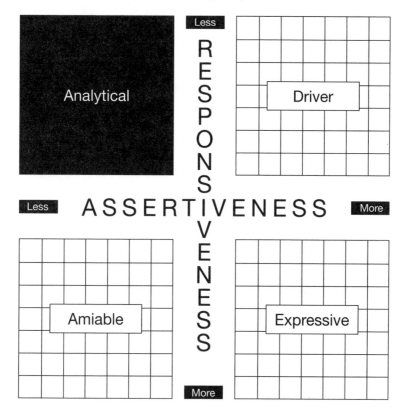

Analyticals are the most perfectionistic of the styles. They value exactness, prefer quality over quantity, want things they're associated with to be *right*. Some styles shoot from the hip. "Ready, fire, aim," advises one well-known management consultant. Analyticals are appalled at such counsel. Their watchword is, "Let's do it right the first time so we don't have to do it over." They set very high standards and are willing to do the time-consuming work needed to achieve or exceed them. These people are sticklers for detail since they're convinced that rigorous attention to every aspect of a project, no matter how insignificant, contributes to a quality outcome. Quick fixes are an anathema to Analyticals—even when a quick fix is all that a situation requires.

Because of their perfectionistic tendencies, Analyticals are often very hard on themselves—and they can be equally hard on others. Their exacting standards tend to make them sparing with positive feedback. Analyticals need to guard against this tendency, because it can be demoralizing to live or work with someone who is heavy on criticism and light on compliments.

People of this style crave data; the more, the better. When you see them converting that data into useful information, you understand the truth of the saying, "Knowledge is power." The danger, of course, is that Analyticals can become so bogged down with data collection that they're apt to miss out on opportunities that require a quick response.

The Analytical is known for being systematic and well organized. At best, this style is adept at building highly effective processes that produce consistently outstanding results. At worst, the Analytical's methodical bent can degenerate into excessive regulation and a by-the-book mentality.

It's very out-of-character for an Analytical to act impulsively. When facing risks, the people of this style prefer to be prudent. Many take *calculated* risks, but some are reluctant to do even that. As a rule, they'd rather be safe than sorry.

Don't expect these careful people to be cavalier or impulsive about decision making. With each decision they want to make the best possible choice. They examine more options than others do. They research alternatives with exceptional thoroughness. When the investigation is finally concluded, they may take an unusually long time mulling over their options before finally arriving at a decision. They're likely to agonize over even minor decisions. Becoming more decisive is an important growth step for many people of this style.

When it comes to time management, the Analytical is a strange mix. Many are punctual for appointments but tardy in meeting deadlines. It's easy to see why people of this style might have a tendency to miss the due date on projects. The Analytical's perfectionistic quest for quality leads her to set exceedingly high standards. At the same time, she tends to work at a slower pace than most people. These tendencies often produce a superior outcome but can cause missed deadlines, unfinished tasks, and bottlenecked projects.

This is the most introverted of the styles. Analyticals are private people who are often seen by others as aloof. They tend to let others take the social initiative. Once contact has been made, it takes more time to get to know them than is the case with people of the other styles. But those who know them well often think it's worth the time and effort.

The Analytical likes to be alone or with just a few other people. If possible, he leaves the big gatherings and cocktail parties to others; he'd rather stay home and read a book. As the Analytical philosopher Henry David Thoreau wrote, "I have a great deal of company in my house; especially in the morning when nobody calls."

A person of this style is rarely linked closely to the grapevine but may be tapped into the Internet. An Analytical who has an office can usually be found in it—and the door will probably be closed. This type of person needs to be prodded to manage by walking around. In fact, she typically prefers working alone to working with others. Despite the Analytical's solitary nature, she tends to be loyal when the going gets rough. Though not thought of as a "people person," in crunch situations the Analytical often goes out of her way to assure that employees are treated fairly.

Analyticals are the quietest of the styles. They tend to speak less often than people of other styles—except when delving into excessive detail on a topic of special interest to them. When the Analytical talks, the volume is low, the pace is slow, and there's little inflection in the voice. People of this style like to think things through before speaking. They often continue thinking as they speak; scanning their minds for the right word or phrase to communicate content accurately. This can lead to frequent hesitations that others often find annoying. It's no wonder that people of this style favor written over spoken communication.

In terms of content, an Analytical's conversation is typically more task-oriented than people-oriented. He approaches issues logically and, even in casual conversation, is apt to break what he's saying into points: "In the first place . . . ," "Second . . . ," and so forth. Analyticals strive for accuracy and expect it in others. They want people to provide them with considerable detail, and assume that others need to have all the fine points spelled out, too. When they explain something, they can overwhelm people with excessive minutia.

When analyzing an issue, Analyticals have a tendency to magnify the complexity involved and may be reluctant to make a clear-cut recommendation. Harry Truman, one of our more assertive presidents, used to say he wanted a one-armed economist—he was frustrated by Analytical advisers who said, "On the one hand this, but on the other hand that."

Analyticals are similar to Amiables in their tendency to be indirect when making a request or stating an opinion. Sometimes when asking a question, an Analytical is really making a statement. "Do you think it would be wise to . . . ?" may mean "I'd like you to take this action."

These people's body language is low key. They tend to lean back in their chair even when making a point. Analyticals don't gesture much, and when they do, their gestures tend to be smaller, less flowing, and less emphatic than is common. And they tend to make less eye contact and have less facial expressiveness than people of the other styles.

Analyticals don't wear their feelings on their sleeve, and sometimes are seen by others as cold or detached. They're not given to demonstrating a great deal of enthusiasm: They may sometimes feel as deeply about an issue as anyone, but they'll probably talk about the facts of the case rather than their feelings about it. Sometimes they're out of touch with their own feelings; their heads shout so loudly that they can't hear what their guts are saying. Because they show so little emotion, others often find them hard to read.

During conflict, others may get carried away by emotion, but Analyticals are apt to become emotionally detached. They often act as though a rational approach will cool an overheated situation. It often has the opposite result. Expressives, in particular, become even more upset when an Analytical tries to get them to talk calmly and rationally during brouhaha. When people of this style are too conflict-avoidant, important issues are tabled, problems are left unattended, and significant opportunities may be missed.

No one is completely true to type. The average Analytical will have most of the characteristics described here but not all of them. So when working with an Analytical, be alert to the characteristics of this style but also look for behaviors that may be unique to this person.

As with each of the styles, there are pluses and minuses to the Analytical's way of doing things. When people do this style poorly, it's a nonproductive way of working. However, Analyticals who use their style effectively are on a well-traveled pathway to success.

Since about 25 percent of the people you interact with are Analyticals, you'll be dealing with these folks every day. In Part Two of this book and in the Appendix for your style, you'll learn how to develop stronger work relationships with these quiet and industrious people. Incidentally, Bob, a co-author of this book, is an Analytical.

CHAPTER 8

Make the Most of Your Gifts

A *GIFT* IS a significant natural aptitude. The salient characteristics of your people style are among the gifts you were endowed with. Making the most of these assets is key to fulfillment and success. You'll make the most of your gifts when you do the following:

- Note the gifts—the potential strengths—of your style.
- Develop those gifts into actual strengths.
- Capitalize on those strengths.

NOTE THE POTENTIAL STRENGTHS OF YOUR STYLE

Significant tendencies of your people style are listed in Figure 8-1. They're likely to be some of your important gifts.

DEVELOP THESE GIFTS INTO STRENGTHS

A gift is the seed of a strength. However, the gift must be developed in order to become an actual strength. Here, in brief, is how to convert a gift—a potential capability—into a viable asset:

Figure 8-1
Potential strengths of each people style.

ANALYTICAL	DRIVER
Logical	Efficient
Systematic	Decisive
Thorough	Pragmatic
Prudent	Independent
Serious	Candid
AMIABLE	**EXPRESSIVE**
Cooperative	Persuasive
Supportive	Enthusiastic
Diplomatic	Outgoing
Patient	Spontaneous
Loyal	Fun-loving

- *Listen/read.* In the process of growing your gift into a strength, you'll undoubtedly need to acquire some know-how. People often gain this information by reading how-to books and manuals, taking classes, and/or being instructed by a knowledgeable practitioner.

- *Observe.* If you've ever tried to put together assemble-it-yourself furniture, you've probably experienced the limitations of written how-to instructions. So it's often advantageous to supplement the verbal directions by observing an exemplar actually doing the ability you wish to develop.

- *Practice.* Once you have a fairly specific understanding of how to perform an ability, you'll need to practice it repeatedly in order to develop it into a bona fide strength. However, the saying, "Practice makes perfect," is misleading. When practicing, many people do the behavior by rote—without thinking about what they're doing. But this kind of practice does not make perfect. Quite the opposite. Instead of leading to perfection, rote practice tends to make *permanent* the current less-than-desirable level of ability.

Effective practice entails mindful repetition—paying attention to and learning from what you are doing. Mindful repetition fosters improvement as you learn from your successes and your failures. Even when you are highly gifted, it takes an enormous amount of attentive practice to achieve excellence in your specialty.

FIND WAYS TO CAPITALIZE ON YOUR STRENGTHS

Your strengths are what you've got going for you, so it makes sense to make the most of them. In trying to find work that's compatible with their style, people sometimes choose a field in which there are a large number of positions that are well suited to their style. Thus, many Analyticals, especially those who are mathematically inclined, become accountants, and many Expressives are drawn to fields like sales or entertainment. However, you can probably find a niche in just about any vocation that will suit you well.

Many people are drawn to a job that's a good fit with their natural gifts. So there's often a fairly good match between people's natural assets and their entry-level position. However, as the Peter Principle predicts, when a person succeeds at doing what she's good at, she'll likely be promoted—often from excellent performance on one rung of the organizational ladder to mediocrity at a higher level. The Gallup Organization asked more than 1.7 million employees, "What percentage of a typical day do you spend playing to your strengths?" Less than 20 percent responded, "most of the time." So the overwhelming majority of people are miscast for most of the work they do. Furthermore, Gallup's researchers found that the "longer an employee stays with an organization and the higher he climbs the traditional career ladder, the less likely he is to strongly agree that he is playing to his strengths." And, as you might predict, researchers found that people who are mismatched to their jobs are significantly less productive, less customer-focused, and more likely to leave their place of employment than those whose abilities are well matched to their work.

AVOID OVERRELYING ON YOUR STRENGTHS

Although it's advisable to capitalize on your strengths, people sometimes overdo a good thing by relying excessively on those strengths. That tendency dawned on consultant Paul Mok while reading *The Count of Monte Cristo* by Alexandre Dumas. The line, "Any virtue carried to the extreme can become a crime," was an eye-opener for him. In that sentence, Mok found an explanation for the problem that was undermining the effectiveness of many people in his executive coaching practice. These executives "were overusing their strengths, employing them even when they were inappropriate, using them to the hilt—and beyond. And when used to excess, these strengths backfired—exploded in their faces."

Here's how strengths of each style create problems when overused or misapplied.

Drivers' Strengths Overused or Misapplied

Drivers are forceful; they're movers and shakers, make-it-happen type of people. In the process of achieving their goals, however, they sometimes come on too strong and may be viewed as pushy, domineering, and authoritarian. When in overdrive, they're apt to run roughshod over people's feelings and their turfs as they ramrod their ideas and objectives through. If they push their forcefulness excessively, their effectiveness may drop precipitously due to the resentment and resistance generated by their hard-hitting ways.

In addition to their forcefulness, Drivers have other tendencies that, when used well, are strengths. But, when overused or misused, those abilities undermine their effectiveness. Figure 8-2 lists some potential strengths of Drivers that become weaknesses when used poorly or inappropriately.

Figure 8-2
Drivers' strengths become weaknesses when overused.

Strengths		Overused
Independent	→	Poor collaborator
Results-oriented	→	Impersonal
Candid	→	Abrasive
Pragmatic	→	Shortsighted

Expressives' Strengths Overused or Misapplied

Spontaneity is one of the Expressive's obvious strengths. But overly spontaneous people can be difficult to work with. When Expressives do what they're drawn to at the moment, they tend not to deliver on existing commitments, whether it's attendance at an important meeting or the timely completion of a project. After being let down by a string of broken commitments, those left holding the bag are understandably resentful.

Along with their spontaneity, Expressives have other characteristics that are strengths when employed effectively. When overused or misused, though, these qualities tend to be dysfunctional. Figure 8-3 lists potential strengths of Expressives that become weaknesses when used inappropriately.

Figure 8-3
Expressives' strengths become weaknesses when overused.

Strengths		Overused
Articulate	→	Poor listener
Fast-paced	→	Impatient
Visionary	→	Impractical
Fun-loving	→	Distracting

Amiables' Strengths Overused or Misapplied

Amiables are standouts at working harmoniously with others. However, if harmonious and cooperative behavior is excessive, there's a propensity to avoid conflict at almost any cost. When Amiables overemphasize their agreeable nature they're apt to sweep unpleasant facts under the rug and avoid taking stands on important issues. If an Amiable yields to this temptation, others may begin to doubt that they can count on him in controversial situations.

In addition to their harmonizing behaviors, Amiables have other characteristics that, when employed effectively, are strengths. When overused or misused, however, these qualities become weaknesses. Figure 8-4 lists potential strengths of Amiables that become weaknesses when used ineffectively.

Figure 8-4
Amiables' strengths become weaknesses when overused.

Strengths		Overused
Diplomatic	⟶	Conflict avoider
Cautious	⟶	Risk averse
Supportive	⟶	Permissive
People-oriented	⟶	Inattentive to task

Analyticals' Strengths Overused or Misapplied

The quest for quality is a major asset of Analyticals. If the pursuit of quality degenerates into perfectionism, however, it becomes a liability. The compulsive perfectionist often sets lofty standards that go well beyond any functional purpose. Taken to the extreme, no task is so irrelevant that it can't be redone and no report is so inconsequential that it can't be revised again and again. This endless nitpicking tends to make the perfectionist perennially late with projects. In an economy where speed in decision making and implementation are increasingly essential to success, the snail's pace of the perfectionist is counterproductive.

In addition to their quality orientation, Analyticals have several other attributes that are strengths when used effectively. However, when overused or otherwise misused, these qualities become weaknesses. Figure 8-5 lists potential strengths of Analyticals that become weaknesses when overused or misapplied.

Figure 8-5
Analyticals' strengths become weaknesses when overused.

Strengths		Overused
Prudent	⟶	Indecisive
Painstaking	⟶	Nitpicky
Task-oriented	⟶	Impersonal
Systematic	⟶	Bureaucratic

PREVENT YOUR MAJOR WEAKNESS FROM DOING YOU IN

A Gallup poll found that 87 percent of the population believes that fixing their weaknesses is the best way to attain outstanding performance. Although that's a popular strategy, it's a poor one when overemphasized. Shoring up your weak spots can help stave off failure but it won't lift you above run-of-the-mill performance. As Marcus Buckingham, a former executive of the Gallup Organization, emphasized, "You will excel only by maximizing your strengths, never by fixing your weaknesses."

This is not to suggest that you ignore your weaknesses. After all, a major weakness is a potential cause of failure. The people styles approach to self-development encourages you to focus primarily on capitalizing on your strengths while making sure that your major weakness does not cause your performance to plummet.

In dealing with your weaknesses the challenge is to focus narrowly on *one crucial weakness*—the one that could most damage your performance. Experience has shown that when people try to root out several weaknesses at the same time, they rarely succeed at uprooting any of them. Executive coach Marshall Goldsmith notes that the leaders he works with are inclined to make two mistakes when trying to pin down the salient weakness they need to work on. First, they resist focusing on just one shortcoming. If the feedback they receive mentions seven deficiencies, many people want to tackle all seven at once. So, Goldsmith says, "My first task is to tell them, 'Don't overcommit,' and get them to believe it."

The second mistake occurs in their selection of which deficiency they should work on. Let's assume the feedback overwhelmingly indicates that the person's foremost problem is anger. "Objectively speaking," Goldsmith says, "it's a no-brainer. . . . We need to change that first. You'd think that would be obvious. What's interesting, though, is how often the people I work with try to ignore that in-your-face problem and instead [want to] tackle one of the other flaws." It is crucial to focus your corrective efforts on your most troublesome weakness.

Don't Underestimate the Effort Needed to Eliminate Your Weakness

The flaw that undermines your performance repeatedly has been with you for years and has acquired the force of habit. So, it won't be overcome easily. Social science research found that humans predictably err by underestimating what it takes to successfully change undesirable behavior. The phenomenon known as the *planning fallacy* often plagues efforts to change a dysfunctional pattern of behavior. Goldsmith notes that people generally underestimate the following:

- The time needed to overcome the weakness

- The effort required

- Distractions like unexpected problems (and opportunities) that sidetrack them from the planned improvement

- After overcoming a flaw, how much maintenance will be required to preserve the gains for the rest of their lives

So, before you commit to overcoming a weakness, make sure you've counted the cost and are committed to seeing this important project through.

Team with One or More Complementary Partners

When you make a realistic assessment of all that's entailed in overcoming a weakness, you may decide that you're not ready to take on such a difficult project. But you want to avoid the negative consequences associated with that weakness. In these circumstances, your best bet is to team up with one (or more) complementary partner(s).

A complementary partner is someone who is strong where you are weak and will supplement your efforts to achieve a goal. There are innumerable examples of complementary pairings in the business world. The founders of the Hewlett-Packard Company were undoubtedly one of the most famous business teams in recent history. As portrayed in Michael Malone's *Bill & Dave*, the two leaders had different styles. Hewlett was the more introverted of the two; Packard was more outgoing. Also, they had compensating business abilities. As Dave Packard put it, "Our abilities tended to be complementary. Bill was better trained in circuit technology, and I was better trained and more experienced in manufacturing processes. This combination of abilities was particularly useful in designing and manufacturing electronic products."

This chapter presented two central emphases of the people styles approach to self-development:

1.   Make the most of your gifts.

2.   Prevent your major weakness from doing you in.

It's a proven part of the trail to success and fulfillment.

CHAPTER 9

Backup Styles: Extreme, Inappropriate, and Inflexible Behavior

SIDNEY WALDHEIM woke up thinking about the sales meeting he'd be leading in a few hours. "Sales are down for the quarter," he mused," but everyone is trying hard. What's needed is an 'up' meeting that will be a real motivator."

While he was dressing, it was impossible not to notice the glowering silence of his wife, Alicia. She was still angry about something he did yesterday, but wouldn't discuss it. Sidney had no idea what he'd done to upset her.

Sidney was steaming inside—Alicia's silent treatment nearly always got to him. Knowing that breakfast at home would be unpleasant, he decided to skip it. Instead, he rushed to his car and barreled off to work. He tried to think about the upcoming meeting, but his mind kept careening back to Alicia's icy anger. His body tensed, and he absentmindedly pressed harder on the accelerator. About halfway to the office, he heard the siren, saw the flashing lights, and was motioned to the side of the road. The officer said he was driving 56 mph in a 35 mph zone. This traffic violation would put him in the assigned-risk category and his insurance costs would be significantly higher.

Sidney's head was throbbing when he got to the office. "What a way to start the day," he grumbled to himself. His phone rang. It was Matt, his regional sales manager. Matt tersely informed Sidney that his district had the worst performance in the region for the fourth straight month.

Matt didn't come right out and say it, but Sidney could read between the lines that he had better turn things around quickly "or else."

Talk about stress! Sidney's glands pumped adrenaline into his already-hyped-up system. His muscles were tense, his nerves were on edge, and he had a monster of a headache. He popped two Advil and stalked into the sales meeting. Stress was now dictating Sidney's behavior. He jettisoned his plan to be upbeat. Instead, he told his salespeople what a lousy job they were doing. He told them they were lazy. And he threatened, "If you don't sell more, I'll find people who will."

Back in his office, Sidney felt a bit better. He'd gotten rid of much of his stress. Where did it go? Into each of the salespeople at that meeting. Sidney dumped his load of stress all over them, and now they had to cope with that on top of all the other stresses they were already dealing with. As you can imagine, no one left the meeting with a soaring motivation to sell. Instead, some were angry, some were hurt, others were worried. But no one was pumped up to go out and sell.

When Sidney arrived home after work, he headed for the den and turned on the TV. But mainly he mentally replayed the events of the day. "They deserved it," he told himself. But he knew his behavior had cost him. As he thought about the debacle, he shook his head and muttered aloud, "I'd have been farther ahead today if I'd stayed in bed."

Sidney, an Expressive, had moved into his *backup style*. His response to the overdose of stress was predictable. So were the results—poor decisions, strained relationships, and lowered performance.

No style handles excessive stress graciously. Each has its predictable and unproductive way of reacting to too much pressure. This chapter will help you understand your own backup style, as well as the backup styles of the people you relate to. We'll define what is meant by the term *backup style* and describe the backup behavior that's typical of each people style. Then, you'll see that although backup behavior relieves some stress for the short term, it has very costly side effects and is highly contagious. Finally, we describe secondary backup—the puzzling reversal of behavior that occurs when stress is so excessive and prolonged that one's initial backup behavior doesn't provide sufficient relief.

CHARACTERISTICS OF A BACKUP STYLE

A person's backup style is an automatic reaction to an overload of stress, which results in an extreme, inappropriate, and inflexible distortion of the person's normal style-based behavior. As Sidney's experience indicates, operating from one's backup undermines a person's effectiveness and raises havoc with his relationships.

Extreme, Inappropriate, Inflexible Behavior

When a person is in backup, his style-based behaviors become *more extreme.* When Sidney became stressed-out, the highly assertive and emotive sales manager became much more assertive and more emotional than usual. In fact, backup behavior is so excessive that it's often called *out-of-the-box behavior.* Figure 9-1 shows why that label is appropriate.

People's speech and actions when in backup are *inappropriate*; what

Figure 9-1
Backup styles

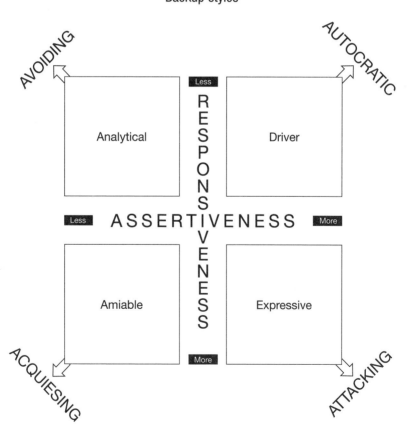

they say and do is unsuitable for the situation and ignores the needs and feelings of others.

Backup behavior is also *inflexible*. However adaptable a person may normally be, when in backup, she rigidly clings to extreme and inappropriate behavior regardless of the damage to her performance or the harm to her relationships.

A Protective Reaction Triggered by Excessive Stress

One's backup style is a protective mechanism that's set off by *excessive stress*. It's not that stress is a bad thing in and of itself. The late Hans Selye, M.D., regarded as the world's leading stress researcher, emphasized that suitable levels of stress add zest to life. On the one hand, he found that optimal levels of stress contribute enormously to one's performance. That's why athletes psych themselves up for a competition. On the other hand, Selye's research revealed that *excessive stress* erodes one's performance and causes such wear and tear on the body that it can be a major factor in all manner of diseases.

A backup style is a "quick and dirty" stress reduction mechanism that's built into each person's physical makeup. When stress becomes excessive, the person is propelled out of her normal style into her backup style. This temporarily slows the buildup of stress and may even diminish it somewhat. However, backup behavior is not the only way of moderating stress, and it's definitely not the best way. People pay a high price in negative side effects for the temporary relief that's provided by their backup behavior.

An Automatic Reaction

Like the knee-jerk response that occurs when a physician taps your knee with a hard rubber mallet, the movement into one's backup style is an automatic reaction rather than a conscious choice. So it occurs without thought or premeditation. Even when you are not aware of being overstressed, your subconscious gets the picture and propels you into backup, thereby limiting the escalation of stress.

Although the shift to one's backup style is instinctive, there's no need to let it run your life. In the next chapter, we'll outline preventive measures that will enable you to significantly decrease the amount of time you spend in backup. You'll also learn damage-control strategies—ways to limit the negative consequences that occur when you or another person are in backup.

THE FOUR BACKUP STYLES

When in backup, people push their style-based tendencies to the hilt. Figure 9-1 shows that when in backup, normal behavior tends to become more extreme:

- *Expressives* (who normally are highly assertive and emotionally demonstrative) *attack*.

- *Drivers* (who normally are highly assertive and emotionally re-strained) become *autocratic*.

- *Amiables* (who normally are less assertive and more emotive than most people) *acquiesce*.

- *Analyticals* (who are less assertive and less emotive than most people) *avoid* participation and emotional involvement.

Here's a description of each of these dysfunctional ways of communicating and how people typically react to each of them.

Expressives in Backup: Attacking

As we saw with Sidney, when these assertive and emotionally expressive people get stressed out, they become even more assertive and more emotional. They often resort to strong and abusive language, a loud, perhaps shouting voice, and vehement and possibly even belligerent gestures as they lambaste you or your point of view—or both—with criticism or sarcasm. The Expressive's backup behavior is more explosive than that of other backup styles, but compared to the others it tends to be relatively short-lived. Almost immediately after the Expressive has blown his stack, he's ready to resume normal interactions as if nothing had happened.

But something pretty dramatic and unpleasant had happened. Many people are doubly upset by the Expressive's backup mode. They disliked the hot-tempered attack on them when the Expressive was in backup. And they are turned off by the Expressive's assumption that now that he's gotten things off his chest at their expense, the relationship should proceed as if nothing amiss had happened. But rash statements that an Expressive makes in backup often rankle long after the incident is past. Few people can recover from a tongue lashing as quickly or graciously as the Expressive expects.

In defense of their backup behavior, some Expressives say, "Sure, I go on a rampage now and then. I get angry quickly, but I also get over it quickly." Other Expressives feel badly about having made exaggerated verbal attacks that hurt other people's feelings.

Drivers in Backup: Autocratic

When experiencing excessive stress, these normally strong-willed people become even more controlling. In backup they're more unbending than usual and are likely to try to impose their thoughts and plans on others. They sometimes raise their voice—or they may speak in a quiet but hard and unyielding manner.

The steely imperiousness of Drivers in backup is a turn-off for people of every style. The normally fast-paced Drivers tend to decide and act even quicker when in backup, which puts enormous pressure on the slower-paced styles. But no one likes to be on the receiving end of the "bulldozing" behavior of a Driver in backup.

In defense of their backup behavior, some Drivers say, "I may become autocratic when I'm stressed, but at least I don't 'lose it.'" Other Drivers regret that they've been so overbearing.

Amiables in Backup: Acquiescing

In periods of low stress, Amiables are quiet, friendly, and cooperative people who like to relate to others with minimal interpersonal tension. Excessive stress increases the Amiables' efforts to avoid conflict by appeasing others. In backup, Amiables go overboard in appearing cooperative and in trying to minimize interpersonal tension.

It's often difficult to know when an Amiable has moved into backup. When an Expressive is in backup, everyone within earshot knows it. When a Driver is highly stressed, people are soon aware of his highhanded ways. But an Amiable slips into backup unobtrusively. She may still be smiling and seem as agreeable as ever. Whatever you propose, you'll probably hear the Amiable say something like, "Sure, that's fine." Or a simple, "OK."

Your first clue that an Amiable is in backup is often a gut feeling that something is wrong, though you can't put your finger on the reason you feel that way. Then, if you carefully observe the Amiable's body language you'll note that there has been a subtle change. Although you may hear agreeable words, the "music"—the body language—has changed. The tone of voice, facial expression, and gestures are perfunctory and empty of commitment. These indicators typically signal that there's a lot that this Amiable isn't telling you about resentment and lack of support for your project. Although genuinely supportive under normal circumstances, Amiables in backup often respond with compliance rather than genuine cooperation and may have no intention of doing what they agree to do. When Amiables do put words to their frustration, they're apt to merely hint at it.

Although it's less obvious than with other styles, an Amiable in backup is as rigid as anyone else. Perhaps you've sensed that an Amiable is stressed out and that her reaction may be related to something that you have done. So you ask whether you've done anything that was upsetting to her. Even though it's obvious that something is wrong, the Amiable in backup will probably be very inflexible about insisting that everything is all right and there's no need to talk about the relationship.

Amiables take longer to move into backup than the more assertive styles. Once in backup, however, Amiables tend to remain in backup quite a bit longer. Though slow to anger, they are also slow to forgive and forget. There's no quick "Let bygones be bygones" for Amiables. As the poet Dryden cautioned, "Beware [of] the fury of a patient man."

Expressives and Drivers have little patience with the peace-at-any-price behavior of an Amiable in backup. Analyticals can understand the desire to avoid conflict but dislike the way the Amiable who is in backup goes about it.

In defense of their backup behavior, some Amiables say, "What's wrong with being cooperative even when I'm stressed? Rather than cause a ruckus or be overly controlling, I don't hassle other people when I'm stressed out." Other Amiables realize that all backup styles, including their own, are unpleasant for other people and regret that their backup behavior resulted in unpleasantness for others.

Analyticals in Backup: Avoiding

Analyticals are quiet, emotionally reserved people. When they experience an overload of tension, they withdraw further into themselves, withholding both their thoughts and their feelings from others. Although they may be hurt and angry, they fume inwardly, while outwardly, they can become as unresponsive as a stone. With a poker face, monotone voice, and little body movement, Analyticals either duck issues entirely or discuss them with cold, detached logic. In backup, when they are physically present with someone, they are often perceived as personally absent from the interaction.

Sometimes Analyticals in backup feel that they just can't deal with other people right now and seek refuge in being alone. They may manufacture reasons for leaving a conversation or meeting, or they may stalk angrily out of the room.

Drivers, who like to tackle things head-on, are frustrated by the Analytical's avoidance when in backup. The more feeling-oriented styles, Expressives and Amiables dislike the extreme emotional withdrawal of an Analytical in backup. As a frustrated Expressive complained, "I can deal with hate, I can deal with anger, I can deal with despair, I can deal with anybody who is feeling anything, but I can't deal with *nothing*."

In justification of their backup behavior, some Analyticals say that remaining unemotional when they're stressed is far better than making a scene. Other Analyticals realize that they're not their normal selves when in backup and regret the negative effect that their emotional withdrawal has on other people.

CONTAGIOUSNESS OF BACKUP BEHAVIOR

An especially troublesome aspect of backup behavior is that it's incredibly catching. It's bad enough when one person in a conversation is propelled into out-of-the-box behavior. But the extreme, inappropriate, and exceptionally inflexible behavior of a person in backup typically sends other people's stress soaring, too. So, when one person moves into backup, there's a high likelihood that others will soon be triggered, setting off a vicious cycle of increasingly toxic behavior that may drag all parties to the conversation into the quagmire of dysfunctional communication.

In her book, *Fierce Conversations*, Susan Scott describes her experience with this vicious cycle:

> When I'm triggered, I have two ingrained reactions, two automatic
> hardwired responses. One is to exit the conversation by clamming up

(the silent treatment). . . . The other is to make accusations and hurl blame. I'm not proud of this. It's just what every fiber of my body wants to do. Of course, the instant I am triggered, my reaction triggers everyone else in the conversation. Then they do whatever they do when they're triggered, and we quickly arrive at endgame. It's over. Not pretty. We've all seen it happen.

SECONDARY BACKUP

After people shift into backup, their tension generally decreases, and before long, they return to using their normal behavior. But occasionally, the stress continues to build and the person is catapulted into a *secondary backup style that is out-of-the-box behavior at the opposite end of the assertion continuum.*

President Nixon's experience during the Watergate crisis illustrates how people move from their normal style to their primary backup style and then, when the pressure isn't relieved, into secondary backup. The normal behavior of Nixon—a Driver—could be characterized as more assertive and less emotionally disclosing than most people's. But the stress of the Watergate investigation thrust Nixon out of his normal Driver style into his autocratic backup behavior (see Figure 9-2). For months he told people what they could and couldn't do and what he would and wouldn't do. But the external pressures kept mounting and finally propelled Nixon into his secondary backup style—avoiding. He retreated from the public eye and isolated himself from people. He refused to meet with his cabinet or even see his attorneys. Like Nixon, when anyone is in the secondary backup style, he is extremely ineffective.

KEY POINTS IN IDENTIFYING BACKUP BEHAVIOR

Most people's backup behavior follows the patterns just described. However, with backup behavior, as with everything else in the people styles model, exceptions do occur. Sometimes the exceptions are a response to one's environment. An Expressive in a corporate environment that

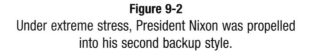

Figure 9-2
Under extreme stress, President Nixon was propelled
into his second backup style.

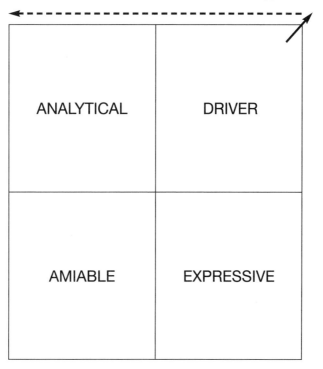

frowns on the emotional fireworks characteristic of this backup style may be less attacking than usual. A Driver told us that he grew up in a household where being autocratic was not allowed. His reaction to excess stress is to avoid.

You will probably encounter some out-of-the-box behavior in every significant relationship, as well as in many business and casual relationships. The goal of this chapter is to help you to understand the dynamics underlying backup behavior and to recognize when excess stress has catapulted you or others into backup. You probably want to know what to do about these dysfunctional interactions. The next chapter gives specific prescriptions for dealing with your own backup behavior, as well as for handling those occasions when others are in backup.

CHAPTER 10

Coping with Backup Behavior

THIS CHAPTER OFFERS practical guidance about what to do when you or someone you are with is in backup. First, we'll show how you can deal more effectively with your own backup tendencies. Then you'll learn how to cope with situations in which the person you are with is in backup.

REDUCE THE NUMBER OF TIMES YOU ARE IN BACKUP

Since people are triggered into backup by excess stress, you can decrease the likelihood of shifting into dysfunctional behavior by improving your stress management. It's much easier to avoid moving into backup than it is to cope with it once it is controlling your behavior. Although it's not within the scope of this book to teach stress management, we can remind you of two strategies for maintaining your equilibrium despite the pressures of daily life:

1. *Keep tabs on your stress level, and when it surges, find ways to reduce it.* For example, don't plan time schedules that are too tight; don't overcommit; reduce the stressors in your physical environment; improve or avoid draining relationships. We realize that these things are easier to say than to do—but they are effective in reducing your stress.

2. *Identify the kinds of events and the types of people that trigger your overreactions.* Then, when you find yourself with one of those

people or in one of those circumstances, you'll be better prepared to handle the situation. Forewarned is forearmed.

PRACTICE DAMAGE CONTROL WHEN YOU ARE IN BACKUP

Although effective stress management can help you greatly reduce the amount of time you spend in backup, it won't completely banish out-of-the-box behavior from your life. Here are four ways to contain the damage when you find yourself in backup.

Take a "Time Out" for Yourself

When a child loses self-control, parents may call a "time out," thereby creating an alone period in which the child can pull himself together. Many adults find that this is a useful strategy for themselves. When stress begins to affect their behavior negatively, they reschedule as many of the day's meetings and appointments as feasible to create a period of alone time in which they can regain their composure. We're not suggesting that it's easy for adults with days jam-packed with commitments to suddenly clear the decks for an afternoon or a day—especially during the work-week. But, when you stop to think about it, rescheduling goes on all the time in most places of business. And avoiding the negative consequences of interacting from your backup style is as compelling as most reasons for re-calendaring meetings. It would undoubtedly have been difficult for Sidney Waldheim to postpone his sales meeting at the last minute (refer back to Chapter 9). But that would have been a piece of cake compared to what it took to patch things up with his salespeople.

Calling a time-out may seem like the avoidance behavior of an Analytical in backup. However, there are fundamental differences. When in backup, an Analytical is indifferent to the negative impact this behavior may have on others. By contrast, when a person puts himself into a time-out, he's attempting to spare others from unpleasantness of his backup behavior. Furthermore, when an Analytical in backup removes herself from discussion of a topic, she generally makes no mention of completing the discussion in the future. When a person schedules a time-out for himself, he negotiates a period in a day or so—when the adrenaline will have settled down—to complete the discussion.

Decrease Your Use of Backup Behavior

There will be occasions when you are stressed out but it's just not realistic to take a time-out. In those situations, it's possible to reduce the worst manifestations of your backup behavior. In the last chapter we pointed out that *the movement into one's backup style* is an automatic reaction, not a conscious choice. However, *once you are in backup, it's possible to regain control of your behavior.* You've undoubtedly witnessed this phenomenon. One of us recently saw an Expressive manager in blatant backup with a subordinate. Suddenly, the company's president appeared on the scene. The manager instantly shifted into fairly normal behavior. If that manager could control his behavior when the president walked into the room, he could control it when only the subordinate was present. Even when greatly stressed, it is possible to exercise more self-control than most people realize. If you have to interact with someone when you are in backup, discipline yourself to reduce your use of the more off-putting aspects of your backup style.

Don't Save Your Backup Behavior for Loved Ones

Ironically, it's not uncommon for people to employ more constructive behavior at work than with the people they're closest to. They sometimes mitigate their backup behavior at work but resort to their full-blown backup tendencies in the more casual atmosphere of the home. Their assumption seems to be that family members should be more accepting than co-workers. Of course, we all need a place where we can relax and "let down our hair" a bit, and one's family often provides that haven. But that's no excuse for unleashing your worst behavior on your loved ones.

Avoid Making Decisions When in Backup

When "under the influence" of backup style, your judgment is severely impaired—and when your judgment is malfunctioning, it's no time to solve problems or make decisions. Decisions based on an abnormal pressure to avoid, acquiesce, dictate, or attack are bound to turn out poorly. Unfortunately, when people are in backup, they generally experience a much stronger than normal impulse to make decisions. This can be a very costly way of dealing with excess stress.

Obviously, decisions can't be put off forever. Rather than making poor decisions while in backup, it's usually best to do whatever it takes to get out of backup as quickly as possible. Then make your decision. If a decision is particularly pressing, it may be expedient to delegate the decision to someone who is in full control of their faculties.

PRACTICE DAMAGE CONTROL WHEN OTHERS ARE IN BACKUP

One of the most difficult interpersonal challenges we face is dealing constructively with others when they're in backup. Here's how to make the best of these difficult situations.

Expect That People Won't Always Be at Their Best

Marcus Aurelius, the Roman emperor and philosopher, wrote, "Every morning when I leave my house, I say to myself, 'Today I shall meet an impudent man, an ungrateful one, one who talks too much. Therefore do not be surprised.'" He wasn't frustrated by people not living up to his expectations because he didn't have unrealistic expectations.

Recognize When the Other Person Is in Backup

The sooner you realize that someone is in backup, the easier it is to deal with the situation. That's rarely a problem when an Expressive or Driver is in backup. There is nothing subtle or unobtrusive about their out-of-the-box behavior. But with Amiables and occasionally with Analyticals, it can be difficult to spot the sometimes subtle differences between normal and backup behavior. Here are two ways of cluing in to the fact that people of these less assertive styles are in backup:

1. The person's style-based behavior may not seem much more extreme but it has become significantly more *inflexible.*

2. The person's behavior is *getting on your nerves* (to a greater degree than usual).

Don't Get Hooked by the Other Person's Backup Behavior

As we've noted, backup behavior is highly contagious and tends to quickly trigger dysfunctional reactions in others. So, when you see that someone is in backup, immediately take steps to guard against moving into backup yourself. One way to maintain your emotional equilibrium is to *reframe* your thinking about the other person's behavior. Reframing is the discipline of looking at a situation from a different point of view.

Here's how to reframe someone else's out-of-the-box behavior. When the person you are with is in backup, *switch your attention from the unpleasantness of that person's disagreeable behavior to what is triggering that behavior—an enormous buildup of stress.* That takes considerable self-discipline—but it can be done. Remind yourself that the person's movement into rigid and frustrating behavior was an automatic response, not a conscious choice. It's a safety valve that's hardwired into her nervous system to protect her from the ravages of dangerous levels of stress. Put yourself in that person's shoes. You know how miserable it is to have so much stress that you are no longer yourself. You'll find that when you really understand what the other person is going through, much of the stress you are experiencing will dissolve.

Don't Do Business with Someone Who Is in Backup

Avoid discussing significant issues when the other person is in backup. The more crucial the transaction, the more important it is to avoid talking about it when the other person's interpersonal ability and judgment are compromised.

When Others Are in Backup, Don't Try to Talk Them out of It

There's an understandably strong tendency to ask people to stop using their backup behavior. When an Expressive is in backup, people often say, "For heaven's sake, stop shouting, will you? Let's talk this over like two rational human beings." When an Analytical in backup withdraws into his shell, people often say, "Get it off your chest." When a Driver becomes more intense and directive than usual, people are likely to say, "Relax, take it easy." When an Amiable is acquiescing, people may say, "Come on, speak up! It's obvious that something is upsetting you." These kinds of statements, which are meant to improve a tense situation, usually have the opposite effect.

We're not suggesting that you make yourself a dumping ground for other people's stressed-out behavior. Obviously, when someone is propelled into backup an inordinate number of times, the situation needs to be confronted. However, wait until the person is out of backup before dealing with the issue.

FINAL THOUGHTS ABOUT BACKUP BEHAVIOR

Backup episodes—extreme, inappropriate, and inflexible behavior—will occasionally disturb virtually all of your important relationships as well as some of your less significant ones. The understanding of backup styles that you gained in the last chapter and the methods of dealing with them that you learned in this chapter will help you manage with these difficult situations more constructively.

PART TWO

Style Flex: A Key to Improved Relationships

"You never know till you try to reach them how accessible men are; but you must approach each man by the right door."
—HENRY WARD BEECHER, *Proverbs from Plymouth Pulpit*, 1887

CHAPTER 11

The Style Flex Solution
to People Differences

YOU HAVE YOUR own ways of relating to people and accomplishing things. You've spent a lifetime developing these habits and are comfortable using them. They're now second nature to you, and for the most part they work well for you. But the people you live with and work with have their own very different ways of relating and accomplishing things. They've spent a lifetime developing those habits and are comfortable using them. Their ways of doing things have become second nature to them, and for the most part, they work well for them.

When two people of different styles live or work together, one or both must adjust. If neither adapts to the other, communication will deteriorate, cooperation will decline, the relationship will be stressed, and in work situations productivity will inevitably slump.

Sometimes the clash of styles is so destructive that one of the individuals is fired. That's what happened to Robert P. Tyler Jr., who was president and COO of Simmons Company. *BusinessWeek* reported that Tyler's boss, Grant G. Simmons Jr., was "swift to make a decision, almost to a fault," while Tyler was "deliberate almost to a fault." Tyler was fired because of what was termed the "incompatible management styles" of the executives.

Although it can be a challenge to bridge the gap between different people styles, no style is incompatible with any other style. *When people of different styles don't get along, the problem isn't incompatibility; the problem usually is inflexibility.* People of very different styles can collaborate fruitfully when one or both of them make an effort to adapt to the other.

Some years ago, Donald Peterson became president of Ford Motor Company and Red Poling became executive vice president. The automotive giant was on the brink of bankruptcy. It had just lost $2.2 billion, the largest single-year loss to that date in the history of American industry. Many analysts thought the company couldn't be turned around. Despite all the urgent actions they needed to take, Peterson and Poling set time aside to work at meshing their styles. Each had his style profiled. And each was coached on how to get in sync with the other's preferred ways of working. Having learned to synchronize their very different skills and styles, Peterson and Poling became one of the most effective leadership teams of the decade. They steered Ford clear of bankruptcy. And after six years of the Peterson-Poling collaboration, Ford's profits surpassed General Motors' for the first time in sixty-two years. The next year, Ford's profits broke all previous industry records. That's some achievement— going from the largest single-year loss to the greatest single-year profit in seven years! Although many factors contributed to Ford's phenomenal resurgence, a major contributor was the way its top executives made the most of their different working styles.

INTERPERSONAL FLEXIBILITY

Interpersonal flexibility is the ability to adapt to a wide variety of people in ways that are relatively stress-free for them. A person with high flexibility is adept at noting the way the person she's with prefers to interact. She has developed a fairly broad repertoire of behaviors that enable her to get in sync with all sorts of people. She typically manages her half of relationships in ways that are comfortable to the other person. The flexible person's approach is captured in the sentence: "I'll do what I can to make it easy for others to relate to me."

It's instructive to compare high interpersonal flexibility with its opposite. People with low interpersonal flexibility are "tone deaf" to the ways other people like to be treated. They're set in their ways and consistently rely on a narrow range of responses, regardless of their suitability to the occasion. Inflexible people are locked into responses that are characteristic of their own style, even when those behaviors turn people off and are self-defeating.

Low-flex people typically are confident that *their way is the right way*.

They're like the elderly cellist in one of William Saroyan's stories who had but one string left on his instrument. He played the same note from morning until night. His wife finally mentioned that other cellists kept moving their fingers from one position to another. The old man replied, "Of course other players keep moving their fingers. They are trying to find the right place. I have found it!" However complacent people with low flexibility may be, others soon tire of their inappropriate and often repetitive behavior. Consultant Stuart Adkins says, "My-way-not-your-way is the most tension-producing, dissatisfying, time-wasting, energy-draining, relationship-breaking, activity known to man, woman or child."

Basic Flex

There are two major components of high interpersonal flexibility. First, a flexible person treats others the way virtually everyone wants to be treated. This way of relating to others is called *basic flex* because it's so critical to constructive interactions and is recommended for *all* interpersonal communication. Basic flex involves treating people honestly, fairly, and with respect. You'll learn more about it in Chapter 15.

Style Flex

The other major aspect of interpersonal flexibility is *style flex—the temporary adjustment of a few of your behaviors to make the interaction more comfortable for the other person.* Some aspects of this definition deserve elaboration.

Adjusting Your Behavior   When it becomes clear that a relationship would work better if some changes were made, the question becomes, "*Who will make the changes*—the other person or me?" People usually assume the other person is the one who should change. So in the quest for improved relationships, people typically try to change their spouse, their kids, their parents, their peers, their manager, their reports, and others who are important to their happiness and success. As Mark Twain observed, "Nothing so needs reforming as other people's habits."

But trying to improve a relationship by reforming the other person seldom works. *The primary leverage you have for improving a relationship is your own behavior.* Things look up when you shift the emphasis from "How can I get you to change?" to "What changes will *I* make?" You can't control other people's behavior. But you can control your own. You can make a positive contribution to the relationship by getting more in sync with the other person's way of interacting. It may seem like bad news that in order to improve a relationship you'll often need to unilaterally adapt to the other person's manner of doing things. However, taking the initiative in improving the relationship will generally create three positive outcomes for you.

First, you don't have to wait for the other person to come around to your manner of doing things in order to relate effectively or function productively with that person. That could be a v-e-r-y long wait. Making a few changes in your behavior will enable you to immediately make some improvements in the relationship.

Also, your ability and willingness to adapt to the other person can help you achieve your goals. When Fred Turner began working at McDonald's fast-food headquarters, he was charged with evaluating the performance of individual restaurants in the chain. Turner's first evaluation resulted in the most thorough report ever made on a single drive-in—a single-spaced, seven-page report. But Ray Kroc, McDonald's Expressive founder, wouldn't read the highly detailed report. Rather than gripe to himself about his boss's rigidity, the young employee flexed his style. Turner, who later became chairman of the corporation, condensed the report to one page and tailored it specifically for Kroc's use. According to John Love's history of the company, the revised report had such enormous impact that it did much to define the future of the entire fast-food industry.

The third benefit of changing your behavior to improve the relationship surprises many people. When you make it easier and more comfortable for another person to work with you, that person often changes his behavior in ways that you appreciate. What starts out as a one-sided effort often winds up as a mutual contribution to improving the relationship.

The point we're making bears repeating: *Style flex involves taking the initiative for improving the relationship.* It entails unilaterally changing some aspects of your manner of doing things to make it easier and pleasanter for the other person to relate to you. It doesn't matter who the other person is—your manager, a peer, a supplier, a customer, someone who reports to you; a member of your family, or a friend—a flexible person is prepared to take the first step toward enhancing the relationship.

Adjusting Just a Few Behaviors   Once you take responsibility for managing your half of a relationship, you'll want to know how to flex your style. Here, in brief, is what to do. Begin by noting key behavioral differences between you and the other person. Then adjust a few carefully selected aspects of your body language and way of saying things to more closely match the other person's typical manner of relating and working. *Select no more than two to three types of behavior to adjust.* Experience shows that most people can't effectively make more than two or three kinds of adjustments at a time.

Clark, an Analytical, decided to flex toward his manager's Driving style in an upcoming meeting. He was aware that his own slow pace and discussion of minutiae often triggered his manager's impatience. So during this meeting Clark spoke more rapidly and kept his focus on the main points. As hoped, the meeting went more smoothly than previous meetings with his boss. Although Clark anticipated that this new approach to the meeting would be somewhat more compatible with his boss's style, he was surprised that a change of only two types of behavior would have as much impact as they did.

People are often dubious that relationships can be improved by making a mere two or three adjustments. Yet, after a two-decade-long research project on relationships, psychologists Clifford Notorius and Howard Markham concluded, "Little changes in you can lead to huge changes in the relationship."

Flexing Your Style Only at Key Times   As people learn to flex their style, some go overboard and try to flex much of the time. However, as poet Carl Sandburg pointed out in his tale about a chameleon, excessive adaptability can be hazardous to your well-being. Sandburg's fictional chameleon got along very well for a time, adjusting moment by moment to every aspect of his environment. However, one day the chameleon had to cross a Scotch tartan. It died on the plaid fabric, heroically trying to blend with all the colors at once.

Instead of contributing to rapport, chameleonlike behavior generally creates distrust and tension in others. So only flex your style when it is appropriate. Guidelines presented in the next chapter will help you to determine when to flex your style and when not to.

NOT MANIPULATION OR CONFORMITY, BUT FLEXIBILITY

People sometimes develop mistaken ideas about style flex. Some associate it with manipulation. Others equate it with conformity. There are practical, personal, and ethical differences between style flex and these problematic ways of interacting with others.

Manipulation

In training sessions, when we talk about consciously adjusting one's behavior to match the way another person likes to interact, some people get very upset. "Manipulation!" they claim in an accusatory tone. It's a serious charge.

The Random House Dictionary of the English Language says that to manipulate is "to manage or influence skillfully, especially in an unfair manner." Much manipulation is "being 'nice' to people at their expense."

Many books have been written on how to manipulate your way to success. There are at least three important reasons for not succumbing to this temptation:

1. *To manipulate others is to harm yourself.* In *Man, the Manipulator*, psychologist Everett Shostrom wrote, "Manipulation not only harms others, it is also self-defeating." He and his colleagues state that, ". . . to manipulate another is to reduce oneself to a 'thing'. . . . The manipulator devalues and thus defeats himself as a person by his manipulative action." Fritz Perls, the founder of gestalt therapy, put it this way, "I call neurotic any man who uses his potential to manipulate others instead of growing up himself."

2. *Manipulation is more likely to work against you than for you.* Although the manipulator may reap short-term gains, the long-term consequences of manipulation are generally very negative. Sooner or later, people discover the deception. When that happens, the manipulator's influence evaporates, leaving anger and suspicion in its wake. People are doubly angry; they hate being taken for a sucker as much as they dislike having someone else gain advantage at their expense. The manipulators' reputation is tarnished by his own actions. His use of devious means ultimately costs him whatever influence he once had. As the saying goes, "Time wounds all heels."

3. *Manipulation is unethical.* It's an unscrupulous attempt to con people into bypassing their higher faculties of mind and spirit. Manipulators "use" people. They treat people as objects to be exploited rather than persons to relate to. That goes against the

teachings of all the world's great religions and noblest ethical teachings.

Manipulation is a loser's game. Style flex, when used to create mutually beneficial relationships, is a winner's mode of operation.

Conformity

There are a number of reasons for not withholding your point of view when important issues are discussed. For one thing, a pattern of concealing your thoughts seldom does much for you and often does much harm, especially in long-term relationships. One of the main reasons people conceal their opinion is to get along better with others. But if you repeatedly downplay, conceal, or misrepresent your point of view to blend in with the person or group you are with, your relationships are bound to deteriorate over time. People will sense that there's no point in communicating with you because they will have no way of knowing what you really think. And many will conclude that talking with you is a waste of time because it's unlikely that you will level with them.

Then there's the problem of what to do when you are in the presence of people with conflicting opinions. You can remain silent, of course. But people will soon lose their respect for you if you repeatedly sit on the sidelines when important issues are discussed. As has often been observed, when you try to please everyone, you please no one. In the meantime, you lose just about everyone's trust.

Furthermore, when you think one thing but say or imply another, your nervous system takes a shot. Lewis Thomas, the noted physician, says, "We are biologically designed to be truthful to each other." In *Doctor Zhivago*, Boris Pasternak writes, "Your health is bound to be affected if, day after day, you say the opposite of what you feel. Our nervous system isn't just a fiction; it's a part of our physical body. It can't be forever violated with impunity."

Then too, conformity is psychologically harmful. Nathaniel Branden, a psychologist who specializes in self-esteem, says that when we behave in ways that conflict with our convictions, our self-respect plummets. Psychiatrist Erich Fromm adds, "If someone violates his moral and intellectual integrity, he weakens or even paralyzes his total personality."

Finally, when important issues are at stake, it's unethical to withhold your views. If you have something to say, and if it is an issue that can improve quality, slash time, save money, serve customers better, or give employees a fairer deal, it's your responsibility to speak out. As the saying goes, "Silence isn't always golden; sometimes it's just yellow."

Flexibility

People sometimes get the idea that style flex is just a pretentious name for conformity. They assume that it entails meekly capitulating to other people's opinions and compliantly acquiescing to their wishes.

When done well, style flex is nothing of the sort. Experts on interpersonal communication distinguish between the *content* and the *process* of an interaction. *The content of a conversation is WHAT is said*—the information that's exchanged, the proposals that are discussed, the decisions that are made. *Process refers to HOW people are communicating:* the tenor of the conversation, the intensity of body language, the amount of air time each person uses, and so forth. Style flex is a way of contributing positively to the process component of communication. *It's not about suppressing your point of view.*

When it comes to presenting your ideas, style flex entails communicating on the other person's wavelength. For example, when an Expressive flexes appropriately to an Analytical, *he tailors his approach, not his position.* Rather than dilute the content he wants to get across, he adjusts his part of the interpersonal process. He'll undoubtedly moderate his normal level of assertiveness to be more in sync with the Analytical's lower level of forcefulness. And he will probably be more factual and less emotive than usual.

This is so important, it merits repeating: Style flex is about enhancing the interpersonal process of a conversation; it is not about diluting your statements or avoiding difficult conversations. As a matter of fact, style flex is especially useful when there's a significant difference of opinion. When there's controversy about content, the last thing you want is needless stress in the process component of the interaction. By creating a less stressful interpersonal process through style flex, you can pave the way for a constructive discussion of difficult issues.

In short, it's important to distinguish between style flex and conformity. Style flex is not about pretending to agree with other people's ideas. Rather, style flex entails getting in sync with another person's manner of relating without stifling your own point of view.

The how-tos of style flex are spelled out in the next three chapters.

CHAPTER 12

Four Steps to Better Relationships

GINA ALLEN HAD a lot riding on the budget meeting with her manager, Joe Patterson. If some new items weren't approved and increases granted for others, Gina's plans for her division would be hamstrung.

Cost containment was a major priority in this year's budgeting process. Not a good year to ask for increases. However, the new expenditures Gina was proposing would pay for themselves in less than three years. After that, significant savings would be realized each year. But all of Gina's planning would be for naught unless she cleared the budgeting hurdle.

No one had ever suggested that Gina's working relationship with Patterson was smooth. Once, after a particularly tense encounter, Gina told her husband, "The interpersonal chemistry definitely is not good." Through executive development, Gina learned a more useful way of describing the problem: She saw that she and Patterson were experiencing a clash of styles. Gina is an Expressive; Patterson is an Analytical. Neither is very flexible, and their rigid ways of interacting severely hamper their relationship.

For the past four years, Gina's budget presentations to Patterson had not gone well. The more enthusiastically Gina waxed about her plans, the more disinterested Patterson became. Gina's colorful visuals received good reviews from some people, but they didn't impress Patterson one bit. Patterson's disdain was evident in his comment that he could be "persuaded by facts," but he couldn't be "swayed by flash."

Two points that were stressed in the executive development session caused Gina to take a different approach to the upcoming budget meeting. One was that *how* a proposal is presented can be as crucial to its getting a good hearing as to *what* the proposal contains. The other idea that intrigued her was this: "When a relationship isn't going well, don't do more of the same; try something different."

What Gina decided to do differently was to use her newly acquired style flex skills in the crucial budget meeting. During an executive development session, Gina had learned that when five of her colleagues filled out the People Styles Assessment Inventory on her, she profiled as an Expressive. It was obvious to Gina that Patterson is an Analytical. Therefore, Gina asked Roger, one of her associates and an Analytical like Patterson, to help her plan a more effective approach to the upcoming meeting. They settled on three things that Gina would do differently in order to have a meeting that would be more congruent with Patterson's mode of operation.

First, Gina would "open in parallel"—flex to her manager's style from the very beginning of the meeting. Instead of her usual way of trying to build rapport by telling a story or two, she would demonstrate more of a task orientation. Gina planned to keep introductory comments brief and move directly to the purpose of the meeting. It would be a serious, low-key beginning.

Next, Gina's presentation would be logical and thorough. It would be supported by a written summary and backed by a couple of detailed appendices. Roger helped Gina develop the presentation and prepare the summary and appendixes. Patterson would have all the data he could possibly want.

Gina also decided to rein herself in a bit. She planned to talk less and listen more. Instead of immediately rebutting Patterson's concerns as she usually did, Gina would encourage her boss to explain his reservations more fully. Once she fully understood Patterson's point of view, she would acknowledge points of agreement and rely on facts and logic when discussing their differences.

Gina liked the plan but was concerned about implementing it. Though she was only making three changes in the way she would interact, two of the changes were fairly encompassing, and they weren't behaviors that came easily for her. So Gina and Roger roleplayed the meeting. Roger took the part of Patterson. The first practice didn't go well, so they discussed improvements and tried again. This time they were satisfied. Gina told Roger, "I'm as ready as I'll ever be."

Gina thought she did quite well at flexing her style in the meeting with Patterson. She was aware of occasional lapses; but, by and large, she successfully implemented the plan and was pleased with the outcome. Rapport was the best it had ever been in their meetings. Patterson didn't even make cuts in the budget. Gina concluded that the behavioral changes she made to get on Patterson's wavelength would come in handy in future meetings.

Style flex worked for Gina. This is not to say that by flexing your style you will inevitably achieve your goals. That's neither possible nor desirable. If, by using a certain method, you could automatically get other people to do your bidding, their freedom as human beings would be destroyed. And the quality of decisions would plummet. When we say that style flex works, we mean that there's a high likelihood that rapport will be better and that, as a result, the two of you will achieve a better outcome.

If style flex is such a contributor to productive interactions, the obvious question is, "How do you do it?" This chapter outlines the steps of style flex.

STYLE FLEX: A FOUR-STEP PROCESS

Gina followed a four-step process for her successful budget meeting:

- Step 1: *Identify.* Gina knew her own style, and she identified Patterson as an Analytical.

- Step 2: *Plan.* Gina selected three types of behavior to change in order to get more in sync with her boss's preferred ways of doing things. She knew that it would be difficult to do some of the things she planned in the give-and-take of the meeting. So she did a couple of dry runs with an Analytical colleague.

- Step 3: *Implement.* During the meeting with Patterson, Gina made the few carefully selected changes that got her more in sync with Patterson's way of working.

- Step 4: *Evaluate.* During the interaction, Gina "took the pulse" of the meeting from time to time to see if she should make any midcourse corrections. When the meeting was over, she mentally reviewed the process and the outcome, so she could learn from the experience.

Let's take a closer look at what's involved in each of the four steps.

Step One: Identify

Style flex begins with an accurate awareness of your own style. The initial self-assessment of one's style may be faulty. In part, that's because your people style is about how you come across to other people—not what you are like inside. If you haven't received feedback on your style from others as yet, get it now, using the aids we provided in Chapter 5.

Obviously, to flex effectively, it's important to correctly identify the style of the person you'll be relating to. Chapter 13 provides guidelines for style recognition.

Step Two: Plan

Some people are turned off by the idea of planning for an upcoming conversation. Several people have told us, "It's pretty bad if you have to plan how you are going to relate to a person. It's so . . . calculated" (or words to that effect). However, everyone does some planning for communication with others. We create agendas for meetings. We know that Helen is a "morning person" so we schedule an appointment with her early in the day. As we drive to work, we sometimes mull over an important conversation that we'll have later on in the day. Whether on the giving or receiving end, most people prepare for their participation in performance reviews or other important performance discussions. And the planning we do often pays off in more productive conversations.

We plan our nonwork interactions, too—even the most intimate ones. Before proposing marriage, many people spend considerable time thinking about where they'll propose and what they'll say. When angry words are exchanged before leaving for work, people are well advised to think about what they'll say and do to get the relationship back on track when they return home.

In the planning step of style flex, you simply incorporate your knowledge of people styles into the planning you'll be doing anyway to enhance important interactions. With experience, you'll often be able to do the style flex planning in your head, on the spur of the moment, while you're talking with the person. At the beginning, though, or when the stakes are especially high, or when an interaction is apt to be quite stressful, it's advisable to do the planning before the conversation begins.

To help you plan better, we've created an appendix for your style that provides specific suggestions about what to do when flexing to each of the people styles. If you are:

- An *Amiable*, turn to Appendix I, p. 155.

- A *Driver*, turn to Appendix II, p. 169.

- An *Expressive*, turn to Appendix III, p. 187.

- An *Analytical*, turn to Appendix IV, p. 202.

When you finish reading this chapter, you may want to take a few minutes to familiarize yourself with this invaluable resource.

As noted in the last chapter, style flex deals with the *process* of an interaction. In addition to the process aspects of the interaction, you'll have a more effective conversation if you think ahead about how to approach the *content* that will be discussed.

Step Three: Implement

In this step, you will be interacting with the other person, usually face to face, but sometimes on the phone or in writing. As you relate to the person, flex your style in the two or three ways that you believe will improve the transaction.

Step Four: Evaluate

Two types of evaluation are presented here to help you continually improve your ability to flex your style.

Monitoring   During a conversation, do an occasional mental check to see if your behavior is having a positive impact on the interaction. Is it helping the other person work more comfortably with you? If not, you can make on-the-spot adaptations to improve the situation.

After-the-Conversation Critiquing   From time to time, and especially after important conversations, take a moment to evaluate how effectively you communicated.

First, note what *went well*:

- What specifically did you do that the other person responded to positively?

- Which of your changed behaviors seemed to have the most impact?

- Is this something you want to do more often with this person?

- Is this something you'd want to consider doing with others of this style?

Next, focus on what, if anything, you did that hampered the conversation:

- What specifically did you do that triggered tension in the other person?

- Was the problem due to:
  - Misidentification of the person's style?
  - Poor planning?
  - Ineffective implementation?
  - Behaviors unrelated to people styles?

Finally, look at *the results* of the interaction:

- Given the content discussed, was the person more at ease than normal?

- Was the interaction:
  - More productive than usual?
  - About the same as usual?
  - Less productive than usual?

The evaluation step helps you improve your ability to flex your style. It also will enrich your understanding of each of the four styles. When people first learn this model, they often develop a simplistic idea of each style. A more realistic understanding of how the styles play themselves out in daily life comes from practicing style flex and learning about people styles from each experience. As you mull over the ways the other person behaved when you were meeting, you gain a richness of understanding that can't be obtained any other way.

WHEN TO FLEX YOUR STYLE

Here are some guidelines.

Not All the Time

We've seen that style flex is the *temporary* adjustment of a few behaviors. When a person overdoes style flex, it often backfires. When someone is "trying too hard" in a relationship, they're likely to raise rather than reduce the other person's tension. The remainder of the chapter notes the types of situations that are likely to be enhanced by style flex.

Open in Parallel

As its name suggests, opening in parallel entails flexing your style at the beginning of a conversation. Getting in sync with the other person's way of relating at the outset can enhance the whole conversation. Psychiatrist Leonard Zunin, in his book *Contact: The First Four Minutes,* points out that there's a sense in which people "restart" their relationship every time they meet. A key to enhancing your relationships is to make each fresh start a positive one. Furthermore, to a large extent, the beginning of a conversation sets the tone for the rest of it. Sociologist Erving Goffman's research demonstrated that *shortly after a conversation has begun it's possible to predict with considerable accuracy how effective it will be.* That's why opening in parallel is one of the prime uses of style flex. This is not to suggest that you open in parallel all of the time. However, you can make the most of many conversations by getting in step with the other person at the outset.

Just-in-Time Flex

It's often a good plan to open in parallel and then, after a few minutes, relax your efforts. Keep monitoring the interaction, though, and if the other person's tension begins to increase, resume flexing your style. Then ease into your natural conversational mode after a few more minutes. A manager we worked with calls this "just-in-time flex."

When an Important Matter Is Being Discussed

Your style has a major impact on your communication. In fact, each people style is, in part, a communication style. Our experiences in interviewing the bosses and colleagues of executive counseling clients revealed that a person's manner of communicating is an even more significant concern than we had realized. If, when making a point, you don't flex toward the other person's style, you'll often be less persuasive than if you communicate on his wavelength.

When the Other Person Is Experiencing Considerable Stress

If you note signs of greater-than-normal stress in a person you're with, use style flex to avoid generating additional tension. To the degree the problem is style-based friction, your adjustments should correct the situation. Even when the stress is related to different points of view or to matters totally unrelated to you, flexing your style should contribute to a better interaction.

When the Person You Are with Is Especially Rigid

Some people are especially set in their ways. If you're working with an unusually rigid person, you'll often need to flex more than usual in order to have a productive process and a positive outcome. By contrast, when the person you are dealing with is highly flexible, you won't have to put as much effort into flexing your style. Of course, you'll want to do your part in promoting good communication, but you won't have to work as hard at it since the other person is doing much to bridge the interpersonal gap. Some of the most enjoyable communication occurs when two highly flexible people unconsciously make subtle adjustments that keep them in tune with each another.

CHAPTER 13

How to Identify Someone's Style

SHERLOCK HOLMES WAS famous for his powers of observation. In one rather typical case, after just a few minutes with his client, the fictional detective noted much that was missed by his companion, Dr. Watson. With feigned modesty the famous sleuth said, "Beyond the obvious facts that he has at some time done manual labor, that he is a Freemason, that he has been in China, and that he has done a considerable amount of writing lately, I can deduce nothing."

Watson was astonished. None of these facts had been communicated verbally. How was it possible for his detective friend to perceive these things?

Holmes reeled off the observations that led to his conclusions. The client's right hand was a size larger than his left. That suggested he once had done manual labor. The particular kind of breast pin he wore indicated that the client was a Freemason. The tattoo of a fish on the right wrist was of a type done only in China. Another clue suggesting a stay in that country was a Chinese coin dangling from the client's watch chain. There was a large shiny patch on the man's right cuff as well as a smooth patch on the left elbow where it probably rested on the desk as he wrote.

On another of the many occasions when Dr. Watson didn't grasp the significance of what was right before his eyes, Holmes told his companion, "You see but you do not observe." Holmes was underscoring the fact that observation entails more than merely looking at something. It is a disciplined search for relevant clues that can reveal information that others who are viewing the same situation are likely to overlook. Or, if they do happen to notice the object or behavior, they're not likely to comprehend its significance.

This chapter on style identification will help you sharpen your powers of observation in ways that will help you understand your colleagues and friends better. You will learn to separate the *observation of behavior* from *making inferences about the behavior.* Then you'll discover the types of behavior to pay attention to when identifying another person's style, how to fine-tune your assessment of the person's style, and how to verify the accuracy of your assessment. The chapter closes with further tips for improving your ability to identify someone's style.

SEPARATE OBSERVING FROM INFERRING

Style identification is based on the observation of behavior. As described in Chapter 2, *behavior is what a person does that can be seen and heard and therefore is observable.* Behavior includes posture, gestures, facial expressions, the actions we take, and so forth. Behaviors are observable: They're on the outside of a person for all the world to see and hear.

There are many inner qualities that lie beneath the behavioral surface: thoughts, feelings, attitudes, motives, beliefs, values. *These inner qualities cannot be observed.* No one can know for sure what's taking place in someone else's inner world. We can only infer—guess at—what someone else is thinking or feeling.

As you read about the distinction between *observing* behavior and *making inferences,* the difference probably seems very clear and perhaps elementary. However, *when asked to observe and describe behavior, people often report their inferences.* In our workshops, for example, before defining and giving examples of the distinction between observation and inference, a trainer often explains that he will do some *behaviors* and afterward will ask the participants to describe the behaviors they observe. The trainer will then take some action such as stomping across the room while shouting and shaking a fist. When asked what behaviors they observed, most people tell the trainer, "You were angry." *Without realizing it, they stated their inferences* (he was angry) *instead of reporting the trainer's behaviors* (stomping across the room, shouting, and shaking a fist).

When it comes to identifying a person's style, discipline yourself to focus strictly on behavior—on what the person says or does. Avoid the tendency to jump from observation of behavior to conclusions about the person's thoughts or feelings.

NOTE THE PERSON'S DEGREE OF ASSERTIVENESS AND RESPONSIVENESS

All observation is selective. We have too much sensory data coming at us at one time to process all of it. Difficult as it is to believe, communication researchers estimate that a person is bombarded with about ten thousand sensory perceptions a second. As a result, there's more data in any interpersonal situation than you can possibly attend to.

In response to this deluge of data, your mind selects some stimuli to pay attention to and ignores the rest. When a sensory impression registers, it's because you've focused on it rather than on other data coming at you at the same time. Consequently, all human perception is selective perception.

Style identification takes advantage of this natural process of selective perception. When trying to identify someone's style, you are on the lookout for certain types of clues. Since style is determined by a person's level of assertiveness and responsiveness, you concentrate on clues related to those key dimensions of behavior.

Degree of Assertiveness

Seven types of behavior, noted in Figure 13-1, are especially useful indicators of a person's level of assertiveness.

Seven categories of behavior may seem like a lot to remember when you first practice style recognition. Fortunately, *assertion is a syndrome*—a collection of behavioral characteristics that typically cluster together. Thus, if you observe a person exhibiting several characteristics of greater-than-average assertiveness, there's a good likelihood that the person often exhibits additional indicators of higher-than-average assertiveness.

Here's another way to identify whether a person is in the more or less assertive part of the population. Focus on three pairs of words: *more/less, faster/slower, louder/softer*. The more assertive styles (Drivers and Expressives) speak *more*, gesture *more*, and demonstrate *more* energy than most people. They talk *faster* and move *faster* than half the population. They speak *louder*.

The less assertive styles (Amiables and Analyticals) demonstrate *less* energy and *less* movement, and they tend to speak *less* than the average

Figure 13-1
Behavioral indicators that are useful for identifying a
person's degree of assertiveness.

Indicators of Assertiveness

	Less Assertive	More Assertive
Amount of talking	LESS	MORE
Rate of speaking	SLOWER	FASTER
Voice volume	SOFTER	LOUDER
Body movement	LESS, SLOWER	MORE, FASTER
Energy expressed	LESS	MORE
Posture	LEANS BACK	LEANS FORWARD
Forcefulness of gestures	LESS	MORE

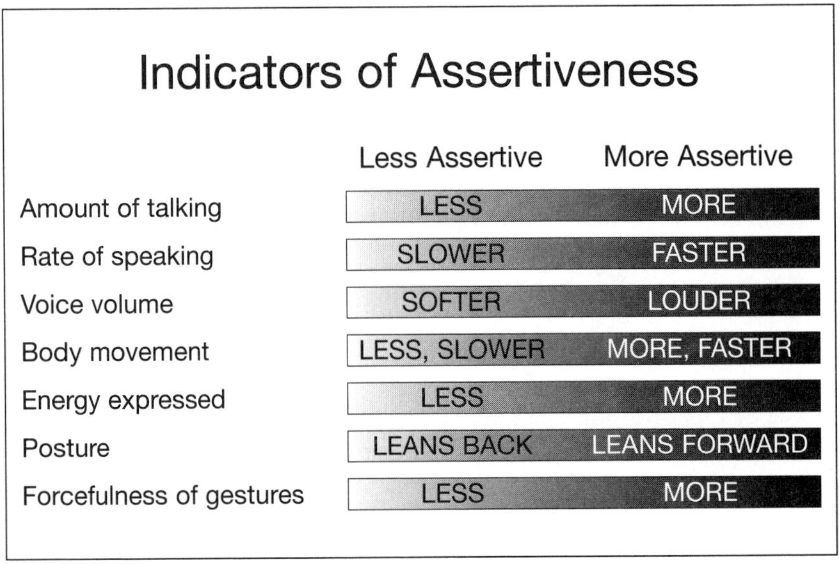

person. They are somewhat *slower* moving and they talk *slower*. Their voices are usually *quieter*. In brief:

Less Assertive Styles	*More Assertive Styles*
Less	More
Slower	Faster
Quieter	Louder

Degree of Responsiveness

Once you've gauged a person's degree of assertiveness, you'll want to estimate his degree of responsiveness. In other words, does the person show more or less emotion, and is he more responsive to other people's emotions than half of the population?

The feelings of more-responsive people (Amiables and Expressives) are quite transparent. These emotionally demonstrative people have *more* facial animation and *more* vocal inflection than most people. Their gestures and posture tend to be *more* flowing than average. And they tend to be *more* aware of other people's feelings than half of the population.

The less-responsive styles (Analyticals and Drivers) are less emotionally disclosing than half of the population. It's often difficult to "read" what they are feeling. As the saying goes, they have "a stiff upper lip." They have *less* facial animation and *less* vocal inflection than most people. They gesture *less* and their gestures and posture tend to be *less* flowing than average. Furthermore, they tend to be *less* aware of other people's feelings than half of the population.

The answers to three questions will help you identify a person's level of responsiveness.

	Less Responsive Styles	*More Responsive Styles*
How much facial animation?	Less	More
How much vocal variation?	Less	More
How flowing are the gestures?	Less	More

When you've determined someone's level of assertiveness and level of responsiveness, you can make a tentative identification of her style (see Figure 13-2).

VERIFY BY CHECKING AGAINST THE DESCRIPTION OF THAT STYLE

Once you've made a tentative identification of a person's style, you can review the "portrait" of that style in Chapter 6 (for a Driver or an Expressive) or Chapter 7 (for an Amiable or an Analytical).

FINE-TUNE YOUR ASSESSMENT

So far, we've talked about determining which half of the assertiveness continuum and the responsiveness continuum represents a person's typi-

Figure 13-2
A people styles grid for use when making a tentative identification of someone's style.

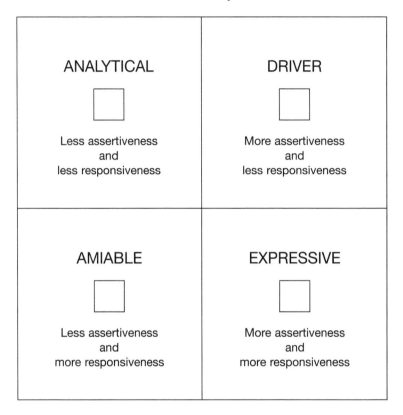

cal behavior. However, there are recognizable differences in assertiveness and responsiveness within each style. Thus, it's often possible to determine which *quarter* of each continuum is representative of a person's typical behavior. That enables you to place that person in a *subquadrant* of their people style. When you are able to fine-tune style identification this much, you can do an even better job of planning the specifics of flexing your style.

To determine a person's subquadrant, figure out whether the person is more or less assertive than half of the population:

- If the person is in the *more assertive half,* ask yourself if she is more or less assertive than *75 percent* of the population.

- If the person is less assertive than half, ask yourself if this person is more or less assertive than *25 percent* of the population.

Next, assess whether the person is more or less responsive than half of the population:

- If the person is in the *more-responsive half,* ask yourself if she is more or less responsive than *75 percent* of the population.

- If the person is in the *less-responsive half,* ask yourself if she is more or less assertive than *25 percent* of the population.

You now have all the information you need to determine someone's subquadrant.

In Figure 13-3, there is a miniature grid inside of each quadrant, thereby creating sixteen subquadrants. Each subquadrant has a two-word name such as Analytical DRIVER. The *second word* designates the person's *quadrant*—in this case, the *driver* quadrant. That's the most important information, so *we print the quadrant name in capital letters.* The first of the paired words identifies the subsection of that quadrant and is written in capital and lowercase letters—in this example, the Analytical subquadrant.

Although it can be useful to know which subquadrant you are in and which subquadrant the other person is in, much of the time that level of specificity isn't necessary. We are repeatedly impressed by how helpful the broad categories of "left of the line" or "right of the line" and "above the line" or "below the line" are in helping us understand others.

TIPS FOR IMPROVED STYLE IDENTIFICATION

Thus far, we've described the basic steps of style identification. Here are a few additional tips that can enhance your style recognition skills.

Let the Other Person Take the Lead

Although a person's style is apparent in most situations, it's likely to be most clearly manifested when he takes the lead in the conversation. If you

Figure 13-3
The sixteen subquadrants.

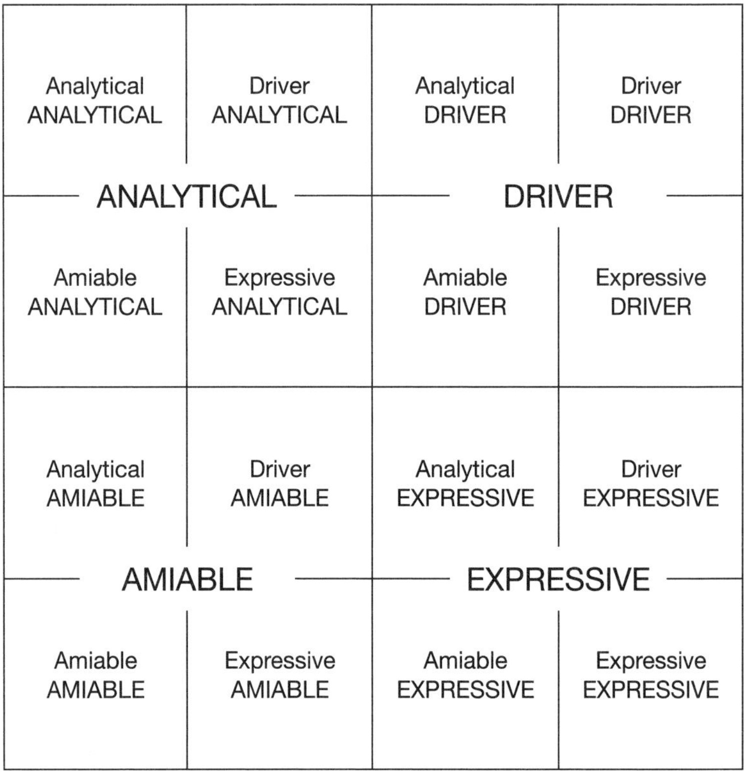

Analytical ANALYTICAL	Driver ANALYTICAL	Analytical DRIVER	Driver DRIVER
—— ANALYTICAL ——		—— DRIVER ——	
Amiable ANALYTICAL	Expressive ANALYTICAL	Amiable DRIVER	Expressive DRIVER
Analytical AMIABLE	Driver AMIABLE	Analytical EXPRESSIVE	Driver EXPRESSIVE
—— AMIABLE ——		—— EXPRESSIVE ——	
Amiable AMIABLE	Expressive AMIABLE	Amiable EXPRESSIVE	Expressive EXPRESSIVE

come across too strongly with your own style-based behavior, the other person may respond more to your manner of relating rather than behave in ways characteristic of his style. So, when trying to identify someone's style, temporarily take a back seat in the conversation.

Pay Attention to Body Language

Since people styles is a behavioral model, the best clues for identifying someone's style are nonverbal. Regrettably, there's a strong tendency in our society for people to overlook body language clues. To become proficient at style recognition, train yourself to be more observant of people's gestures, posture, facial expression, rapidity and loudness or softness of voice, and so forth.

Don't Be Misled by Style Labels

As we saw in Chapter 5, style labels can facilitate understanding and are often essential for communicating about styles. But the labels can also lead to misunderstandings. For instance, when the word *Driver* is used, people may conjure up visions of a tyrant with whip in hand—even though some Drivers excel at empowering others. Also, one of the most frequent mistakes in style identification comes from assuming a person is a Driver when, in reality, she is an Expressive. One reason so many Expressives are misidentified as Drivers is that to many people, the word *Expressive* doesn't convey the high level of assertiveness that's characteristic of this style, while the word *Driver* seems to impart that meaning. Some people think that all highly assertive people are Drivers, whereas half of the people in the more assertive part of the population are Expressives. So don't let the names of the styles skew your identification of a person's style.

Treat Your Initial Identification as a Working Hypothesis

Don't be overconfident about your initial perception of someone's style. Continue to take in new information about the person's assertiveness and responsiveness. Check your hypothesis against specific clues about the style you think the person may be (Chapters 6 and 7).

Then test your hypothesis in action by flexing to your assessment of that person's style. If flexing your style makes it easier for the other person to relate to you, you've made a reasonably accurate assessment of the person's style. If style flex doesn't improve the interaction, you may have misdiagnosed the person's style. Keep observing and experimenting, and you'll undoubtedly figure out what you can do to make it easier for that person to relate to you.

Recognize That Knowing Styles Is Just a Starting Point

Knowledge of styles is the *beginning* of wisdom about a person. We are constantly amazed at how much the people styles concept has helped us better understand, relate to, live with, sell to, and work with people.

When a person's style is accurately identified, it provides a surprising amount of useful information about constructive ways of relating to him. Nevertheless, it's important to remember that style only pertains to certain aspects of a person's life. Each of us is far more than our style. Thus, while the identification of a person's style sheds light on many important characteristics of that person, it is just one useful step of what can be a long and exciting journey of understanding and appreciation of another person.

CHAPTER 14

Flexing in Special Situations

FLEXIBILITY INVOLVES adjusting your behavior to meet the demands of a situation. Other people's styles are important variables but not necessarily the only variables to be considered. Participants in our workshops often want to know how to deal with style issues when other factors complicate the situation. In this chapter, we'll respond to six of the questions most frequently asked about flexing one's style:

1. How do I flex to my manager?

2. How do I flex to someone who reports to me?

3. How do I flex to a group?

4. What if the other person's style preferences are different from what's needed to do the task?

5. What if I can't figure out the other person's style?

6. What if I want to improve the relationship with someone whose style is the same as mine?

FLEXING TO YOUR MANAGER

People sometimes wonder how to flex their style in meetings with their manager, since the stakes are generally higher in that relationship than in most others at work. There's more to lose if you try something and it doesn't work. However, it's unwise to ignore the way people styles affect this important relationship. Since your manager is one of the most crucial people in your work life, it makes sense to build a more effective work relationship by getting in sync with the way he prefers to work.

Figuring out how to flex to your manager is pretty simple. First, locate your manager and yourself on a style map. That can give you some basic ideas about how to flex to him or her. Then, further customize your flex by observing some of your manager's strongest preferences. What types of employee behavior seem most pleasing to your manager? What type of behavior seems especially frustrating?

Make the most of times when it is appropriate to discuss how your manager would like you to work with him. It could be during a periodic progress review or a performance appraisal, at the beginning of a project, or at a time when you are given new responsibilities. At times like these, ask your manager, "How would you like me to work with you?" If you're not getting clear-cut suggestions, ask questions like: "How often do you want me to fill you in on what I am doing?" "Would you prefer a detailed analysis, a brief summary with recommendations, or some other approach?" It often helps to use examples. "In my last report, did I give too much or too little information?" "Do you have any suggestions about how I could present information like this in a way that would be more useful to you?"

FLEXING TO THE PEOPLE YOU MANAGE

Some managers are surprised at the suggestion that they try to get more in sync with their employees' ways of working. But it's an unusually good way of improving your employees' effectiveness and consequently your own productivity.

Most applications of the people styles concept to those who report to you are so straightforward as to require no comment. However, two things are worth emphasizing. First, whenever possible, *give people the freedom to do things their way.* It's common practice to try to change people's fundamental way of doing things. According to Graig Nettles, that's what the New York Yankees' coaching staff did to his teammate, pitcher Tommy John. "They tried to turn him into a power pitcher rather than a player who won with finesse. Here's a guy who's been getting by on what he's been doing for fifteen years, and they want to change him." Tommy John finally said he wanted out and was traded to California. Nettles concluded, "Tommy is as good a pitcher as he's ever been. He should still be pitching for the Yankees. It was stupid, all the way around."

You'll never get peak performance from your associates if you expect them to do everything the way you'd do it. An Expressive sales manager kept trying to get all his people to behave like Expressives on their calls. He finally backed off when an Amiable on his team, who couldn't do things the manager's way, was the company's highest producer year after year. Savvy managers encourage their people to use their own style and capitalize on their natural strengths, rather than attempt to make them into pale imitations of themselves.

Second, when appropriate, *use style flex in team meetings.* In the next section we describe how to do that.

FLEXING TO A GROUP

Much of your time at work is probably spent in meetings. People often ask, "How can I flex my style in a meeting where people of several styles are interacting with one another?"

When flexing to a group, follow the same four steps you would use when flexing to an individual: (1) identify, (2) plan, (3) implement, and (4) evaluate. Begin by identifying the style of each person in the group. Drawing a style map and locating group members on it will help you with the planning. Once you've identified the members' styles and you've planned how to flex to the group, you implement the plan and then evaluate both the process and the results.

Al Lewis headed the information systems department of a large manufacturing corporation. Here's how he used style flex to improve the performance of his management team.

Al contacted us because of his frustration at not being able to get the managers he supervised to contribute many ideas at their weekly meetings. It was at these meetings that problems were noted, decisions made, and action plans designed. It seemed to Al that he did all the thinking, contributing, and problem solving. No one else seemed willing to jump in with their reactions or their ideas, or even present their problems.

Other team members confirmed that this was an accurate picture of the situation. Al wanted a team-building session that would generate more participation in these meetings.

Together, we designed a team meeting based on the four steps of style flex. Step 1 is to identify. Since Al knew the people styles concept, he identified the style of each team member and located each person on a grid. He then proceeded to Step 2: planning. Al decided to flex only on the assertiveness dimension in his team meetings (as shown in Figure 14-1). He chose to make four changes:

1. Stop being the first person to give his ideas (as had been his custom).

2. Decrease his own participation by speaking only every third time he wanted to say something.

3. Use listening skills to draw out the ideas of others.

4. Decrease the number of items on the agenda so there would be more time to discuss each item. The greater amount of time might be necessary not only to allow for more discussion, but also to slow the pace of the discussion to better match the slower pace of his less assertive team members.

Al also planned to have a process observer at several team meetings. The process observer would monitor two team meetings before changes were made to establish a baseline. This person would serve as observer in several consecutive meetings where efforts would be made to increase participation.

Step 3, implementation, was the tough one. Although Al was trying to modify only a few behaviors, he was going against the grain of his Expressive EXPRESSIVE style. With great effort, he managed to refrain from speaking first throughout the meeting. He also talked only one-third as much as previously, and he used reflective listening skills from time to time. Al was amazed at how stressful this was for him and how tired he was at the end of the meeting.

Step 4, evaluation, occurred at the end of the team's meeting and was led by the process observer. She reported that Al had generally done what he said he would. But there was almost no increase in other people's participation. The meeting consisted primarily of long, awkward silences. All members agreed that it was a terrible meeting. Al hoped, however, that it was one of those situations where behavioral changes tend to make outcomes worse before they improve.

Figure 14-1
Styles grid of Al's team.

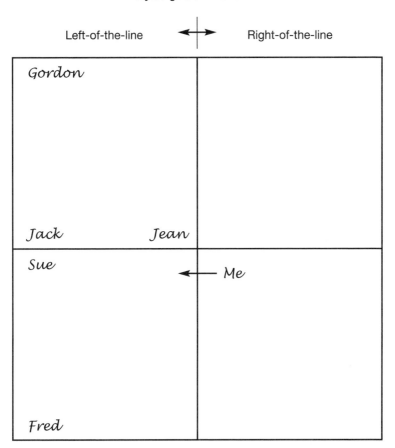

At Al's urging, the team decided to continue the experiment for four more sessions. One of the first signs that Al's participative efforts were paying off was when one team member said, "Al has done his part; now it's up to us to make some changes." Each member of the team committed to one or two behavioral changes in the next meeting. These were written on an easel pad and pages were taped to the wall in several subsequent meetings. By the fourth meeting, the group had hit its stride, and there was no turning back. The process observer estimated that the amount of team participation increased by more than 70 percent, and Al reported that the commitment to implement team decisions improved significantly.

About five years later, Al told us, "It was a bit of a struggle at the time, but that effort to use style flex in team meetings had tremendous payoff. Our department has grown rapidly in the past several years. Our new mode of operation helped us manage the changes, and it readied team members for the many opportunities for promotion which resulted from that growth."

FLEXING TO A PERSON AND TO A TASK

Sometimes what's called for in flexing to another person undercuts your effectiveness in doing the task that the two of you are working on. Here are some guidelines we've found helpful when the requirements of the task are very different from what's called for in flexing to your co-worker.

First, build rapport by flexing to the person. To the degree possible, avoid using behaviors that might be detrimental to achieving the task when flexing to the person. Once rapport is established, flex to the task. Alternate between flexing to the person and flexing to the task as needed.

Here's an example. Shelly, an Amiable, was assigned to a project with Tony, an Expressive. They had worked together on two previous projects, and on both occasions had gotten on each other's nerves. After learning about people styles, Shelly saw that much of the problem was due to their very different ways of working. This time, she planned to create a better relationship by flexing to Tony's Expressive style.

The project they were to work on entailed meticulous examination of a large amount of information on customer purchasing trends. Detailed work with data seldom is a strong suit of Amiables (Shelly's style), but of all the styles, the Expressive (Tony's style) is least suited for it, so Shelly thought she was in a double bind. On the one hand, she was afraid that if she got in sync with her Expressive co-worker, the project would flounder. On the other hand, she feared if she became as detail-oriented as the job required, a key working relationship could be further damaged.

Here's what Shelly did to complete the project successfully while improving her relationship with Tony. When they worked together, Shelly "opened in parallel." She was determined to flex to those behaviors of her co-worker that could be an asset or at least have a neutral impact on doing this particular task. She decided that in flexing to Tony she would step up her pace by speaking and moving faster. She avoided joining

Tony's tendency to focus mainly on the big picture while giving only scant attention to details. Although that characteristic could be valuable in some situations, it would be very detrimental to this project.

Once rapport with Tony was established, Shelly flexed to the task. She was aware that they needed to have a good system for analyzing the extensive data. Since this wasn't a strong point for either Shelly or Tony, she suggested they ask an Analytical teammate to join them. When the system was in place, Shelly and Tony had to spend days at the repetitive and detailed work of inputting each customer's data. Predictably, Tony soon got bored with the work.

When Tony began to get bogged down from the monotony of the task, Shelly would once again flex to her co-worker. In addition to increasing the assertiveness of her posture and gestures and stepping up the pace at which she spoke and worked, Shelly found ways to get in sync with Tony's fun-loving side. She told a few jokes—a stretch for her—and found other ways to make the work more fun. Since this was not her customary behavior and was therefore taxing for her, she tapered off those efforts as Tony again became more comfortable with her and with his work on the project. Throughout their work together, Shelly monitored both Tony's mood and their working relationship. When either condition needed attention, she flexed to his style. Otherwise, she concentrated primarily on working with the data (see Figure 14-2).

It took a lot of Shelly's energy to flex back and forth between her co-worker and the project. But Shelly thought the results justified the effort. The project was a solid success, and the relationship was stronger than ever. As Shelly put it, "This project was far better than the other two in which Tony and I got so stressed out with each other." Shelly found that over time she became more adept at flexing to Tony; on later projects, it took much less effort on her part to flex her style. Also, as the relationship became increasingly congenial, Tony accommodated more to Shelly's way of doing things.

WHEN YOU CAN'T IDENTIFY A PERSON'S STYLE

There may be times when you want to flex to another person but are having trouble identifying the person's style. How do you proceed?

Even if you can't figure out a person's style, you may be able to peg

Figure 14-2

What's needed to flex to a task may be very different from what is called for when flexing to the person you are working with.

his or her location on *one* of the two key dimensions of style-based behavior: assertiveness or responsiveness. Miguel, an Amiable, wanted to flex to Krystal, a co-worker, but he couldn't determine her style. However, it was clear to him that she was more assertive than he. That told him a lot about what he could do to get more in sync with her. He could pick up the pace a bit, state his opinions more directly, or use some other type of behavior that would help him temporarily increase his assertiveness.

Sometimes when you can't recognize a person's style, he or she is located in one of the four central subquadrants of the grid. If you are in one of the central subquadrants yourself, there's probably no need to flex your style to someone located that near to you on the grid. If you are in one of the outer subquadrants, flex toward the middle of the grid.

Here are some other ways to flex when you're not sure of a person's style:

- If you are in one of the outer subquadrants, tone down some of your extreme behaviors. If you are in one of the corner subquadrants this can be especially important.

- If you see that the other person is becoming stressed, make a guess as to what behaviors triggered the stress and modify those behaviors for a while.

- If (1) the relationship is especially strained and (2) you've been unsuccessful in several other attempts to work more constructively with the person, consider doing the opposite of what you normally would do. Thus, if you are typically quiet and unassuming, you might temporarily become more assertive. If you're highly assertive, you might ease off a bit and listen more. If you are quick to express your feelings, moderate your expression of feelings somewhat. Or if you tend to keep your feelings to yourself, let them out a bit more.

RELATING TO A PERSON WHOSE STYLE IS THE SAME AS YOURS

Throughout this book we've shown that style-based differences often trigger interpersonal tension. The similarities between you and a person of the same style can also become a source of friction, if they're not handled well.

For example, when there's a style-based clash between two Drivers, it's usually because they're both bringing high levels of assertiveness to the interaction. The solution is for one person to listen more, to speak more provisionally, and to be a bit less directive than usual.

When there's a style-based clash between two Expressives, a similar way out is often appropriate. When there's too much assertiveness in an interaction, one person needs to listen more, speak more provisionally, and moderate her directness. More than any style, Expressives love the limelight. If the conflict is about who will take center stage, one of the parties may have to be temporarily more self-effacing.

When Amiables get frustrated with each other, it may be that each is waiting for the other to give his ideas. If neither person is contributing a sense of direction, there's apt to be no progress, no goal achievement, no sense of accomplishment. The solution is for one person to exert more leadership—provide more goal orientation, more of an action focus, and more decisiveness.

When Analyticals irritate one another, the reason may be that they are so indecisive or so perfectionistic that they miss one important deadline after another. As the organization pressures them for completion, they may aggravate each other more and more. The solution is for at least one of them to be more decisive and more pragmatic about the quality that's needed. Another problem that Analyticals can have with one another is that, even more than people of other styles, these people have a need to be right. When that's the issue, it helps to listen better, speak more provisionally, and try to create a mutual outlook on what's being discussed.

A general guideline for what to do when you are in a style clash with a person of your own style is to moderate your behavior toward the opposite corner of the grid:

- *Driver*: Flex toward the Amiable quadrant

- *Expressive*: Flex toward the Analytical quadrant

- *Amiable*: Flex toward the Driver quadrant

- *Analytical*: Flex toward the Expressive quadrant

This chapter has shown how to apply style flex to special situations and to certain types of relationships. As you integrate the people styles approach into your life, you'll undoubtedly see important applications to such work activities as goal setting, performance appraisals, delegation, coaching, planning, time management, and so forth. We've found that the people styles concept helps us find ways to improve many facets of our work life. We'll discuss applications to family life in Part Three.

CHAPTER 15

Three Keys to Good Relationships

WE HAD BEEN TEACHING style flex for several years, and follow-up evaluations six months later had indicated that using style flex helped most people make significant improvements in their relationships. Some told us about breakthroughs they'd made in difficult work relationships. Others described the positive contribution that style flex has made in relationships with their spouse and children.

However, we found that some people who used style flex were not successful in improving their relationships. When we investigated these situations, it became obvious that, by itself, style flex is not sufficient for enhancing relationships. To be optimally effective, style flex must be undergirded by a "Do unto others as you would have them do unto you" orientation.

THE UNIVERSALITY OF THE GOLDEN RULE

The Golden Rule integrates much of society's wisdom about human behavior. For example, Hillel, a renowned Jewish scholar of the first century of the Common Era, addressed a major problem facing his people. At that time, pious Jews were expected to live up to 613 commandments—365 negative and 248 positive. It was impossible for most people to remember all the laws, let alone follow them. Hillel's ingenious solution was to sum up all the commandments in a single guideline:

Do not unto thy neighbor what is hateful unto thee; that is the whole law. All the rest is commentary.

This principle of human conduct, often referred to as the Golden Rule, is found in the scriptures of each of the major world religions:

- *Buddhism.* Hurt not others in ways that you yourself would find hurtful—*Udana-Varga*, 5, 18

- *Brahmanism.* This is the sum of duty: Do naught unto others which would cause you pain if done to you.—*Mahabharata*, 5, 1517

- *Christianity.* So in everything, do to others what you would have them do to you, for this sums up the Law and the Prophets.—Matthew 7:12 and Luke 6:31

- *Confucianism.* Surely it is the maxim of loving-kindness: Do not unto others that you would not have them do unto you.—*Analects*, 15, 23

- *Islam.* No one of you is a believer until he desires for his brother that which he desires for himself.—*Sunnah*

- *Taoism.* Regard your neighbor's gain as your own gain, and your neighbor's loss as your own loss.—*T'ai Shang Kan Ying P'ien*

- *Zoroastrianism.* That nature alone is good which refrains from doing unto another whatsoever is not good for itself.—*Dadistan-i-dinik*, 94, 5.

It's remarkable that people living in so many radically different cultures would arrive at the same guideline for relating constructively to others. The Golden Rule is as close to a universal guide to conduct as you'll find.

Today, however, many people doubt that this age-old precept can be an effective interpersonal guide in the rough and tumble environment of business. Fortunately, it has been field-tested in one sector of business after another and has been linked to outstanding performance. J. C. Penney, who built one of the nation's largest retail chains, installed this tenet as a key operating principle of his company. He was fond of insisting, "The Golden Rule is still golden." The philosophy of Worthington Industries is contained in a single sentence: "We treat our customers, employees, investors, and suppliers as we would like to be treated." Marion Laboratories' CEO, Ewing Kauffman, created this fast-growing and high-performing organization by rigorously applying the Golden Rule. Whenever asked why he emphasizes the Golden Rule in the management of his company, he said, "It's just good business practice." The success of Mary Kay Ash's cosmetics firm in its first two decades astounded business analysts and competitors alike. She ran her remarkable corporation by what she referred to as "golden rule management." This guideline, one of the world's oldest and best-known prescriptions for relating to people, works wonders in today's global economy.

HOW VIRTUALLY EVERYONE WANTS TO BE TREATED

To gain a clearer understanding of how the Golden Rule applies to contemporary relationships, we asked hundreds of participants in our people styles workshops to list the three main ways they like to be treated. We were astonished to find that in workshop after workshop, the same three responses predominated. People want to be treated:

1. Respectfully

2. Fairly

3. Honestly

We then observed leaders who were exemplars in forging strong work relationships. We found that they demonstrated high levels of these attributes. Conversely, people who tended to have troubled relationships were usually gravely deficient in one or more of these qualities. Here's why these three types of behavior are so essential to developing and maintaining vital relationships.

Respectfully

Respect is essential to building constructive relationships. Perhaps that's why many successful corporate leaders maintain that respecting others is good business. IBM's former CEO, Thomas Watson Jr., said that his corporation's approach to people management is based on "the simple belief that if we respected our people and helped them respect themselves, the company would certainly profit."

Respect is based on the fact that every other individual is, above all else, a *person*. Respect is expressed through nondisparaging communication and by putting others at ease through using good manners. True respect is the outer garment of goodwill.

Treating Each Individual as a Person   Some people are surprised at the suggestion that they demonstrate respect for everyone they meet. These people protest, "A person has to earn my respect." Those who don't measure up are ignored. Or they're treated with disdain or contempt because, "They don't deserve my respect."

However, the kind of respect we're talking about has nothing to do with competence or incompetence. It's not something reserved for the deserving. Respect is what's due another person simply because he or she is a person.

Obviously, a person's level of competence is important. Underperformance must be confronted. In the workaday world, when competent coaching and confrontation don't improve someone's performance, she may have to be fired. However, even in the midst of difficult conversations about deficient performance, it's important to treat people respectfully.

Communicating Without Put-Downs   Respect or disrespect is often conveyed in the way we talk with one another. In T. S. Eliot's play *The Confidential Clerk*, Elizabeth tells her husband:

> It's very strange, Claude, but this is the first time I have talked to you without feeling very stupid. You always made me feel that I wasn't worth talking to.

Claude replied:

> And you always made me feel that your interests were much too deep for discussion with me. . . .

When you speak, make sure your manner is respectful rather than patronizing. Even when there is a significant difference of opinion, mature people manage to express their disagreement without conveying disrespect for others or for their ideas.

Using Good Manners   What people commonly refer to as *good manners* are really cultural norms—commonly agreed-upon ways of relating to one another. By defining what is appropriate conduct, these cultural norms make it possible for us to interact much more easily and efficiently. When we greet a co-worker in the morning, we don't have to figure out what to say or do. We can just give a conventional, "How're you doing today, Michelle?" She knows you aren't looking for an in-depth medical report or a detailed disclosure of her current mood. "Just fine, how are you?" is all she needs to say. Not a deep conversation—but it is an easy way to acknowledge one another's presence.

The existence of cultural norms is a precondition of coordinated social behavior. We would not be able to run corporations or any other type of organization without some norms regarding appropriate interpersonal behaviors. These cultural norms are much more important than most of us realized when we were taught to say "Thank you" to Aunt Harriet for a birthday present.

Cultural rules for relating to one another make interactions safer psychologically—another reason why good manners are important. Psychologists remind us that human beings are quite vulnerable psychologically. Even people with strong egos may, at times, feel slighted, discounted, left out, put down, disliked, or rejected by other people. No one needs to be told how unpleasant those feelings are. Or that they seriously interfere with relationships and productivity.

Dr. Edgar Schein, an organizational psychologist, says that when you examine the cultural rules for social interaction, you'll find that their primary function is to protect people from feeling too vulnerable. Observing the social amenities helps people feel secure at a very fundamental emotional level. Jonathan Swift, the author of *Gulliver's Travels,* once said,

> Good manners is the art of making those people easy with whom we converse. Whoever makes the fewest persons uneasy has the best manners. . . .

What this boils down to is that when a person acts discourteously, the other is apt to feel uneasy and emotionally vulnerable. If this happens very often, you can bet that the person on the receiving end of the ill-mannered behavior will not be inclined to help the discourteous person succeed. In the long run, bad manners are bad business.

Wearing the Outer Garment of Graciousness   Unfortunately, some people's behavior gives good manners a bad name. Author Dorothy Parker observed, "Those who have mastered etiquette, who are entirely, impeccably right, would seem to arrive at a point of exquisite dullness." When a person's manners are merely an empty formality, they are a barrier to vital relationships.

The spirit behind an action is usually evident in the behavior itself. There's a world of difference between mere politeness and true graciousness. *Graciousness* combines an awareness of social norms with genuine consideration of the feelings of others. It's a sensitive and creative way of expressing kindness in the ebb and flow of daily life. Graciously respectful behavior toward another person is the outer garment of the inner spirit of goodwill.

Fairly

When we asked people how they want to be treated, *fairly* was another of the three characteristics that were commonly mentioned. Unfortunately, well-intentioned people don't always agree on what's fair. Two principled people may disagree on what's a fair wage if one is a union member and the other is a company executive.

Although there's no way to determine what would be absolutely fair in any situation, two questions can help you be reasonably fair in your dealings with others. First, ask yourself: Am I using a win–win approach?

In most situations, it's appropriate for everyone to seek to win. But the usual assumption about winning is that for someone to win, someone else has to lose. A win–win approach requires a shift in thinking. Instead of you *or* me, the emphasis is on you *and* me. The person taking a win–win approach seeks a *mutually beneficial* outcome.

After you've come up with what seems to be a win–win approach, you can test its fairness by asking yourself a question that is central to the ethics of philosopher Immanuel Kant: Would I be willing to be the recipient of my action?

If not, don't do it.

Once you have determined what is fair in a situation, you still have to act on it. Often, that's not easy because it means rising above self-interest or the interest of a group you are associated with. Being fair ultimately requires the moral fiber to be just and impartial when you could press your own advantage. Jock Conlan, a Chicago White Sox outfielder, had an enviable reputation for being fair-minded. Years ago, during a game with the St. Louis Browns, a base umpire fainted from heat exhaustion. Both teams agreed that Conlan should take the base umpire's place. He officiated the rest of the game, wearing his White Sox uniform.

Good relationships are forged by treating people "fair and square." That means seeking win–win approaches and making sure the scales aren't tipped unduly in your direction. It involves tough-minded impartiality when making the hard calls.

Honestly

True honesty is not something that comes easily; it's a rigorous moral achievement. George Washington once said, "I hope I shall always possess firmness and virtue enough to maintain what I consider the most enviable of all titles, the character of an honest man."

Honest people consistently do three things. First, they steadfastly refuse to make misleading statements. They don't lie. They don't embellish the facts. They don't twist the truth to their advantage. They don't say, "The project is going fine," when it's critically behind schedule. They don't say, "Your job is secure," when they know it could be cut any month. When honest people make a statement, they believe it themselves.

Second, honest people are forthright. They don't withhold important information. They do not conceal problems from their manager. They give straight feedback to employees on a timely basis. Many people who abhor lying fall far short of true honesty because, for a variety of reasons, they don't divulge information that's important to other people.

Honest people communicate the facts truthfully even when it's to their disadvantage to do so. This behavior may seem naive. But we're talking about the tough-minded honesty of a person who is fully aware of possible negative consequences of telling the truth but who has the moral fiber to speak out nonetheless.

Finally, truly honest people are genuine. They don't seem to be other than who they really are. They don't put on airs. To use a phrase that was popular a few decades ago, "What you see is what you get."

Sometimes people who are strong on honesty are weak on respect. However, the person who is genuinely flexible says what he truly believes and, at the same time, treats others with respect. A person who excelled at this was Roger Williams, the founder of the state of Rhode Island and probably the strongest champion of religious freedom in colonial America. A vigorous advocate of liberty and justice, Williams called for better treatment of the Indians. He also spoke out strongly against the community's religious persecution. In letters to those who differed with him, he stated his position clearly, then typically wished his opponent well, stating his desire that the ways of God might be more fully disclosed to them both. A biographer said of this forthright man, "His personal relations with men of all parties were marked by both frank controversy and friendliness. . . . Williams had learned the high art of carrying on a battle of ideas without loss of respect, esteem and affection." The Bible refers to this ability as "speaking the truth in love."

Strong relationships are built by being *consistently* honest, fair, and respectful of others. Being respectful only now and then, being fair only some of the time, and being honest only when the spirit so moves you is not a formula for building positive relationships. Make these three qualities an ever-present part of the way you relate to others.

PART THREE

People Styles and Family Relationships

"The family is the nucleus of civilization."
—ARIEL AND WILL DURANT

CHAPTER 16

The Art of Loving Someone Very Different from Yourself

CARL JUNG, ONE OF THE towering figures of modern psychology, wrote, "It is very often the case . . . that an introvert marries an extrovert for compensation, or another type marries a countertype to complement himself." If you are in a long-term intimate relationship, there's a 95 percent probability that your partner's style is different from yours. We base that estimate on more than three decades of observing the mix of styles in couples we meet, as well as on self-reports of people in our workshops. Just as there's no better or worse style, there's no better or worse combination of styles in a loving relationship.

Karl Menninger, the famous psychiatrist, said that it's amazing how many "marital partners live out their lives in complete ignorance of one another's nature." This book and especially the rest of this chapter will help you avoid this relationship pitfall. To help you personalize this chapter to your couple relationship, put yours and your partner's names in the appropriate quadrants (or if you can identify them, the subquadrants) of the style map in Figure 16-1.

THE CHALLENGE OF CREATING LASTING COUPLE RELATIONSHIPS

More than nine out of ten people in our culture believe that love is the most important contributor to happiness. Yet, forming an intimate and

Figure 16-1
The family styles grid.

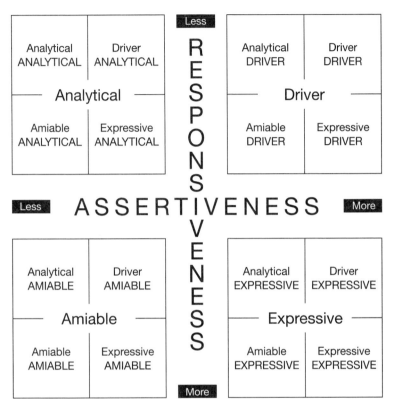

enduring bond with someone has never been easy, and today it's more difficult than ever. Societal values that once supported long-term couple relationships have eroded. And the stress of modern living creates additional difficulties for couples.

Also, in our day, a love that's "til death do us part" usually must last many decades longer than it did a few centuries ago. When the marriage ritual containing that phrase was first written, people seldom survived their twenties. Most marriages continued until the death of one of the mates, but since life expectancy was so short, those unions tended to last but a few years. Today, many people live into their eighties and nineties, and when an intimate relationship lasts "til death do us part," it may extend for fifty or sixty or more years.

Most romantic relationships today don't go the distance. Forty-three percent of first marriages break up within fifteen years. Many couples that do stay together lose their affection for one another and live together in mutual boredom or maintain interpersonal distance by living parallel lives. Psychotherapist Erich Fromm said, "There is hardly any activity . . . which is started with such tremendous hopes and expectations, and yet, which fails so regularly, as love."

Style-based differences are often an important part of the stresses associated with intimate relationships. But you can make style-based differences work *for* rather than against your relationship. As G. K. Chesterton said, "I have known many a happy marriage but never a compatible one."

THE FOUR PHASES OF INTIMATE RELATIONSHIPS

Long-term couple relationships generally evolve through a succession of phases:

- Phase I: Attraction

- Phase II: Frustration

- Phase III: Adjustment

- Phase IV: Devotion

The borders between the phases are not distinct and well defined. There's typically an amalgamation of the two phases at the boundaries.

Every couple moves through each phase at its own pace. Only a minority of couples make it through all four phases. The prevalence of disappointment and frustration in Phase II induces many couples to separate. Others throw in the towel in the Phase III challenge of adjusting to their partner—or they endure a less-than-satisfactory relationship for the rest of their lives. Happily, some couples navigate each phase rather well and enjoy the culmination of love in Phase IV—Devotion.

We've found that integrating the people styles model with the four phases of loving relationships provides a big assist for couples who are dealing with the difficulties posed by significant and deeply ingrained behavioral differences. Let's look at the challenges and opportunities that couples face in each of the four phases of a loving relationship.

Phase I: Attraction

The phrase "opposites attract" has been part of the folk wisdom of our culture for generations. Contemporary behavioral scientists refined that maxim a bit: When it comes to people styles, folks of *different* styles (not necessarily opposite ones) generally attract each another. For clarity of illustration, the next example will be of a couple whose location on the people styles grid is opposite each other.

Kathy, an Amiable, and Jack, a Driver, met at work, and their differences soon drew them together. Kathy was impressed by Jack's purposefulness. His decisions were made quickly and rationally. He set realistic goals for himself and worked pragmatically to achieve them. Skillful time management heightened his efficiency. When Jack spoke, he was direct and to the point. Kathy and others sensed his confidence. She admired those qualities, in part, because they weren't her strong points.

Kathy struck Jack's fancy, too. Her open expression as she looked at him, the warmth of her smile, and the contagion of her soft laugh attracted him. She was incredibly easy to talk with. Although Jack was comfortable communicating with people about projects he was involved in, he was less at ease in personal interactions. Kathy specialized in personal relationships. For the first time in Jack's life, it felt perfectly natural to spend long periods of time talking about anything and everything.

When we connect with a partner who has pluses where we have minuses, who is competent in areas where we are weak, and whose emotional makeup is very different from our own, the initial attraction can be very powerful. As Kathy and Jack bonded they felt they had found missing parts of themselves in the other. This dovetailing of traits led them to believe they were "made for each other."

The strength of the attraction that people feel in Phase I ranges from moderate to intense. At the low-key end of the continuum, it may be a time of life when a person thinks she should be married. Of all the people she knows, she's more partial to one. The time is right. And the other person is available. So they settle into an exclusive relationship. In addition to a probable difference in behavioral style, the couple's attraction may be based on factors like physical attraction, financial success, social status, or family pressure.

At the other end of the attraction continuum, the partners are "swept off their feet." They are "crazy" about each other, "head over heels in love." Each feels that he or she can't live without the other. They crave to be together all the time. When apart, they yearn for the other and try to erase the distance by incessant phone calls.

In this state of infatuation, people often commit to a life-long relationship. George Bernard Shaw highlighted the irony of this tendency: "When two people are under the influence of the most violent, most insane, most delusive, and most transient of passions, they are required to swear that they will remain in that excited, abnormal and exhausting condition until death do them part."

Phase II: Frustration

A man and a woman went into a church. They stood at the altar, exchanged their vows, and were made one. They left the church and got into the waiting car. From that moment on, the question was, "Which one?"

This scenario draws a smile of recognition from people because it highlights one of the most challenging realities of intimate relationships: When two people live together, there are *two* sets of habitual behavioral preferences but only *one* relationship. And, in time, differences that once were alluring become points of contention. Carl Jung, the noted psychotherapist, said, "Seldom, or perhaps never, does a marriage develop into an individual relationship smoothly and without crisis; . . . without pain." And in *Intimate Partners*, therapist Maggie Scarf notes:

> It is a fact of marital reality, well known to experts in the field, that those qualities cited by intimate partners as having first attracted them to each other are usually *the same ones that are identified as sources of conflict* later on in the relationship. The "attractive" qualities have, in time, been relabeled; they have become the bad, difficult things about the partner, the aspects of his or her personality and behavior that are viewed as problematical and negative . . . . Thus it is that the admirable, wonderful traits of the partner become the awful, terrible things that one wishes one had realized in time! [Author's italics.]

Living with the partner's "negative" traits for a lifetime can seem intolerable. So each person typically tries to change the other's "bad" qualities, many of which are style-related. But people generally resist efforts to reform them. Additionally, most behaviors targeted for reform are deeply entrenched habits. So, at the outset, nearly all attempts to reform one's partner are destined to fail. With each person resolutely trying to change the other and each tenaciously resisting the change effort, you have a formula for frustration, an agenda for conflict.

To make matters worse, people of different styles handle conflict differently. You'll recall from Chapter 8 that in conflict, Drivers become autocratic, Expressives attack, Analyticals clam up and avoid emotional involvement, and Amiables acquiesce, but often with a resentful heart. These different ways of dealing with conflict add significantly to the frustration the parties are experiencing. So, when a couple begins arguing about spending or punctuality or childrearing, they sometimes end up fighting about how they are fighting!

The unpleasantness of so much frustration and conflict in Phase II causes many to give up. In fact, most divorces occur in the first two years of marriage.

Although it doesn't feel like it at the time, the frustration phase can contribute significantly to the development of genuine love. For one thing, when it occurs before marriage this rigorous test of the relationship helps you determine whether or not this is the person you'll choose to be with for the rest of your life. Equally important, in order for robust love to develop, romantic illusions must be shed. For love to be real, a person must see her partner as he actually is—his shortcomings as well as his strengths. Before making a lifetime commitment to someone, it's important to understand the difficulties posed by the way that person is different from you. With this grounding in reality you've taken a major step toward forging a rewarding and enduring relationship.

When a couple moves into the next stage of their relationship, both people will still experience frustrations and disappointments but these will occur less frequently. And the couple will usually be better at coping with these aggravations than they were in Phase II.

Phase III: Adjustment

The *adjustment phase* has its own set of difficulties. There's a sense in which a long-term relationship must be rebuilt every day—often in the face of difficulties. This is a period in which one or both partners may be struggling with their jobs, perhaps including setbacks like a stalled career or the trauma of a layoff. Many couples have children during this period and may have conflicting approaches about how to rear them. Couples often become so busy ferrying children and attending their activities that they don't give their own relationship the time and attention it needs. And while they are overbusy with their children, many couples find that they are needed by their own parents, who are entering old age. Then too, difficult financial choices often loom large in Phase III. How big a mortgage or rent can they afford? According to the financial magazines they may read, they probably are not investing nearly enough for their retirement and may never be able to. And they're most likely behind schedule on their saving plan for their kids' college education. The financial issues are thorny and seem to be ever-present. Then there are health problems, menopause, and mid-life crises to deal with.

In Phase III, partners face the challenges of dealing with these types of stresses while shifting their mode of operation from trying to *change* their partner to trying to *adjust* to him or her. It's not easy. Many come to feel that it's not worth the effort. So, there's a spurt in the number of divorces after about twenty years of marriage.

Of course, many couples successfully navigate the whitewater of adjustment. Here are some tips on how to help your relationship mature as you deal with the challenges of this phase of love.

Shift from a Mindset of Judgment to a Mindset of *Acceptance*   In the frustration phase, partners often become very judgmental. The prevalence of criticism inevitably saps a relationship of its vitality. For love to flourish, partners need to be mainly accepting of one another. It helps that people often come to realize that they overreacted in the frustration phase and that things weren't as bad as they had thought. As novelist Albert Camus said, "We . . . deceive ourselves twice about the people we love—first to their advantage, then to their disadvantage."

Then too, insight into your own and your partner's styles can help you become more accepting of your partner's ways of doing things. Charlene, who you met in Chapter 1, was frustrated by Don's highly methodical ways. After taking a People Styles for Couples Workshop, she understood that those tendencies were typical of Analyticals, and that Analyticals make up 25 percent of the population. That helped her take Don's methodical ways more philosophically. She still didn't like recalling all the brand names he favored or putting the spices back in alphabetical order after she used them. But the awareness that Don's strong need for order is characteristic of people of his style helped her be more tolerant of these tendencies. In her effort to be more accepting, Charlene repeatedly reminded herself of a sentence on one of the wall charts in the People Styles Course she took:

"My partner is not wrong—just different."

Realize that Couples in Long-Term Relationships Face a Number of Unsolvable Problems   Daniel Wile, a savvy marriage counselor, says,

"Let's face it: Everyone is the one person on earth you shouldn't get involved with."

He adds,

"There is value, when choosing a long-term partner, in realizing that you will inevitably be choosing a set of unresolvable problems that you'll be grappling with for the next ten, twenty, or fifty years. . . . In fact, a relationship is, in some sense, the attempt to work out the negative side effects of what attracts you to your partner in the first place."

So, part of the art of loving is knowing what to overlook.

Change Yourself, Not Your Partner   Sooner or later, nearly everyone in an intimate relationship tries to change some of his or her partner's ways of doing things. But, as we've noted, people are highly resistant to their partner's efforts to reform them. A sentence that's worth committing to memory is:

"You can only change *your* half of a relationship."

Part Two of this book and the Appendix for your style can help you pinpoint changes in your behavior that can leverage substantial improvements in your relationship.

Fortunately, when you change your behavior, you will thereby influence your partner's conduct. Psychologists at the Kaiser Foundation in California found that a person's behavior tends to "pull" rather predictable responses from others. For example, smiles tend to elicit smiles, tears typically evoke sympathetic behavior, and authoritarian actions usually call forth dependence or resentment. When you change your behavior in ways that are valued by your partner, there's a good likelihood that, in time, your partner will reciprocate to some degree.

Appreciate and Celebrate Your Differences   As we've seen, when it comes to intimate relationships, most of us choose a mate whose strengths offset our weaknesses. This tendency is often referred to as *complementary pairing*. According to our dictionary, *complement* means "something that completes . . . To complement is to provide something that is felt to be lacking or needed; it is often applied to putting together two things each of which supplies what is lacking in the other . . . ."

When determining who will do what tasks, couples typically take advantage of each partner's strengths and interests. But, as the years pass, they tend to take their mate's contributions for granted. They seldom note opportunities to express appreciation. Many drift into what is literally a thankless union. So be alert to the good things your partner is doing. And be quick to respond with heartfelt appreciation. When you manage your differences both well and appreciatively, you may be able to say with a Charles Dickens character, "We are two halves of a pair of scissors when apart; but together we are something."

Phase IV: Devotion

The final phase of love is *devotion*. Three characteristics stand out in this blossoming of a couple's togetherness.

Both Persons Have a Realistic Confidence in the Relationship   They trust the durability of their love. The partners know they can count on each other when the chips are down. They have a hard-won knowledge that, whatever comes, they'll be able to work things out. Their patience with each other in difficult times, their magnanimous concern for each other, their gracious kindness to each other—these have forged a mutual trust and durable love that undergirds their bedrock confidence in the relationship.

They Enjoy a Rich Intimacy   Unlike Phase I intimacy, which is full of youthful exuberance and fireworks, Phase IV intimacy is relaxed and tranquil. This mellower intimacy is fuller and deeper; it has the ripeness of maturity. Partners talk more openly about what is real in their lives— their vulnerabilities and fears, as well as their pleasures and accomplishments. They listen attentively and enjoy significant silences with each other. Decades of frank but sensitive conversation have made them perceptively attuned to one another. They reassure with a touch and communicate paragraphs with a glance. Their union has flowered through the decades without eroding the uniqueness of their distinctive personalities. Indeed, the partners, while remaining markedly dissimilar, have become *one*.

They "Go with the Flow" of the Relationship   Even in this stage of love, the partners accept that there will inevitably be fluctuations in the affection and support that they extend to one another. Writer Anne Morrow Lindbergh notes, "When you love someone you do not love them all the time, in exactly the same way . . . . It is an impossibility."

People who flourish in Phase IV have what Ross Snyder calls "creative fidelity." The partners "bear with their plateaus, their regressions, and imperfectness in such a way that these are transformed into new possibilities." They are for and with their partner "come hell or high water."

The pilgrimage of love requires much resourcefulness and a great deal of heart. Rainer Maria Rilke, the great lyric poet of Germany, writes:

> For one human being to love another: that is perhaps the most difficult of all our tasks; the ultimate, the last test and proof, the work for which all other work is but preparation.

Few things are more demanding than creating a lasting and truly loving relationship. Yet few, if any, are as rewarding.

CHAPTER 17

Style-Based Parenting

YOU MAY RECALL from the last chapter that we authors of this book, an Analytical and an Amiable, are a married couple. Our blended family includes seven adult kids who are distributed across all four people styles. Ditto for our sixteen grandkids. Our immersion in the often-bewildering realities of family life provide us with convincing evidence that we are not experts on childrearing! In the process of applying the people styles model to our family, however, we've learned a few things we wish we'd known many years ago. This chapter summarizes some of these learnings.

ACCEPT THAT RAISING KIDS IS TOUGH

There's a myth that having children helps a marriage. But think about it. In terms of timing, the first child often arrives on the scene after the attraction phase of a couple's relationship has worn off. The new parents need to give the baby much of the attention they once devoted to each other. They're often tired and irritable from being up much of the night with a crying infant. They can't go out as freely as they once did, and the husband may be jealous of all the attention diverted from him to the baby. Daniel Gilbert, a Harvard University professor of psychology, reviewed several studies and concluded that marital satisfaction decreases dramatically after the birth of the first child and doesn't improve until the last child has left home. After examining data from several studies, the most extensive of which involved 13,000 families, Florida State University sociology professor Robin Simon concluded, "Parents experience lower levels of emotional well-being, less frequent positive emotions and more frequent negative emotions than their childless peers." We think that having kids is worth the hassle. But make no mistake; incorporating children into the family unit adds moments of stress and heartache.

MAP YOUR FAMILY

When applying the people styles model to raising kids, it's helpful to create a style map of your family. On the Family Styles Grid (Figure 17-1), write the names of each family member in the appropriate quadrant. Include the other parent (even if he or she is no longer living with you but has continuing contact with the children). If a step-parent or intimate partner is living with either of you, note that person's location on the grid. Write the names in pencil in case further observation and reflection sheds new insights into the family members' styles. (If there's a very young child in your household, put her on your family map, too. Style-based characteristics show up at an early age and persist throughout life.)

When we mapped our family, we did it separately at first. Then we discussed our reasons for positioning each person where we did. As a result, each of us made some minor revisions. If you and your partner don't reach complete agreement on a given family member's style, discuss what *behaviors* suggest that he is more or less assertive and what *behaviors* suggest that he is more or less responsive. If you still don't agree, maintain an open mind and continue observing that person's behavior.

BIT BY BIT, INTRODUCE YOUR CHILD TO
THE PEOPLE STYLES MODEL

Broaden your child's understanding of himself and others by gradually introducing him to the people styles model. If you tailor your input to the child's age and avoid using people styles terminology, you can orient the child to some of the model's basic concepts when he's quite young.

Figure 17-1
The family styles grid.

With preschoolers, for example, you can notice what activities they enjoy and do well. Then give them positive feedback and perhaps some coaching on how to further develop those strengths. You can also plan additional activities that will enable them to enjoy and make the most of these natural competencies.

Additionally, you can help them understand interpersonal dynamics better by using people style insights couched in children's vocabulary to discuss a problem that they're having with another child. For example, you might say to an Expressive daughter whose sister is an Analytical:

> Have you noticed that Claire likes to play more quietly than you do? She's happy when she is curled up with a good book while you like to be more active and busy with lots of activities.

When the child is age 6 to 8, you can give a somewhat more advanced explanation of people styles:

> I know it hurts that your best friend doesn't want to come over to our house any more. Joe is a gentle kind of kid who doesn't say much. You talk more than he does. And you tell him what to do a lot. Maybe you can think about what would be more fun for him when the two of you are together. If you do a few things differently, you and he might become good friends again.

ACCEPT YOUR CHILD'S STYLE

A child's style is part of her genetic makeup. Style-based characteristics entered the world with her and are an essential part of who she is. Psychological theorist Isabel Myers Briggs, who uses the word *type* where we would say *style*, writes, "If parents understand and accept their children's type, the children have a spot of firm ground to stand on and a place in which to be themselves. But if children suspect that their parents want them to be different—to go against their own type—then the children lose hope."

Some parents, however, are disappointed with their child's style and try to reshape their child in fundamental ways. As one of T. S. Eliot's characters said: "You know, Claude, I think we . . . made the same mistake . . . . We wanted Colby to be something he wasn't."

Glenn Taylor, a Driver and hard-charging executive with a Fortune 100 company, made a similar mistake. Glenn viewed Ryan, his teenager, as an underdeveloped Driver who needed to be toughened up in order to become the forceful, hard-hitting son he wanted. But Ryan, an Amiable, preferred jamming with his musical friends to being the jock and hard-charging go-getter his father envisioned. The more Glenn tried to turn his laid-back son into a younger version of himself, the more Ryan's confidence eroded and the more he withdrew from his father. The ongoing struggle not only poisoned the father–son relationship; it also sparked a conflict between Glenn and his wife, who put herself between the two as her son's protector.

Sometimes a parent will attempt to remake a child whose basic makeup is similar to her own.

Marge O'Connor, an Analytical, has a daughter, Joan, who is also an Analytical. Early on, Marge commented to a friend, "If Joan doesn't start speaking up more and getting more involved, I'll be beside myself." The friend reminded Marge that her daughter wasn't four years old yet. "Besides," she added, "you've been a quiet one all your life." "That's the reason I so hate to see it in her," Marge replied.

When Joan became a teenager, Marge was concerned about "all the good experiences that Joan is missing." Soon, Marge was carping at her Analytical daughter to take part in the school play, be in the church choir, join the girl's soccer team, invite friends for a sleepover, and so forth. As often happens, this well-intentioned badgering boomeranged, and Joan became even more withdrawn and her previously close relationship with her mother was badly frayed.

In one after another of the numerous books that therapist Sheldon Kopp wrote, he portrayed the misery and despair he experienced because of his parent's efforts to remake him into the kind of person he could never be. Here's a brief passage from *An End to Innocence*, in which Kopp describes the effect of his parent's nonacceptance of his basic temperament:

> For most of my life I did not understand that much of my needless
> social difficulty resulted from trying to live up to my parent's expecta-
> tions. They saw me as a flawed [Expressive], unpopular only because I
> "preferred being miserable." In truth, I am a consummate [Analytical]
> who was innocently trying to push against the grain of my natural tem-
> perament. I was destined to feel inadequate so long as I tried to be
> something other than myself.

We're not suggesting that parents provide no guidance to their children. What we're talking about is different from teaching manners, having standards about the amount of TV viewing time, setting reasonable expectations about school performance, and establishing norms about such things as chores and bedtimes. The concern we are addressing is a parent's effort to fundamentally remake a child into someone else— someone who would be acceptable to the parent.

Accepting your children's basic nature with all its inherent strengths and limitations is crucial to helping them flourish. The goal of style-based parenting is to raise each child in a way that's congruent with his or her natural style.

ACCEPT YOUR PARENTING STYLE

Your people style has a major influence on your parenting style. And every parenting style has its pluses and minuses. But many of us grew up with the cultural stereotype that mothers should be especially affectionate and supportive: In people styles terms, they should personify the Amiable style. Yet studies show that 25 percent of women are Drivers, 25 percent are Analyticals, and 25 percent are Expressives, so at least 75 percent of all women don't fit the widely held view of what a mother ought to be like! (Men are also divided equally among the four styles.)

It's important to remember that there are many ways of being a good mother, and women of all four styles have learned to make the most of their strengths as they fulfill that significant role. So accept your parenting style—whatever style it is, it's a good one. Make the most of the strengths you bring to this set of responsibilities and keep your weaknesses on a short leash.

In similar fashion, fathers are often expected to be the assertive head of their household and the family disciplinarian—in other words, they should personify something like the Driver style. In some people's minds, some Expressives might fit the bill as well. But 25 percent of fathers are Amiables and 25 percent are Analyticals, so at least 50 percent of all men don't fit the cultural stereotype of what a father should be like. Fortunately, there are many ways of being a good dad, and men of all four styles have learned to make the most of their strengths as they contribute to their children's development. So accept your parenting style as you accentuate the strengths you bring to your relationship with your children.

SYNCHRONIZE YOUR PARENTING STYLE WITH YOUR PARTNER'S

Parenting is complicated by the fact that, in loving relationships, people typically partner with someone whose style is different from theirs. Furthermore, in some families step-parents and significant others—each with their own parenting style—may become part of the already-compli-cated picture. Whatever your domestic situation, there's a good likeli-hood that you'll need to integrate your parenting style with at least one other person. The process of meshing two or more parenting styles is called *co-parenting*.

To be successful at co-parenting, you need to respect your partner's parenting style. Some people, however, are very inflexible about their parenting. They are convinced of the "rightness" of their approach to childrearing and equally certain of the "wrongness" of their partner's approach. When one parent is rigid about the way the children are raised, the other parent often digs his heels in and stubbornly relates to the child in his own preferred way. Psychologists found that once this occurs, the differences in the couple's parenting styles tend to become extreme. Each parent tries to compensate for the "mistakes" made by the other. James, who "believes in running a tight ship," is a strict disciplinarian. To coun-teract James's excessive severity, his wife, Cindy, spoils the children be-hind his back. Swiss therapist Paul Tournier cited several examples of this polarizing tendency and concluded that in this type of situation, "Each parent exaggerates his error in order to balance the opposite error of the other." Before long, the parents are at war with each other and their unfortunate child is the battlefield.

When done well, co-parenting is beneficial to both the child and the parents. Janice, an Expressive, contrasts her approach with that of her husband, Ted, an Analytical. "I'm emotional and outgoing," she says. "He's rational, reserved, and even-tempered. Ted helps our son with his homework and I teach him how to deal with tricky people problems."

Peter, an Amiable, explains, "In our family, my Driver wife, Sally, is more of a disciplinarian and I tend to the lenient side. At first we let our different parenting styles generate lots of friction. But we've learned to turn that point of contention into an advantage. Sally privately lets me know when she thinks I'm being too soft and permissive. And I help her back off a bit when she's expecting too much of the kids. We've become a good counterbalance for each other when dealing with Stacy and Greg."

Both of these couples worked at successfully synchronizing their dif-ferent parenting styles. They respected each other and drew upon each other's strengths. Areas of disagreement were negotiated. By meshing their parenting styles, they provided a well-balanced and fairly consistent influence on their children. Their cooperative approach also proved to be a boon for the couples since it eliminated much potential friction between them and created a more comfortable relationship with their children.

A prominent authority on family life says that raising kids is the hardest job in the world. Obviously, that's an overstatement. But every parent knows that to do it well, a person needs all the help that he or she can get. Although it certainly is not a panacea, we've found that the people styles model is a useful resource with its reminders to:

- Accept that raising kids is tough
- Map your family
- Bit by bit introduce your child to the people styles model
- Accept your child's style
- Accept your parenting style
- Synchronize your parenting style with your partner's

For *Amiables* Only: How to Flex to Each Style

The purpose of this appendix is to coach Amiables on specific things they can do to create more productive relationships with people of each style.

Most of the recommendations are temporary behavioral changes that you can make just for a few minutes, before resuming your more comfortable style-based ways. However, we also mention a few options, such as goal setting, that have more long-term implications.

Since this appendix is a planning aid, don't try to read it straight through. Instead, find the section that applies to the style you want to flex to:

- Analyticals, p. 155
- Expressives, p. 160
- Drivers, p. 163
- Other Amiables, p. 168

Read that section to figure out what you can do to make it easier for persons of that style to work effectively with you. Later, when you want to improve your relationship with someone of a different style, read the section dealing with that style. By working your way through the appendix on an as-needed basis, you'll soon read all the sections and strengthen important relationships in the process.

FLEXING TO ANALYTICALS

As an Amiable, you have much in common with Analyticals. You are similar on one of the two behavioral dimensions of style: Both of you are less assertive than most people. Consequently, Analyticals tend to appreciate your low-key ways.

In flexing to Analyticals, your major challenge is to get in sync with some of their less-responsive behaviors. You can create a more effective working relationship with an Analytical by temporarily using some of the following four types of behavior, within each of which a number of specifics are mentioned. Do several, but not necessarily all, of the suggested specifics. You'll probably think of additional ways to work better with the particular person you have in mind.

Be More Task-Oriented

The Analytical is usually more task-oriented, and the Amiable tends to be more people-oriented. When working with an Analytical, you may want to give increased attention to the task side of things.

1. *Be on time.* Analyticals are more time-conscious than most Amiables. They expect you to be punctual.

2. *Get right to business.* Don't give the impression that you're there to chat. But don't lose your human touch, either. Limit the small talk. It's usually appropriate to spend a little time on openers, but keep it brief and don't make it too personal. Then get right into what you're there to talk about.

3. *Be a bit more formal.* It's easy for an Amiable to slip into a more casual demeanor than Analyticals may consider appropriate. Dress in a businesslike manner (assuming that's compatible with the culture of your company). Don't overuse slang.

4. *Maintain a somewhat reserved demeanor.* Amiables are friendlier than most people. But your Analytical colleagues are more comfortable with you when you maintain a somewhat reserved demeanor in your interactions with them.

De-emphasize Feelings

You can get more in sync with Analyticals by being *less* emotionally disclosing. Be more reserved without becoming cold or aloof.

1. *Decrease your eye contact.* Generally, Analyticals make less eye contact and are less comfortable with it than most people are.

2. *Limit your facial expressiveness.* Analyticals usually have a rather serious facial expression, especially when discussing business. In contrast, Amiables smile easily and often. To flex to Analyticals, have your facial expression be a closer match to your co-worker's seriousness.

3. *Limit your gestures.* Analyticals gesture less than any of the styles. Furthermore, feelings are communicated mainly through gestures and other aspects of body language, so when working with an Analytical, it may make sense to rely less on body English.

4. *Avoid touch.* Analyticals typically feel uneasy when someone touches them. Honor their preferences and avoid touch.

5. *Talk about what you think rather than about what you feel.* Think longer and harder about issues you're discussing with an Analytical. The words you use are important, too. Saying, "*I think . . .*," instead of "I feel . . .," can make a difference. Then follow with factual statements. Analyticals appreciate the change in conversational ambience when you begin using such phrases as, "I've *analyzed* the situation . . . ," "My *objective* in doing this is . . . ," "My *plan* for the next quarter . . . ," "*A logical conclusion* . . . ," or "Let me get some *more information* before I give my opinion on that." Why not use words and phrases that are music to an Analytical's ears?

6. *Don't upset yourself over the Analytical's impersonal and unfeeling manner.* If an Analytical seems distant or disengaged, don't take it personally unless you have reason to believe you've done something to offend. People of this style tend to be somewhat remote and unapproachable. Accept that this is the way these people are and that it's OK for them to be this way. You make things far worse if you create judgmental labels about them in your mind, or start telling yourself how bad they are or how unpleasant they are to work with.

Be Systematic

Analyticals like to be systematic about most things they're associated with. When you work with Analyticals, they find the relationship much more congenial when you are more systematic than usual.

1. *Set high standards.* Stretch as much as you can in setting standards for your work. Just be sure to deliver what you say you will. Analyticals get turned off sooner than most when someone makes a promise and doesn't deliver.

2. *Plan your work.* Analyticals are avid planners and like to work with people who develop detailed, step-by-step, written plans.

3. *Work your plan.* The Analytical thinks of a plan as a rational road to accomplishment—something that should be strictly adhered to. Consider being more organized than usual, without necessarily being as rigorous as the Analytical might wish.

4. *Develop superior procedures.* Analyticals relish outstanding quality. One way they try to achieve outstanding quality is through superior procedures and processes. When it comes to ongoing activities, they like co-workers to discover the best way of doing a task and then create a step-by-step procedure which, when followed, consistently yields excellent results. This rigorous attention to creating procedures doesn't come

easily to Amiables. But you can do it. Chances are, you can find some areas in which new procedures are needed. As you develop them, you are likely to enhance productivity and build stronger ties to the Analyticals with whom you work.

5. *Continually improve procedures.* Even more than most people, Analyticals are concerned with continuous improvement. Support their quest for quality by improving some of the most important procedures in your area.

6. *Be more rigorous in following established procedures.* Analyticals tend to be sticklers for doing things according to set procedures. If you make the effort, you can probably think of procedures that would produce better results if you followed them more consistently. Doing so undoubtedly strengthens your relationship with the Analyticals in your work group.

Be Well Organized, Detailed, and Factual

Analyticals, the most perfectionistic of the styles, are particular about the way things are presented to them. They expect you to be well organized, detailed, and factual in your communication. In presenting ideas or recommendations to Analyticals, you make your case better when you incorporate the following behaviors:

1. *Be prepared.* Analyticals expect you to make good use of their time. Don't wing it; think things through in advance. Dig up all the data you need. Anticipate questions you may be asked. Even for one-on-one meetings, it's often appropriate to create an agenda. Consider getting the agenda to the Analytical in advance; she may want to think about the topics beforehand. Most of the suggestions here are enhanced if you give things more than your customary preparation.

2. *Have a well-organized presentation.* Explain your thoughts systematically. It often helps to present your ideas as a series of points arranged in a logical order. That's what Analyticals often do. You frequently hear them say, "In the first place . . . , In the second place . . . ," and so forth. When communicating with an Analytical, do likewise.

3. *Go into considerable detail.* When making a presentation to people of this style, don't just hit the high points. Analyticals thrive on specifics. They want to make sure all the ground has been covered before they make a decision. You gain credibility with people of this style when they see that you've chased down every detail.

4. *Give a sound rationale for narrowing the options.* Analyticals want to consider all the alternatives. Although this tendency often helps them make good decisions, it also increases their tendency to be inordinately

indecisive. You can help them weed out some of the weaker alternatives by giving them logical and factual reasons for doing so.

5. *Mention the problems and disadvantages of the proposal you put forward.* In addition to mentioning the advantages of the proposition you recommend, tell about the downside, too. The Analytical respects you for doing so. Then, further build your credibility by recommending ways of dealing with the problems and disadvantages.

6. *Show why the approach you advocate is best.* For Analyticals, "best" is a combination of quality, economy, and low risk. You have to figure out the relative weight of each of these criteria for the particular Analytical in the specific circumstances. "Best" for this style includes *long-term benefits* as well as immediate advantages. Discuss the future in terms of probabilities: "Here's a projection of what's likely to happen. . . ." Like you, the Analytical is conservative when it comes to risk, so if possible show why your approach is a fairly safe bet.

7. *Provide accurate factual evidence.* When talking with Analyticals, it's rarely advisable to use someone's opinion or recommendation as evidence. Hard facts persuade these folks. Since they like an objective presentation, avoid emotional appeals. Where others might settle for approximations, Analyticals want meticulously correct information. So be painstakingly accurate in what you report to people of this style.

8. *Stick to business.* Don't digress. As you discuss the business at hand and are reminded of things that are tangential to the discussion, don't pursue these side issues. When the time is up, depart quickly and graciously.

9. *Provide written support materials, and/or follow up in writing.* Analyticals tend to prefer the written word to the spoken. Even so, it's best to make an oral presentation as well. That way you can note reactions and answer the Analytical's questions. At the same time, cater to the Analytical's preference for written communication by preparing well-thought-out support materials and/or a follow-up report. If a decision was reached, you may want to include a step-by-step timetable for implementation.

10. *Be prepared to listen to more than you want to know.* When Analyticals talk, they often present far more information than most people think is necessary. They explain their ideas or discuss progress on projects in what may feel to you like overwhelming detail. This much minutiae may be boring and difficult to follow, but be patient and stay tuned in. Analyticals appreciate your attentiveness. And, there's probably information you need to know buried somewhere in all that detail.

In your initial efforts to flex to Analyticals, you'll probably find it helpful to review the portrait of the Analytical style found in Chapter 7, pages 58–62.

FLEXING TO EXPRESSIVES

As an Amiable, you have much in common with Expressives. You are similar on one of the two basic dimensions of style: Both of you are more responsive than most people. Consequently, Expressives tend to appreciate your warmth, your friendliness, and your focus on people.

Your major challenge in flexing to Expressives is to get in sync with some of their more-assertive behaviors. You should be able to create a more effective working relationship with an Expressive by *temporarily* using some of the following five types of behavior. Within each type or category of behavior, a number of specifics are mentioned. Do several, but not necessarily all, of the specifics within the type of behavior you plan to emphasize. You'll probably think of additional ways to work better with the specific person you have in mind.

Pick Up the Pace

Expressives tend to do everything at a faster pace than Amiables. Often you relate better to Expressives when you increase your pace to be more of a match for theirs.

1. *Move more quickly than usual.* Do whatever you are doing as fast as possible—on the double.

2. *Speak more rapidly than is normal for you.* Also, pause less often.

3. *Address problems quickly.* When problems arise, face them and dispose of them as soon as possible. From the Expressive's point of view, there's no time like the present to resolve a troubled situation.

4. *Be prepared to decide quickly.* Knowing that the Expressive makes decisions quickly, anticipate decisions he wants from you (or will want to make with you) and do whatever preparation you can to speed your decision making.

5. *Implement decisions as soon as possible.* Once a decision is made, try to put it into operation immediately.

6. *Respond promptly to messages and requests,* in person or by telephone.

7. *When writing, keep it short.* Consider "bulleting" key points. Put supporting information in appendixes. Expressives like to keep paperwork at a minimum.

8. *Expect the hurry-up-and-wait phenomenon.* The fast-paced Expressive wants things done yesterday. But after you've knocked yourself out and

met the Expressive's deadline, your work may be ignored for some time as the Expressive takes up another project. Your project, which seemed so urgently needed a short time ago, may gather dust for a few months. On the one hand, it's important not to take these incidents personally: Realize that it's a style-based tendency. On the other hand, if you experience a great deal of hurry-up-and-wait with a particular person, be sure to confront the issue.

Demonstrate Higher Energy

Expressives are high-energy people. When relating to Expressives, there are times when you need to put more vigor into what you say and do.

1. *Maintain an erect posture.* Keep your back straight and lean into the conversation. Keep your head erect, not propped on your hands.

2. *Use gestures to show your involvement in the conversation.* Use larger motions. Be more emphatic with body English.

3. *Increase the frequency and intensity of your eye contact.*

4. *Increase your vocal intensity.* Speak louder than you normally would. Let the intensity of your voice communicate that you are taking the matter seriously. Show conviction through your voice.

5. *Move and speak more quickly.* The behaviors that were mentioned under the heading "Pick Up the Pace" all help you interact more energetically.

Focus on the Big Picture

Expressives want to take a macro view of things. They quickly become impatient when a discussion turns to the nitty-gritty. In fact, of all the styles, Expressives are the least interested in details. Although as an Amiable you aren't nearly as detail-oriented as Analyticals, there are times when you wish to discuss more particulars than the Expressive cares to.

1. *Concentrate on high-priority issues.* You probably have a lot more topics you want to talk about than the Expressive wants to hear about. When briefing an Expressive, radically prune the list of items to discuss.

2. *Present the main points and skip all but the most essential details.* Expressives rarely feel they need anything more than an overview. They will ask for more information if they want it.

3. *Nevertheless, make sure the details are well attended to.* Although Expressives are not particularly interested in hearing about the nitty-gritty that you have to concentrate on, they can become very impatient if someone's inattention to details causes them problems.

Say What You Think

Expressives speak candidly and directly. Amiables are apt to keep their thoughts to themselves and speak somewhat tentatively and indirectly. Here's how you can bridge that behavioral gap.

1. *Speak up more often.* Initiate more conversations. In discussions and meetings, express yourself frequently enough so there's a more balanced give-and-take. Expressives usually want to know where people stand. They would rather not have to try to interpret the meaning of your silence or have to pry thoughts out of you.

2. *Tell more; ask less.* Say "Here's what I think . . . ," rather than "Do you think it would make sense to . . . ?" Say "Please do this" instead of "Could you do this?"

3. *Make statements that are definite rather than tentative.* Avoid words like *try, perhaps, maybe, possibly,* etc. Be specific. Don't say you'll complete a project "as soon as possible." Say it will be done "by 12:00 noon next Tuesday."

4. *Eliminate gestures that suggest you lack confidence in the point you are making.* Don't shrug your shoulders, hold your palms up, or use facial expressions that undercut what you are saying, imply helplessness, or suggest the avoidance of responsibility.

5. *Voice your disagreements.* When Expressives disagree with you, they usually come right out and say so. They expect the same from you. Face conflict more openly. State your opinions frankly but tactfully. At the same time, try to avoid situations where you and the Expressive are battling from entrenched positions. If it gets to that point, the highly competitive Expressive may put more emphasis on winning the argument than on arriving at a common understanding.

6. *Recommend a course of action and sell it with enthusiasm.* Expressives like to be pumped up about the choices they make and the things they do. A careful weighing of the pros and cons of numerous alternatives rarely gives the Expressive the excitement she expects from making a decision. So when it's appropriate, make a specific recommendation. Integrity requires you to mention the disadvantages, but when you can do so with a clear conscience, emphasize the positives. Pull out all the stops; Expressives usually like an emotional appeal.

7. *Don't gloss over problems.* Expressives will be furious if they hear from others what they should hear from you. Beat bad news to the punch. Then give regular, frank reports on your progress regarding the problem situation.

Facilitate Self-Determination

Expressives like to set their own direction. They want to do things their way. Here are some ways Amiables can constructively facilitate an Expressive's sense of self-direction.

1. *Give Expressives as much freedom as possible in achieving their visions.*

2. *As far as practicable, let the Expressive determine how to do projects and achieve objectives.*

3. *Don't be a stickler for rules.* Expressives are prone to stretch or break rules in order to achieve results. Be open to changing or bending the rules when appropriate.

In your initial efforts to flex to Expressives, you'll probably find it helpful to review the portrait of the Expressive style found in Chapter 6, pages 48–53.

FLEXING TO DRIVERS

As an Amiable you differ from the Driver on both of the basic dimensions of style: The Driver is more assertive and less responsive than you are. Thus, you experience more style-based differences with Drivers than with either Analyticals or Expressives, each of which has one basic dimension of behavior in common with you. As a result, you find more types of behavior you can modify when flexing to a Driver than when flexing to any other style.

As you read the types of temporary adjustment of behavior that help you get in sync with Drivers, select carefully the one to four types you think will help you work best with a particular person. It's not easy to change habitual behavior, even for a short time, so be sure to select only one to four types of behavior to work on. Within each type or category of behavior, a number of specifics are mentioned. Do several, but not necessarily all, of the specifics within the behavioral category you plan to emphasize. You'll probably think of additional ways to work better with the specific person you have in mind.

Pick Up the Pace

Drivers tend to do everything at a fast pace. You often relate better to Drivers when you increase your pace considerably.

1. *Move more quickly than usual.* Walk at a faster pace. Do whatever you are doing as quickly as possible—on the double when you flex to a Driver.

2. *Speak more rapidly than is normal for you.* Also, pause less often.

3. *Use time efficiently.* When meeting with a Driver, don't exceed the allotted time. Do your business at a fast clip. Then leave quickly, yet graciously.

4. *Address problems quickly.* When problems arise, face them and dispose of them as soon as possible. From the Driver's point of view, there's no time like the present to resolve a troubled situation.

5. *Be prepared to decide quickly.* Knowing that Drivers make decisions quickly, anticipate decisions they want from you (or will want to make with you), and do whatever preparation you can to speed your decision making.

6. *Implement decisions as soon as possible.* Once a decision is made, try to put it into operation immediately. Drivers are do-it-now people. When you are action-oriented, they're less stressed.

7. *Complete projects on schedule.* More than any other style, Drivers value on-time completion. Don't be casual about deadlines. When you commit to a schedule, especially with a Driver, keep your commitment.

8. *Respond promptly to messages and requests.*

9. *When writing, keep it short.* Consider "bulleting" key points. Put supporting information in appendixes.

Demonstrate Higher Energy

Drivers are typically high-energy people. When relating to Drivers, there are times when you'll need to put more vigor into what you say and do.

1. *Maintain an erect posture.* Keep your back straight and lean into the conversation. Keep your feet flat on the floor. Keep your head erect, not propped on your hands.

2. *Use gestures to show your involvement in the conversation.* As an Amiable, you tend to use loose, flowing gestures. Use more emphatic body English.

3. *Increase the frequency and intensity of your eye contact.*

4. *Increase your vocal intensity.* Speak a bit louder than you normally would. Let the intensity of your voice communicate that you are taking the matter seriously. Show conviction through your voice.

5. *Move and speak more quickly.* The behaviors that were mentioned under the heading "Pick Up the Pace" all help you interact more energetically.

Be More Task-Oriented

The Driver is usually more task-oriented, and the Amiable tends to be more people-oriented. When working with a Driver, you may want to give increased attention to the task side of things.

1. *Be on time.* Drivers are more time-conscious than most Amiables. They expect you to be punctual.

2. *Get right to business.* Don't give the impression that you're there to chat. But don't lose your human touch, either. Limit the small talk. It's usually appropriate to spend a little time on openers, but keep it brief and don't make it too personal. Then get right into what you're there to talk about.

3. *Be a bit more formal.* It's easy for an Amiable to slip into a more casual demeanor than Drivers may consider appropriate. Dress in a businesslike manner (assuming that that's compatible with the culture of your company).

4. *Maintain a businesslike demeanor.* Drivers prefer to keep focused on the task.

De-emphasize Feelings

Drivers are less emotionally aware and less disclosing of their feelings than most people. You can get more in sync with Drivers by being less emotionally disclosing. Be more reserved without becoming cold or aloof.

1. *Limit your facial expressiveness.* To flex to Drivers, have your facial expression be a closer match to your co-worker's seriousness.

2. *Limit your gestures.* When working with a Driver, it usually makes sense to rely less on body English. Talk less with your hands, for example.

3. *Avoid touch.* Below-the-line people, including many Amiables, spontaneously reach out and touch the person they're talking to. Drivers typically feel uneasy when someone touches them. Honor their preferences and avoid touch.

4. *Talk about what you think rather than about what you feel. Think* about issues you'll be discussing with a Driver. The words you use are important, too. Saying "*I think . . .*" instead of "I feel . . ." can make a difference. Then follow up with factual statements. Drivers appreciate the change in conversational ambience when you begin using such phrases as, "I've *analyzed* the situation . . . ," "My *objective* in doing this is . . . ," "My *plan* for the next quarter . . . ," or "A *logical conclusion* . . . ." Why not use words and phrases that are music to a Driver's ears?

5. *Don't upset yourself if the Driver seems impersonal.* These people are so focused on task and are so time-conscious that you may feel you are just another piece of equipment the Driver is using to get the job done. Don't take it personally—unless, of course, you've done something to offend. Accept the fact that many people of this style are fairly impersonal in their manner of working.

Be Clear About Your Goals and Plans

Drivers are the most goal-oriented of the styles. They also take a more planned approach to their work than most people. The Amiable is more apt to take a fairly casual approach to goal setting and planning. This can become a point of tension between the two styles.

1. *Engage in goal setting.* A Driver expects you to have a very clear and specific understanding of what you are trying to achieve.

2. *Set stretch goals.* Don't think Drivers are content if you show them a set of run-of-the-mill goals and objectives. They expect you to raise your sights and commit to meaningful goals. At the same time, Drivers are realists. So set stretch goals that are achievable.

3. *Plan your work.* The Driver doesn't want you to waste time crafting ornate plans. Just come up with a simple, straightforward, results-oriented guide to action.

Say What You Think

Drivers tend to speak up and express themselves candidly and directly. Amiables are more likely to keep their thoughts to themselves and speak somewhat tentatively and indirectly. Here's how you can bridge that behavioral gap.

1. *Speak up more often.* Initiate conversations more often. In conversations and meetings, express yourself frequently enough so that there's a more balanced give-and-take. Drivers usually want to know where people stand. They would rather not have to try to interpret the meaning of your silence or have to pry thoughts out of you.

2. *Tell more; ask less.* Say "Here's what I think," rather than, "Do you think it would make sense to . . . ?" Say, "Please do this," instead of, "Could you do this?"

3. *Make statements that are definite rather than tentative.* Avoid words like *try, perhaps, maybe, possibly,* etc. Be specific. Don't say you'll complete a project "as soon as possible." Say it will be done "by 12:00 noon next Tuesday."

4. *Eliminate gestures that suggest you lack confidence in the point you are making.* Don't shrug your shoulders, hold your palms up, or use facial expressions that undercut what you are saying, imply helplessness, or suggest the avoidance of responsibility.

5. *Voice your disagreements.* When Drivers disagree with you, they usually come right out and say so. They expect the same from you. Face conflict more openly, stating your opinions frankly but tactfully. At the same time, try to avoid situations where you and the Driver are battling from entrenched positions.

6. *Don't gloss over problems.* Beat bad news to the punch. Then give regular, brief, frank reports on your progress regarding the problem situation.

Cut to the Chase

Amiables are interested in some kinds of information that Drivers could care less about. These very-time-conscious people may get very stressed if you talk about things they don't think they need to know.

1. *Concentrate on high-priority issues.* Drivers seldom want to be briefed on as many topics as an Amiable may want to discuss. For example, in weekly meetings with his reports, a Driver probably wants to hear only about exceptions from what is expected: problems, potential problems, and better-than-anticipated performance—not all the areas of a subordinate's responsibilities. Be very disciplined about reducing the number of topics you initiate in conversations with Drivers.

2. *Present the main points and skip all but the most essential details.* Drivers rarely feel they need anything more than an overview. They'll ask for more information if they want it.

3. *If in doubt, leave it out.* This guideline reiterates the previous two. It's worth repeating, though, because when you eliminate from the conversation those things that Drivers may think are extraneous, you greatly reduce their stress and impatience.

Be Well Organized in Your Communication

Drivers expect you to be well organized, brief, practical, and factual. As an Amiable, by contrast, you tend to be more casual and informal when you talk. So, when presenting ideas or recommendations to Drivers, you make your case better when you incorporate the following behaviors.

1. *Be prepared.* Drivers expect you to make good use of their time. Don't wing it; think things through in advance. Anticipate questions you may be asked. Most of the suggestions here are enhanced by using more than your customary preparation.

2. *Have a well-organized presentation.* Explain your thoughts systematically. It often helps to present your ideas as a series of points arranged in logical order.

3. *When making recommendations, offer two options for the Driver to choose between.* Provide information that helps the Driver assess the probable outcome of each alternative.

4. *Focus on the results* of the action being discussed. Very early in the discussion of a course of action, describe the outcomes that could be

achieved by the approaches you advocate. Then, factually demonstrate that the outcomes you project are both desirable and achievable.

5. *Emphasize that you are recommending pragmatic ways of doing things.* Demonstrate to these practical people that the options you present are very workable, no-frills ways of getting the results they want.

6. *Provide accurate factual evidence.* When talking with Drivers, it's rarely advisable to use someone's opinion or recommendation as evidence. Hard, accurate facts persuade these folks, so keep your presentation objective. Don't rely on sentiment or emotional appeals. As the detective on TV's *Dragnet* series used to say, "Just the facts . . . just the facts."

In your initial efforts to flex to Drivers, you'll probably find it helpful to review the portrait of the Driver style found in Chapter 6, pages 43–48.

Be Careful in Relating to Other Amiables

When people of the same style work together, they may be too similar! They lack important differences that occur when people of two or more styles collaborate. Some style-based differences can be useful at times in developing productive work relationships. Thus, when relating to another Amiable, you may sometimes find it advantageous to temporarily use behaviors that are more characteristic of one of the other styles. For example, when two Amiables are working together, they may be more productive if one becomes more time-conscious and goal-oriented, calling attention to milestones and deadlines. Also, Amiables tend to create exceptionally harmonious working relationships. When two Amiables are collaborating, it's often helpful if one strongly asserts a different point of view when that's appropriate. Similarly, Amiables are so people-oriented that when they are engaged in a project, they may become less productive because of spending excessive time on interpersonal issues. Or, they may come up with a rather bland recommendation because of not wanting to rock the boat.

Therefore, in relating to another Amiable make sure you don't overuse style-based tendencies or use them when it's inappropriate to do so. Also, look for times to add some of the strengths more characteristic of the other styles by temporarily modifying some of your behavior.

For *Drivers* Only: How to Flex to Each Style

The purpose of this appendix is to coach Drivers on specific things they can do to create more productive relationships with people of each style.

Most of the recommendations are about temporary behavioral changes that you can make for just a few minutes, before resuming your more comfortable style-based ways. However, we also mention a few options that have more long-term implications.

Since this appendix is a planning aid, don't try to read it straight through. Instead, find the section that applies to the style you want to flex to:

- Expressives, page 169
- Analyticals, page 175
- Amiables, page 180
- Other Drivers, page 185

Read that section to figure out what you can do to make it easier for persons of that style to work effectively with you. Later, when you want to improve your relationship with someone of a different style, read the section dealing with that style. By working your way through the appendix on an as-needed basis, you'll soon read all the sections and strengthen important relationships in the process.

FLEXING TO EXPRESSIVES

As a Driver, you have much in common with Expressives. You are similar on one of the two behavioral dimensions of style: Both of you are more assertive than most people. Consequently, Expressives tend to appreciate your energetic, fast-paced ways.

In flexing to Expressives, your major challenge is to get in sync with some of their more-responsive behaviors. You're able to create a more effective working relationship with an Expressive by *temporarily* using some of the following types of behavior, within each of which a number of specifics are mentioned. Do several, but not necessarily all, of the suggested specifics. You'll probably think of additional ways to work better with the particular person you have in mind.

Make Personal Contact

Expressives like to have personal contact with those they work with. It's important to them that they get to know you and that you get to know them personally. Drivers need to remind themselves to take the time and make the effort to establish personal contact with Expressives they work with.

1. *Don't seem aloof.* Expressives are apt to see the more reserved Drivers as aloof and distant. Without overdoing it, demonstrate more warmth in your words, your tone of voice, and your facial expression.

2. *Be more casual and informal than usual.* Expressives are inclined to informality. The more formal tendencies of a Driver may make you seem somewhat impersonal. Let your hair down a bit in this conversation.

3. *At the outset, touch base personally.* The Expressive is put off by an immediate plunge into the agenda. Take a few minutes to build rapport at the beginning of a conversation. Show Expressives that you're interested in them as people. Give them an opening to talk about themselves. For example, you can inquire about their personal interests or their opinions on a topic that's being widely discussed.

4. *Disclose something about yourself.* Expressives are the most talkative of the styles, so you may have to look for an opening to get in a word about yourself. You don't have to go on at length, but do let them get to know you better.

5. *Talk about what's going on with other people, too.* The gregarious Expressive is interested in knowing the latest about people he knows.

6. *Look for opportunities for conversations that are not task-related.* When a meeting ends, there may be a few minutes for the two of you to catch up on one another's life. The goal is to be appropriately though not excessively sociable.

Focus More on Feelings

Expressives are very much in touch with and disclosing of their feelings. Whatever those feelings are, they influence and sometimes even dominate the Expressive's decisions, actions, and responses to others. Since Drivers are much less emotive, getting in sync with an Expressive's feelings is a key to working effectively with her.

1. *Be aware of what the Expressive is feeling.* It's not that an Expressive's emotional cues are subtle; they'll probably come across loud and clear. But everyone has selective perception, and the Driver is likely to become engrossed in the *content* of the conversation and miss the emotional component even when it's quite obvious. Since Expressives' emotions have major impact on what they do, it's crucial to stay in touch with what they're feeling.

2. *Acknowledge the Expressive's feelings.* When Expressives are up about something they're working on, acknowledge the feelings: "You're excited about the way project X is going." When they're down, reflect those feelings, too: "You're frustrated that just when you got Sandy trained, she was transferred to another department, and now you have to start breaking in a new rep."

3. *Don't overreact to the Expressive's highs and lows.* Expressives have greater mood swings than any of the styles. When they're high, they are energetic and excited about what they're doing. When they're low, they feel discouraged and unappreciated. As a Driver you are more even-keeled in emotional terms. Don't read too much into the Expressive's extremes of feeling, unless they persist over time. An Expressive's feeling states are more fleeting than most people's; he'll probably be in a very different mood shortly.

4. *Show more feelings yourself.* If you are delighted about something, say so. If you are disappointed, let that be known. When you are annoyed, talk about your feelings as well as what is bugging you. Say something like, "I'm irritated that you missed this deadline." Let your body language convey more of your feelings, too. For example, when expressing feelings, put more inflection in your voice.

5. *Demonstrate more enthusiasm.* When relating to an Expressive, showing enthusiasm is a particularly important way of disclosing more feeling. Though Expressives get dispirited at times, they are the most enthusiastic of the styles. When trying to sell an idea to an Expressive, your enthusiasm itself may be more persuasive than a logical presentation of the facts of the case. If you don't show excitement about the idea, the Expressive is apt to think you lack confidence in it. Also, whenever you're genuinely enthusiastic for the Expressive's projects and victories, share that feeling.

6. *Don't read too much into an Expressive's volatile verbal attacks.* Remember, under normal circumstances, people of this style are very emotive and more given to exaggeration than any of the styles. When the Expressive is angry, emotions and exaggerations tend to become more pronounced. Try not to take the angry comments literally. Expressives

have more temper to control than most people, so don't assume that the derogatory things said in a fit of anger accurately communicate their thinking. However, if the verbal abuse becomes excessive, find a way to put an end to it.

Cooperate with the Expressive's Conversational Spontaneity

It's important to realize that when Expressives talk, they're often "thinking out loud." Expressives sometimes ask, "How will I know what I'm thinking unless I say it?" Above-the-line styles tend to get their ducks in order before they speak. If either you or the Expressive doesn't adapt to the style-based differences in verbal spontaneity, communication snafus are likely.

1. *Allow enough time for the conversation.* Although Expressives' speech is fast-paced, their tendency to tell stories and skip from one topic to another can be quite time-consuming, so don't impose tight time constraints on your meeting with an Expressive.

2. *Keep a balance between flowing with an Expressive's digressions and getting back on track.* With Expressives you can expect to have long, wandering conversations. If you try to keep these highly assertive people from getting sidetracked onto other subjects, you're apt to end in an unproductive power struggle. However, after they've digressed for a while, you sometimes need to tactfully get the conversation refocused.

3. *Spend time in mutual exploration.* Once Expressives are sold on an idea, they may not want to explore other options. Similarly, Drivers are likely to have their own point of view. When two highly assertive people argue from fixed positions, the result can be an unproductive "dialogue of the deaf." To avoid this, listen carefully to the Expressive's ideas and converse in such a way that there's a mutual discussion of the problem and possible solutions.

4. *Be patient with overstatements.* With their tendency to be dramatic, Expressives are liable to exaggerate to make a point. Unless a more accurate understanding of a particular matter is essential to the discussion, don't press for accuracy. Concentrate instead on the idea the Expressive is trying to get across, and let the conversation move on.

5. *Be tactful in responding to contradictions in what the Expressive says.* Since Expressives are thinking things through while they talk, they may make contradictory statements in the same conversation without realizing it. If the conflicting thoughts are not germane to what's being discussed, just overlook the discrepancy. If it's central to what is being talked about, find a diplomatic way to get at the actual meaning of the Expressive's statements.

Be Open to the Expressive's Fun-Loving Side

Expressives are the most playful and fun-loving of the styles. They like to mix pleasure with business. If you lighten up a little when working with an Expressive, you may be able to get more done than if you stick strictly to business.

1. *Don't get impatient if the Expressive indulges in a few jokes.* When you are ready to get down to business, an Expressive is apt to regale you with jokes. Instead of getting upset at what might seem like a waste of time, relax and enjoy the humor. However, there's no need for you to get into the act with jokes of your own unless you choose to.

2. *Be relaxed about a certain amount of fooling around.* Even in the midst of serious business, an Expressive may engage in horseplay. Go with the flow for a while. It may be the release that the Expressive needs before focusing again on the business at hand.

3. *Try to create a more pleasant atmosphere for your conversation.* Sitting behind a table in a sterile conference room or talking across a desk in someone's office is not the Expressive's cup of tea. If the weather and location permit, talk while taking a noontime stroll, or over breakfast or lunch at a favorite bistro. Put your mind to it, and you'll find more options than you expect.

Give the Expressive Recognition

Expressives, even more than most people, like recognition.

1. *Show appreciation for the Expressive's contribution.* Expressives thrive on sincere compliments. For the Expressive, it's even better if the appreciation is expressed publicly.

2. *Let the Expressive be in the spotlight.* By and large, people of this style find it easy to be the center of attention. Try to find ways for them to get the recognition they enjoy while making sure everyone on a project gets the credit they deserve.

Communicate on the Expressive's Wavelength

When speaking with an Expressive, realize that information you find convincing may carry little weight with the Expressive. Here are some ways to communicate on the Expressive's wavelength.

1. *Summarize face-to-face communication in writing.* Expressives like to talk things over face-to-face. If that's not possible, try using the telephone. When you reach a definite conclusion in your face-to-face meeting or phone call, paraphrase it. Then, when the issue is important, follow up immediately with a *brief* written summary of what was decided.

2. *Try to support the Expressive's vision.* People of this style are dreamers—in both the best and the worst senses of the word. They often have a vision of a better future for their department or organization. But their vision may be unrealistic or poorly aligned with the direction of the corporation. When you can, help Expressives inject realism into their proposed ventures. And on those occasions when you can't conscientiously support their visionary proposals, be respectful as well as clear in expressing your opposition.

3. *Steer clear of the nitty-gritty.* Mention even fewer details than you normally would. When Expressives want to know more, they'll ask. However, when details are of crucial importance, make sure they are not glossed over.

4. *Don't overdo facts and logic.* What seems like a desirable amount of facts and logic to a Driver undoubtedly seems like overkill to an Expressive. Edit out of your conversation any facts or logic that aren't absolutely essential to making your point.

5. *Highlight recommendations of others*—especially recommendations of people the Expressive knows or respects. The testimony of a friend or of people who have successfully used the same approach probably carries more weight than tables of statistics or other impersonal evidence.

6. *Demonstrate concern about the human side.* When possible, invite the Expressive's input before a decision is made. Discuss the effect on people of new policies, procedures, processes, and projects. For example, when discussing a new practice, in addition to pointing out its cost-cutting advantages, be sure to add a comment such as, "Most people will like the way it cuts down on the excessive overtime they've been complaining about."

7. *Recommend a particular course of action.* Rather than present Expressives with options, it's often best to help them get enthused about what you think is the best alternative.

8. *Provide incentives when possible.* Everybody likes an incentive, but few people are as motivated by them as Expressives.

Provide Considerable Freedom

Like Drivers, Expressives want to do things their own way. These free spirits want to avoid as many restraints as they can.

1. *Help Expressives put their personal stamp on what they do.* They want their work to be a form of self-expression. Regarding the things they are involved with, they want to be able to say, "I did it my way." However, Drivers are sometimes very insistent about how they want things done.

When possible, avoid pressuring the Expressive into doing things your way.

2. *Empower Expressives to do new things.* They hate doing the same old things in the same old ways. Look for ways to help them inject some novelty into their work. Also, try to find new approaches to the way the two of you work together.

3. *Be willing to improvise when you can.* You are probably much more organized than your Expressive colleague. You may be used to planning your work and working your plan. However, for the Expressive, planning is a drag and following a plan feels like being put in a straitjacket. Be open to the possibility of winging it from time to time.

4. *Cater to their physical restlessness.* Expressives hate to sit still even more than you do. Don't just sit and talk with an Expressive for long periods; create reasons to get up and move around a bit. Also, since Expressives don't like the confinement of a desk-type job, when it's in your power help them find projects or roles that enable them to release some of their physical energy.

5. *Avoid power struggles.* The Expressive is more assertive than most people. You are, too. Because of that, the two of you have much in common. However, when two such assertive people work together, there's always the danger that sparks will fly. If that begins to happen, temporarily find ways of being less assertive. Listen more, and listen better. Decrease your vocal intensity, phrase your ideas more provisionally, and be more negotiable.

In your initial efforts to flex to Expressives, you'll probably find it helpful to review the portrait of the Expressive style found in Chapter 6, pages 48–53.

FLEXING TO ANALYTICALS

As a Driver, you have much in common with Analyticals. You are similar on one of the two basic dimensions of style: Both of you are less responsive than most people. Consequently, Analyticals generally appreciate your focus on task and your objective approach to things.

In flexing to Analyticals, your major challenge is to get in sync with some of their less-assertive behaviors. You should be able to create a more-effective working relationship with an Analytical by temporarily using some of the following four types of behavior, within which a number of specifics are mentioned. Do several, but not necessarily all, of the specifics within the types of behavior you plan to emphasize. You'll probably think of additional ways to work better with the specific Analytical you have in mind.

Slow Your Pace

Analyticals walk slowly, talk slowly, decide slowly. To fast-paced Drivers, it seems they do everything at a snail's pace. But to the Analytical, the fast pace of a typical Driver is very uncomfortable. It throws Analyticals off their stride. If you want to work better with those thorough and deliberate people, slow down and get more in sync with their natural rhythm.

1. *Talk slower.* When Drivers talk at their natural pace, Analyticals often have to strain to keep up. Why put yourself at that disadvantage when making a point?

2. *Don't create unnecessarily tight deadlines.* Few Drivers understand how very stressful it can be for Analyticals to do things at a rate that would be only mildly uncomfortable for the Driver. Then, too, as the Analytical knows full well, there are many times when haste merely makes waste.

3. *When it comes to making decisions, don't rush the Analytical unnecessarily.* Realize that your style and the Analytical's are very different when it comes to making decisions. Compared to most people, you make choices quickly and easily. For the Analytical, decision making is a slow, more difficult, and more stressful process. If you add a time crunch to the scenario, the Analytical's stress may go even higher. There are times when these slow deciders need a nudge. But if time is not of the essence, let them make decisions in their own way: deliberately.

4. *Take time to be more thorough.* Analyticals like to do things slowly and thoroughly. When working with Analyticals, look for situations where you can increase your productivity as well as rapport by taking a more thorough approach than you normally would.

Listen More, Listen Better

Drivers tend to speak their minds; Analyticals are apt to keep their opinions to themselves. If the Driver is also a poor listener, which is often the case, the Analytical is apt to clam up even more. It's hard to have a productive work relationship when one person isn't talking. Drivers don't get the information they need, and the Analytical's active participation begins to dry up. A growing rift settles into the relationship. Though the conversational lopsidedness is certainly not all your fault, it is in your best interest to improve the situation by listening more and better.

1. *Talk less.* When you are with an Analytical who tends to be on the quiet side, make a disciplined effort to talk less. Because the amount of talking you do is habitual, you probably find that it's not easy to decrease it. Drivers who commit to having balanced conversations with Analyticals are usually helped by the method described in Chapter 11.

2. *Provide more and longer pauses to make it easier for the Analytical to get into the conversation.* Analyticals need longer pauses than Drivers, so give them longer and more frequent pauses.

3. *Invite Analyticals to speak.* Request their input on the agenda; ask their opinions on the topics you cover. When explaining your thoughts, draw them into the conversation by checking: "How does this fit with your thinking?" "I'm interested in your point of view on what I've said." "How does this sound to you?"

4. *Reflect back to the speaker the gist of what you hear.* This is a way of acknowledging a person's viewpoint without either agreeing or disagreeing with it. Once you've reflected back what the person has said, pause to see if she wishes to add anything. Then it's your turn to give your response. Begin by stating points of agreement. Choose your words carefully if you disagree with parts of what the Analytical said. If people of this style think they'll get clobbered when they do speak up, you'll hear even less from them in the future.

5. *Don't interrupt.* When you cut off other people in midsentence to add more comments of your own, it's not unreasonable for them to assume you don't value their opinion. That can be a real barrier to constructive work relationships.

6. *Don't finish the other person's sentences.* It can try the patience of a fast-paced Driver to listen to the hesitant speech of a particularly slow-talking Analytical. But patience is exactly what's required for a Driver to flex effectively to an Analytical.

Don't Come on Too Strong

Analyticals, by definition, are less assertive than you. Their body language isn't as forceful. They don't speak as often, and when they do, they're not as emphatic. So when you use your normal Driver behavior, the mismatch in assertiveness may lead the Analytical to think of you as pushy. A relationship certainly isn't enhanced when one person feels he is being pushed around by another. Also, if your way of communicating makes you seem dogmatic, the Analytical may become even more silent than usual, thus depriving you of important information. Here are some things you can do to avoid coming on too strong to Analyticals.

1. *Decrease the intensity of your eye contact.* When speaking to an Analytical, look away a bit more than you normally would. When you do make eye contact, soften your gaze somewhat.

2. *Don't gesture too emphatically.* Drivers often develop some forceful ges-

tures, such as pointing a finger, to underscore a point. This type of gesture tends to be a bit much for most people: It's certainly to be avoided when you are talking to an Analytical.

3. *Decrease your vocal intensity.* Your voice is probably louder than the Analytical's, so you may want to drop the volume a few decibels. Beyond volume, however, Drivers often have an insistent sound to their voice. Once you become aware of your vocal characteristics, you can learn how to sound more casual but still be influential.

4. *Lean back when you make a point.* Do as Analyticals do and lean back when you're talking. Fortunately, when you assume a more laid-back posture, you probably show less intensity in your eye contact, gestures, and voice.

5. *Phrase your ideas more provisionally.* Analyticals often choose language that's quite tentative. Drivers, by contrast, often select words that suggest a more dogmatic stance than they may mean to take. When you use this kind of phrasing with fairly insistent body language, it may sound as if you are trying to rule out any further discussion. These are some phrases that can help you come across in a less dogmatic manner: "Here's an idea off the top of my head." "I'd like to run this up the flagpole." "I like that idea. What if we also . . ." When you don't agree with something, you can take an approach like this: "I'd like to play devil's advocate for a few minutes."

6. *Be more negotiable.* When possible, avoid imposing your solution to a problem on your Analytical co-worker; that's a win–lose approach. A series of win–lose struggles undermines the relationship. Instead, through a win–win style of negotiation or cooperative problem solving, jointly create solutions to the problems you encounter.

Communicate on the Analytical's Wavelength

As with each style, Analyticals have their own preferences about how they'd like things presented to them. If you have an idea you want to get across or a recommendation you wish to make, consider incorporating the following behaviors.

1. *Be prepared.* Analyticals expect you to be well prepared. Dig up all the data they may want. Anticipate questions you may be asked. Even for one-on-one meetings, it's often appropriate to create an agenda. Consider getting the agenda to the Analytical in advance; she may want to think about the topics beforehand. Most of the suggestions here are enhanced by using more than your customary preparation.

2. *Go into great detail.* Analyticals want to delve into the particulars; they thrive on specifics. They want to make sure all the ground has been

covered before they make a decision. You gain credibility with people of this style when they see that you've chased down every detail.

3. *Give a sound rationale for narrowing the options.* Analyticals want to consider all the alternatives. Although this tendency often helps them make good decisions, it also increases their tendency to be inordinately indecisive. You can help them weed out some of the weaker alternatives by giving them logical and factual reasons for doing so.

4. *Mention the problems and disadvantages of the proposal you put forward.* In addition to mentioning the pluses of your recommendation, tell the Analytical about the downside, too. She undoubtedly will respect you for doing so. Then, build your credibility further by recommending ways of dealing with the problems and the disadvantages.

5. *Show why the approach you advocate is best.* For Analyticals, "best" is a combination of quality, economy, and low risk. You have to figure out the relative weight of each of these criteria for a particular Analytical in a particular set of circumstances. "Best" for this style includes *long-term benefits* as well as immediate advantages. Discuss the future in terms of probabilities: "Here's a projection of what's likely to happen. . . ." Since the Analytical is conservative when it comes to risk, if possible show why your approach is a fairly safe bet.

6. *Be accurate.* People of this style are both precise and skeptical. They abhor a superficial gathering of information or careless reporting of it. Where others might settle for approximations, Analyticals want meticulously correct information. So be painstakingly accurate in what you report to people of this style.

7. *Provide written support materials, and/or follow up in writing.* Analyticals tend to prefer the written word to the spoken. Even so, it's best to make an oral presentation as well. That way you can note the Analytical's reactions and answer questions. At the same time, cater to the Analytical's preference for written communication by preparing well-thought-out support materials and/or a follow-up report. You may want to include a step-by-step timetable for implementing any decisions.

8. *Be prepared to listen to more than you want to know.* When Analyticals talk, they often present far more information than most people think is necessary. They explain their ideas or discuss progress on projects in what may feel to you like overwhelming detail. This much minutiae may be boring and difficult to follow. Be patient and stay tuned in; Analyticals appreciate your attentiveness. And, there's probably information you need to know buried somewhere in all that detail.

In your initial efforts to flex to Analyticals, you'll probably find it helpful to review the portrait of the Analytical style found in Chapter 7, pages 58–62.

FLEXING TO AMIABLES

As a Driver, you differ from the Amiable on both of the basic dimensions of style. The Amiable is less assertive and less responsive than you are. So you are likely to experience more style-based differences with Amiables than with either Analyticals or Expressives, both of whom have one basic dimension of behavior in common with you. As a result, there are more types of behavior that you can modify when flexing to an Amiable than when flexing to any other style.

As you read the types of *temporary* adjustment of behavior that can help you get in sync with Amiables, select carefully the one to four types you think will help you work best with a particular Amiable. It's not easy to change habitual behavior, even for a short time, so be sure to select only one to four types of behavior to work on. Within each type or category of behavior, a number of specifics are mentioned. Do several, but not necessarily all, of the specifics within the behavioral category you plan to emphasize. You'll probably think of additional ways to work better with the specific Amiable you have in mind.

Make Genuine Personal Contact

The Amiable wants to be treated as a human being and not as a function or a role only. The Driver, who is more task-oriented than most people, may need to remember to show a sincere interest in the Amiable as a person.

1. *Don't seem aloof.* Be more casual and informal than usual. Without overdoing it, demonstrate more warmth in your words, your tone of voice, and your facial expression.

2. *At the outset, touch base personally.* Amiables are usually uncomfortable with a cold, headlong plunge into the agenda. At the beginning of a conversation, take a few minutes to build rapport. Show that you are interested in the Amiable as a person. Give Amiables an opening to talk about themselves.

3. *Disclose something about yourself.* The Amiable likes to invite you to talk about yourself. Don't brush it off with, "Oh, things are fine." Briefly, let him know some things that are going on in your life.

4. *Make the most of opportunities for conversations that are not task-related.* For example, when waiting for a meeting to begin, don't read a report; use that time to chat with Amiables and others who like more personal contact. When a meeting concludes, you can also create opportunities for social interchange. You'll find many other occasions when you can be in touch with Amiables as people. The goal is to be appropriately though not excessively sociable.

Slow Your Pace

Amiables walk slowly, talk slowly, decide slowly. To fast-paced Drivers, it seems like they do everything at a crawl. But to the Amiable, the fast pace of a typical Driver is very uncomfortable. It throws Amiables off their stride. If you want to work better with Amiables, slow down and get more in sync with their natural rhythm.

1. *Talk slower.* When Drivers talk at their natural pace, Amiables often have to strain to keep up. Why put yourself at that disadvantage when making a point?

2. *Don't create unnecessarily tight deadlines.* Remember, it can be very stressful for the Amiable to do things at your pace.

3. *When it comes to decision making, don't rush the Amiable unnecessarily.* There are times when these slow deciders need a nudge. But unless time is of the essence, let them make decisions on their own schedule.

Listen More, Listen Better

Drivers tend to speak their minds; Amiables are apt to keep their opinions to themselves. If the Driver is also a poor listener, which is often the case, the Amiable is apt to clam up even more. It's hard to have a productive work relationship when one person isn't talking. Drivers don't get the information they need, and the Amiable's active participation begins to dry up. A rift appears in the relationship. Although the conversational lopsidedness is certainly not all your fault, it's certainly in your best interest to improve the situation by listening more and better.

1. *Talk less.* When you are with an Amiable who tends to be on the quiet side, make a disciplined effort to talk less. It's not easy. Drivers who commit to having balanced conversations with Amiables are usually helped by the method described in Chapter 11.

2. *Provide more and longer pauses to make it easier for the Amiable to get into the conversation.* Amiables need longer pauses than Drivers, so give them longer and more frequent pauses.

3. *Invite Amiables to speak.* Request their input on the agenda. Ask their opinion on the topics you cover. When explaining your thoughts, draw them into the conversation with checking questions: "How does this fit with your thinking?" "I'm interested in your point of view on what I've said." "How does this sound to you?"

4. *Reflect back to the speaker the gist of what you hear.* This is a way of acknowledging a person's viewpoint without either agreeing or disagreeing. Once you've reflected back what the person has said, pause to

see if he wishes to add anything. Then it's your turn to give your response. Begin by stating points of agreement. If you disagree with something, choose your words carefully. If people of this style think they'll get clobbered when they speak up, you'll hear even less from them in the future.

5. *Don't interrupt.* When you cut people off in midsentence in order to add more comments of your own, it's not unreasonable for them to assume that you don't value their opinion. That can be a real barrier to constructive work relationships.

6. *Don't finish Amiables' sentences.* It can try the patience of a fast-paced Driver to listen to the hesitant speech of a particularly slow-talking Amiable. But patience is exactly what's required for a Driver who wants to flex effectively to an Amiable.

Don't Come on Too Strong

Amiables, by definition, are less assertive than you. Their body language isn't as forceful. They don't speak as often, and when they do they're not as emphatic. So when you use your normal Driver behavior, the mismatch in assertiveness may lead the Amiable to think of you as pushy. A relationship certainly isn't enhanced when one person feels pushed around by another. Also, if your way of communicating makes you seem dogmatic, the Amiable may become even more silent than usual, thus depriving you of important information. Here are some things you can do to avoid coming on too strong to Amiables.

1. *Decrease the intensity of your eye contact.* The Driver's eye contact is more intense than the Amiable's. When speaking to an Amiable, soften your gaze.

2. *Don't gesture too emphatically.* Drivers often develop some forceful gestures, such as pointing a finger, to underscore a point. This type of gesture tends to be somewhat disturbing for most people: It's certainly to be avoided when you are talking with an Amiable.

3. *Decrease your vocal intensity.* Drop the volume a few decibels. Try to sound less insistent. Once you become aware of your vocal characteristics, you can learn how to sound more casual and still be influential.

4. *Lean back when you make a point.* Do as they do and lean back when you're talking. Fortunately, when you assume a more laid-back posture, you probably show less intensity in your eye contact, gestures, and voice.

5. *Phrase your ideas more provisionally.* Amiables often choose language that's quite tentative. Drivers, by contrast, often select words that sug-

gest a more dogmatic stance than they mean to take. When this kind of phrasing is coupled with a fairly insistent body language, it may sound as if you are trying to rule out any discussion. These are some phrases that can help you come across in a less dogmatic way: "Here's an idea off the top of my head." "I'd like to run this up the flagpole." "I like that idea. What if we also . . ." When you don't agree with something, you can take an approach like this: "I'd like to play devil's advocate for a few minutes."

6. *Be more negotiable.* When possible, avoid imposing your solution to a problem on your Amiable co-worker, for that's a win–lose approach. A series of win–lose struggles undermines the relationship. Instead, through a win–win approach to negotiation or cooperative problem solving, jointly create solutions to the problems you encounter.

Focus More on Feelings

Amiables are expressive of their emotions and sensitive to the feelings of others. You can get more in sync with Amiables by focusing more on feelings—both theirs and your own.

1. *Look at the person you are conversing with* so you can take in body-language cues.

2. *Concentrate on the meaning of the person's body language.* Drivers are apt to give excessive attention to the words that are spoken and overlook important nonverbal cues. As you notice the nonverbal signals, keep asking yourself, "What does this suggest about this person's feelings right now?"

3. *Note how the other person reacts.* Amiables dislike conflict and may not verbalize their disagreement or dissatisfaction. Changes in their body language can tip you off as to how they may be reacting to what is being said. Once you surmise that the other person has negative feelings about a proposal, you can invite his or her reaction: "Some people are leery of this part of the plan. I'm interested in your thoughts about it."

4. *Demonstrate more feelings yourself.* If you are pleased about something, say so. If you are disappointed, let that be known. Let your body language express your feelings more. Put a little more inflection into your voice. Smile a bit more to demonstrate warmth toward the person you are with.

Be Supportive

Amiables are supportive, and they expect others to be supportive in turn. They feel that's the least one human being should be able to expect from another.

1. *Listen empathically so the Amiable feels heard and understood.* Truly listening to someone is one of the most supportive things we can do for that person. Earlier, we emphasized the importance of listening, but it's so important for Drivers flexing to Amiables that it bears repeating.

2. *Express sincere appreciation for the Amiable's contributions.* A number of behavioral scientists say it's desirable to "stroke" a person five times as much as you criticize or give negative feedback. Even more than most people, Amiables thrive on appreciation. Find lots of ways to say, "Thanks for your good work." Also, decrease the number of critical and judgmental statements you make. When you do give criticism, make sure it's constructive.

3. *Lend a helping hand.* Amiables are the most helpful of the styles. They often drop what they're doing to aid someone who's in a pinch. They appreciate it when you spot an opportunity to give them a hand when they're under pressure.

Provide Structure

Amiables tend to be most comfortable and work best in stable, clearly structured situations. Do what you can to contribute to that stability and structure without being overly constraining.

1. When it's within your area of responsibility, *make sure the Amiable's job is well defined and goals are clearly established.* Amiables work best when their roles are clarified and their goals are set.

2. *Help the Amiable plan difficult projects and design complex work processes.* Planning is not the Amiable's forte. When you help develop a sound plan or design an effective work process, an Amiable usually takes it from there.

3. *Reduce uncertainty.* Amiables are not likely to function well in highly ambiguous situations. Try not to put the Amiable in an unstable, rapidly fluctuating situation.

4. *Demonstrate loyalty.* In most cases, Amiables feel a greater-than-average loyalty to the people they work with and the organizations they work in. Consequently, they expect you to demonstrate your loyalty to them, their co-workers, and the organization. Amiables will probably be turned off if they hear you take potshots at employees or the organization. Instead of voicing criticisms, make constructive suggestions for improvement, and make them directly to the people involved.

Demonstrate Interest in the Human Side

Amiables tend to take a people-oriented approach whereas Drivers are prone to be task-oriented. When working with an Amiable, give increased attention to the human side of things.

1. *Invite Amiables' input on matters that affect them.* Although they aren't as demanding as most people, they like to be consulted on matters pertaining to them.

2. *Show that other people support the idea you are advancing.* This people-oriented style is often influenced more by the experiences and opinions of others than by cold facts. Let them know about the positive feelings others in the organization have about your proposal. Provide evidence from experts. Mention testimonies of others who have successfully used a similar approach. If, in the process, the Amiable discovers that there's little risk to the recommended course of action, so much the better.

3. *Discuss the effects of decisions on people and their morale.* Be alert to and speak about the effects on people of new policies, procedures, processes, and projects. For example, when discussing a new practice, in addition to pointing out its cost-cutting advantages be sure to add something like, "Most people will like the way it cuts down on the excessive overtime they've been complaining about."

4. When appropriate, *provide an opportunity for the Amiable to talk with others* before committing to a decision.

In your initial efforts to flex to Amiables, you'll probably find it helpful to review the portrait of the Amiable style found in Chapter 7, pages 54–58.

Be Careful in Relating to Other Drivers

When people of the same style work together, they may be too similar! They lack important differences that occur when people of two or more styles collaborate. Some of these style-based differences can be useful at times in developing productive work relationships. Thus when relating to another Driver, you will sometimes find it advantageous to temporarily use behaviors that are more characteristic of one of the other styles. For example, Drivers are often overly decisive. When a couple of Drivers are working together, they may be more productive if one of them suggests further exploration before making a decision. Also, Drivers tend to be exceptionally independent. When two Drivers are collaborating, it's often helpful if one encourages interdependence by checking out what the other thinks. One of the two Drivers could help them both focus more on long-term impact rather than solely on short-term goals. Similarly, Drivers are so task-oriented that when two of them are engaged in a project, they may become less productive over time because neither one puts in the effort required to maintain a good working relationship. Or, they may come up with an otherwise brilliant recommendation that ultimately fails because they paid scant attention to the human side of the change they wish to implement.

Therefore, in relating to another Driver, make sure you don't overuse style-based tendencies or use them when it's inappropriate to do so. Also, look for times to add some of the strengths more characteristic of the other styles by temporarily modifying some of your behavior. When two highly assertive Drivers work together, there's always a danger that they'll end up in a power struggle. This is the biggest threat to Driver-Driver relationships. If you find that you and another Driver are beginning to butt heads, temporarily find ways of being less assertive. Listen more and listen better. Decrease your vocal intensity, phrase your ideas more provisionally, and be more negotiable.

For *Expressives* Only: How to Flex to Each Style

The purpose of this appendix is to coach Expressives on specific things they can do to create more productive relationships with people of each style.

Most of the recommendations are about temporary behavioral changes that you can make for a few minutes, before resuming your more comfortable style-based ways. However, we also mention a few options that have more long-term implications.

Since this appendix is a planning aid, don't try to read it straight through. Instead, find the section that applies to the style you want to flex to:

- Amiables, page 187
- Drivers, page 191
- Analyticals, page 194
- Other Expressives, page 201

Read that section to figure out what you can do to make it easier for the people of that style to work effectively with you. Later, when you want to improve your relationship with someone of a different style, read the section dealing with that style. By working your way through the appendix on an as-needed basis, you'll soon read all the sections and strengthen important relationships in the process.

FLEXING TO AMIABLES

As an Expressive, you have much in common with Amiables. You are similar on one of the two behavioral dimensions of style: Both of you are more responsive than most people. Consequently, Amiables tend to appreciate your warmth, your friendliness, and your focus on people.

In flexing to Amiables, your major challenge is to get in sync with some of their less-assertive behaviors. You create a more effective working relationship with an Amiable by *temporarily* using some of the following types of behavior, within each of which a number of specifics are mentioned. Do several, but not necessarily all, of the suggested specifics. You'll probably think of additional ways to work better with the particular person you have in mind.

Slow Your Pace

To the Amiable, the fast pace of a typical Expressive is very uncomfortable. It throws Amiables off their stride. If you want to relate better to Amiables, slow down and get more in sync with their natural rhythm.

1. *Talk slower.* Many Expressives talk a lot faster than Amiables. When Expressives talk at their natural pace, Amiables often have to strain to keep up. This is certainly not a user-friendly way of speaking with people. Why put yourself at that disadvantage when making a point?

2. *Don't create unnecessarily tight deadlines.* Remember, it can be very stressful for the Amiable to do things at your pace.

3. *When it comes to decision making, don't rush the Amiable unnecessarily.* There are times when these slow deciders need a nudge. But unless time is of the essence, let them make decisions on their own schedule.

Listen More, Listen Better

Expressives tend to speak their minds; Amiables are apt to keep their opinions to themselves. If the Expressive is also a poor listener, which is often the case, the Amiable is apt to clam up even more. It's hard to have a productive relationship when one person is doing most of the talking. The Amiable's active participation begins to dry up, the Expressive doesn't get the needed information, and there'll probably be a growing rift in the relationship. Although the conversational lopsidedness is certainly not all your fault, it's definitely in your best interest to improve the situation by listening more and better.

1. *Talk less.* When you are with an Amiable who tends to be on the quiet side, make a disciplined effort to talk less. Expressives who commit to having balanced conversations with Amiables are usually helped by the method described in Chapter 11. Although the section in Chapter 11 was written for Drivers, it is equally useful for Expressives.

2. *Provide more and longer pauses to make it easier for the Amiable to get into the conversation.* Amiables need longer pauses than Expressives. So give them long and more frequent pauses.

3. *Invite Amiables to speak.* Request their input on the agenda; ask their opinion on the topics you cover. When explaining your thoughts, draw them into the conversation with checking questions: "How does this fit with your thinking?" "I'm interested in your point of view on what I've said." "How does this sound to you?"

4. *Reflect back to the speaker the gist of what you hear.* This is a way of acknowledging a person's viewpoint without either agreeing or disagreeing with it. Once you've reflected back what the person has said, pause to see if he wishes to add anything. Then it's your turn to give your response. Begin by stating points of agreement. When you disagree, choose your words carefully. If people of this style think they'll get clobbered when they speak up, you'll hear even less from them in the future.

5. *Don't interrupt.* When you cut off others in midsentence to add more comments of your own, it's not unreasonable for those people to assume you don't value their opinion. That can be a real barrier to constructive work relationships.

6. *Don't finish other people's sentences.* It can try the patience of a fast-paced Expressive to listen to the hesitant speech of a particularly slow-talking Amiable. But patience is a prime requisite for an Expressive who wants to flex effectively to an Amiable.

Don't Come on Too Strong

Amiables, by definition, are less assertive than you. Their body language isn't as forceful. They don't speak as often, and when they do, they're not as emphatic. So when you use your normal Expressive behavior, the mismatch in assertiveness may lead the Amiable to think of you as pushy. A work relationship certainly isn't enhanced when one person feels he is being pushed around by another. Also, if your way of communicating makes you seem dogmatic, the Amiable may become even more silent than usual, thus depriving you of important information. Here are some things you can do to avoid coming on too strong to Amiables.

1. *Decrease the intensity of your eye contact.* The Expressive's eye contact is more intense than the Amiable's. When speaking to an Amiable, soften your gaze somewhat.

2. *Restrain your gestures.* Both Expressives and Amiables tend to talk with their hands. However, the Amiable's gestures are much smaller and less dramatic. When talking with Amiables, don't gesture as emphatically as you may be inclined to.

3. *Decrease your vocal intensity.* As a group, Expressives have louder voices than any of the styles. Soft-spoken Amiables find it irritating when

someone speaks to them in a loud voice during a normal conversation. You get through to this style much more effectively when you lower your voice.

4. *Lean back when you make a point.* Do as they do and lean back when you're talking. Fortunately, when you assume a more laid-back posture, you show less intensity in your eye contact, gestures, and voice.

5. *Phrase your ideas more provisionally.* Amiables often choose language that's quite tentative. Expressives, by contrast, often select words that suggest a more dogmatic stance than they may mean to take. This kind of phrasing coupled with fairly insistent body language may sound as if you are trying to rule out any discussion. These are some phrases that can help you come across in a less dogmatic way: "Here's an idea off the top of my head." "I'd like to run this up the flagpole." "I like that idea. What if we also . . ." When you don't agree with something, you can take an approach like this: "I'd like to play devil's advocate for a few minutes."

6. *Be more negotiable.* When possible, avoid imposing your solution to a problem on your Amiable co-worker. Instead, through a win–win approach to negotiation or cooperative problem solving, jointly create solutions to the problems you encounter.

Be Supportive

Amiables are supportive of other people, and they expect others to be supportive in turn. They feel that's the least one human being should expect from another.

1. *Listen empathically so the Amiable feels heard and understood.* Truly listening to others is one of the most supportive things we can do for them. Although we mentioned the importance of listening earlier, it is so important for Expressives flexing to Amiables that it bears repeating.

2. *Express sincere appreciation for the Amiable's contributions.* Amiables thrive on appreciation. Find lots of ways to say, "Thanks for your good work." Also, decrease the number of critical and judgmental statements you make. When you do give criticism, make sure it's constructive.

3. *Lend a helping hand.* Amiables are the most helpful of the styles. They're apt to drop what they're doing to aid someone who's in a pinch. They appreciate it if you spot an opportunity to give them a hand when they're under pressure.

In your initial efforts to flex to Amiables, you'll probably find it helpful to review the portrait of the Amiable style found in Chapter 7, pages 54–58.

FLEXING TO DRIVERS

As an Expressive, you have much in common with Drivers. You are similar on one of the two behavioral dimensions of style: Both of you are more assertive than most people. Consequently, Drivers tend to appreciate your energetic, fast-paced ways.

In flexing to Drivers, your major challenge is to get in sync with some of their less-responsive behaviors. You create a more effective working relationship with a Driver by temporarily using some of the following four types of behavior, within each of which a number of specifics are mentioned. Do several, but not necessarily all, of the suggested specifics. You'll probably think of additional ways to work better with the particular Driver you have in mind.

Be More Task-Oriented

The Driver is usually more task-oriented and the Expressive tends to be more people-oriented. When working with a Driver, you may want to give increased attention to the task side of things.

1. *Be on time.* Expressives are by far the least punctual of the styles—very annoying to most Drivers. When you're working with Drivers, watch your clock (and your calendar!) and be on time.

2. *Be a bit more formal.* Drivers tend toward the conservative in their clothing and grooming. You may want to have a somewhat conservative appearance when working with above-the-line styles. Also, don't be too flip or offbeat in your interactions with Drivers. It's best to take a businesslike approach to your interactions with Drivers—at least until they indicate a preference for a more informal relationship.

3. *Get right to business.* Don't give the impression that you're there to chat. But don't lose your human touch, either. Limit the small talk. It's usually appropriate to spend a little time on openers, but keep it brief and don't make it too personal. Then get right into what you're there to talk about.

4. *Stick to business.* Drivers are the most time-conscious of the styles. And they're not as people-oriented as the below-the-line styles. So they like to keep conversations and meetings short and to the point. The shorter the better. Even in a one-on-one meeting with a Driver, have an agenda and follow it. Don't digress. As you discuss the business at hand and are reminded of things that are tangential to the discussion, don't pursue them. The guideline is, "If in doubt, leave it out." When the time is up, depart quickly, yet graciously.

De-emphasize Feelings

Drivers are less emotionally aware and less disclosing of their feelings than most people. Expressives, by contrast, are more disclosing of their emotions than any style. You can get more in sync with Drivers by being less emotionally disclosing. Be more reserved, without becoming cold or aloof.

1. *Limit your facial expressiveness.* Match your facial expression more closely to your co-worker's seriousness.

2. *Limit your gestures.* The more reserved Driver may be distracted or even a bit disconcerted if you constantly talk with your hands. So, when working with Drivers, tone down the body English a little.

3. *Avoid touch.* Below-the-line people, especially many Expressives, spontaneously reach out and touch the person they're talking to. Above-the-line people, like Drivers, typically feel uneasy when someone touches them. Honor their preferences and avoid touch.

4. *Talk about what you think rather than about what you feel.* Think longer and harder about issues you're discussing with a Driver. The words you use are important, too. Saying "I *think* . . ." instead of "I *feel* . . ." can make a difference. Then follow up with factual statements. Drivers appreciate the change in conversational ambience when you begin using such phrases as: "My *objective* in doing this is . . . ," "My *plan* for the next quarter . . . ," "As I've *analyzed* the situation . . . ," or "A *logical conclusion.* . . ." Why not use words and phrases that are music to a Driver's ears?

5. *Don't upset yourself over the Driver's impersonal and unfeeling manner.* If a Driver seems distant or disengaged, don't take it personally unless you have reason to believe you've done something to offend. People of this style tend to be more impersonal than below-the-line styles. Accept that this is the way these people are and that it's OK for them to be this way. You make things far worse if you create judgmental labels about them in your mind or start telling yourself how unpleasant they are to work with.

Plan Your Work and Work Your Plan

The no-nonsense Driver wants everyone to be clear on goals and how they are going to be achieved. The more spontaneous Expressive is rarely as explicit about these things as the Driver expects. It's often a source of considerable tension.

1. *Convert your dreams into goals and objectives.* Push yourself to commit to a specific result.

2. *Be realistic.* Expressives are great optimists. In their enthusiasm, Expres-

sives often set unattainable goals and objectives. However, Drivers want figures they can count on. So do set stretch goals—and make sure the goals are achievable.

3. *Plan your work.* Drivers are bare-bones planners, but they are planners nonetheless. Expressives have the least affinity for planning of all the styles. But you can do it. The Driver doesn't want you to waste time crafting ornate plans. Just come up with a simple, straightforward, results-oriented guide to action.

4. *Deliver the goods.* When Drivers specify objectives and draw up plans, their direction is set. They take great pride in delivering what they said they would—on standard, on schedule, and on budget. They expect others to do the same. It's not enough to plan your work; work your plan as well. You may be tired of that cliché, but when you heed it, you'll have much better working relationships with Drivers.

Be Well Organized in Your Communication

When you communicate with Drivers, they expect you to be well organized, practical, factual, and brief. Expressives, however, are often poorly organized, somewhat impractical, less factual, and somewhat long-winded. That's a big communication chasm to bridge. When presenting ideas or recommendations to Drivers, you make your case better when you incorporate the following behaviors.

1. *Be prepared.* Drivers expect you to make good use of their time. Don't wing it; think things through in advance. Anticipate questions you may be asked. Even for one-on-one meetings, it's often appropriate to create an agenda. Most of the suggestions here are enhanced by using more than your customary preparation.

2. *Have a well-organized presentation.* Explain your thoughts systematically. It often helps to present your ideas as a series of points arranged in a logical order.

3. *When making recommendations, offer two options for the Driver.* Provide information that helps the Driver assess the probable outcome of each alternative.

4. *Focus on the results of the actions being discussed.* Very early in the discussion of alternative courses of action, describe possible outcomes of the approaches you describe. Then, factually demonstrate that the outcomes you project are both desirable and achievable.

5. *Be pragmatic.* Demonstrate to these practical people that your recommendations are very workable, no-frills ways of getting the results they want.

6. *Provide accurate factual evidence.* When talking with Drivers, it's rarely advisable to use someone's opinion or recommendation as evidence. Hard, accurate facts persuade these folks, so keep your presentation objective. Don't rely on sentiment or emotional appeals. As the detective on TV's *Dragnet* series used to say, "Just the facts . . . just the facts."

Avoid Power Struggles

The Driver is more assertive than most people. You are too. Because of that, the two of you have much in common. However, when two such assertive people work together, there's always the danger that sparks will fly. If that begins to happen, temporarily find ways of being less assertive. Listen more and listen better. Decrease your vocal intensity, phrase your ideas more provisionally, and be more negotiable.

In your initial efforts to flex to Drivers, you'll probably find it helpful to review the portrait of the Driver style found in Chapter 6, pages 43–48.

FLEXING TO ANALYTICALS

As an Expressive, you differ from the Analytical on both dimensions of style. The Analytical is less assertive and less responsive than you. So you may experience more style-based differences with Analyticals than with either Drivers or Amiables, each of whom has one of the basic dimensions of behavior in common with you. As a result, there are more types of behavior you can modify when flexing to an Analytical than when flexing to any other style. As you examine the following temporary adjustments of behavior that help you get in sync with Analyticals, select carefully the one to four types you think will help you work best with the particular person you're relating to. It's not easy to change habitual behavior, even for a short time, so *be sure to select only one to four types of behavior to work on.* Within each type or category of behavior, a number of specifics are mentioned. Do several, but not necessarily all, of the specifics within the behavioral categories you plan to emphasize. You'll probably think of additional ways to work better with the particular Analytical you'll be flexing to.

Slow Your Pace

For the Analytical, the fast pace of a typical Expressive is very uncomfortable. It throws Analyticals off their stride. If you want to work better with Analyticals, slow down and get more in sync with their natural rhythm.

1. *Talk slower.* When Expressives talk at their natural pace, Analyticals often have to strain to keep up. This is certainly not a user-friendly way

of speaking with people. Why put yourself at that disadvantage when making a point?

2. *Don't create unnecessarily tight deadlines.* Remember, it can be very stressful for the Analytical to do things at your pace.

3. *When it comes to decision making, don't rush the Analytical unnecessarily.* There are times when these slow deciders need a nudge. But unless time is of the essence, let them make decisions their way: deliberately.

Listen More, Listen Better

Expressives tend to speak their minds; Analyticals are apt to keep their opinions to themselves. If the Expressive is also a poor listener, which is often the case, the Analytical is apt to clam up even more. It's hard to have a productive work relationship when one person is doing most of the talking. The Analytical's active participation begins to dry up, and the Expressives don't get the information they need. A growing rift appears in the relationship. Though the conversational lopsidedness is not all your fault, it's certainly in your best interest to improve the situation by listening more and better.

1. *Talk less.* When you're with an Analytical who tends to be on the quiet side, make a disciplined effort to talk less. Expressives who commit to having balanced conversations with Analyticals are usually helped by the method described in Chapter 11. Although the section in Chapter 11 was written for Drivers, the method is equally useful for Expressives.

2. *Provide more and longer pauses to make it easier for the Analytical to get into the conversation.* Analyticals need a longer pause than Expressives, so give them longer and more frequent pauses.

3. *Invite Analyticals to speak.* Request their input on the agenda; ask their opinion on the topics you cover. When explaining your thoughts, draw them into the conversation by checking: "How does this fit with your thinking?" "I'm interested in your point of view on what I've said." "How does this sound to you?"

4. *Reflect back to the speaker the gist of what you hear.* This is a way of acknowledging a person's viewpoint without either agreeing or disagreeing with it. Once you've reflected back what the person has said, pause to see if he wishes to add anything. Then it's your turn to give your response. Begin by stating points of agreement. Choose your words carefully if you disagree with parts of what the Analytical said. If people of this style think they'll get clobbered when they speak up, you'll hear even less from them in the future.

5. *Don't interrupt.* When you cut off others in midsentence to add more comments of your own, it's not unreasonable for those people to assume you don't value their opinion. That can be a real barrier to constructive work relationships.

6. *Don't finish other people's sentences.* It can try the patience of a fast-paced Expressive to listen to the hesitant speech of a particularly slow-talking Analytical. But patience is a prime requisite for an Expressive who wants to flex effectively to an Analytical.

Don't Come on Too Strong

Analyticals, by definition, are less assertive than you. Their body language isn't as forceful. They don't speak as often, and when they do they're not as emphatic. So when you use your normal Expressive behavior, the mismatch in assertiveness may lead the Analytical to think of you as pushy. A relationship certainly isn't enhanced when one person feels she is being pushed around by another. Also, if your way of communicating makes you seem dogmatic, the Analytical may become even more silent than usual, thus depriving you of important information. Here are some things you can do to avoid coming on too strong to Analyticals.

1. *Decrease the intensity of your eye contact.* When speaking to an Analytical, look away a bit more than you normally would. And when you do make eye contact, soften your gaze.

2. *Limit your gestures.* Analyticals gesture less often and less energetically than any of the styles. They are often distracted and even disconcerted by an Expressive's frequent, large, and forceful gestures. So when you are working with Analyticals, tone down your body English considerably.

3. *Decrease your vocal intensity.* Soft-spoken Analyticals find it irritating when someone speaks to them in a loud voice during a normal conversation. You get through to this style much more effectively when you lower your voice.

4. *Lean back when you make a point.* Do as they do and lean back when you're talking. Fortunately, when you assume a more laid-back posture, you show less intensity in your eye contact, gestures, and voice.

5. *Phrase your ideas more provisionally.* Analyticals often choose language that's quite tentative. Expressives, however, may select words that suggest a more dogmatic stance than they mean to take. This kind of phrasing coupled with a fairly insistent body language may sound as if you are trying to rule out any discussion of the matter. These are some phrases that can help you come across in a less dogmatic manner: "Here's an idea off the top of my head." "I'd like to run this up the

flagpole." "I like that idea. What if we also . . ." When you don't agree with something, you can take an approach like this: "I'd like to play devil's advocate for a few minutes."

6. *Be more negotiable.* When possible, avoid imposing your solution to a problem on your Analytical co-worker. Instead, use a win–win style of negotiation or cooperative problem solving to jointly create solutions to the problems you encounter.

Be More Task-Oriented

Analyticals are more task-oriented; Expressives are more people-oriented. Since tasks are performed by people, when used well, either approach can be effective. In working with an Analytical, you may want to give increased attention to the task side of things.

1. *Be on time.* Analyticals are much more time-conscious than the average Expressive. So when working with Analyticals, watch your clock (and your calendar!) and be on time.

2. *Be a bit more formal.* In their clothing and grooming, Analyticals tend to be the most conservative of styles. You may want to have a somewhat conservative appearance when working with them. Also, don't be too flip or offbeat in your interactions with Analyticals. They usually expect a more buttoned-down type of work relationship. Finally, your Analytical colleagues are more comfortable with you when you maintain a somewhat reserved demeanor with them.

3. *Get right to business.* Don't give the impression that you're there to chat. But don't lose your human touch, either. Limit the small talk. It's usually appropriate to spend a little time on openers, but keep it brief and don't make it too personal. Then get right into what you're there to talk about.

De-emphasize Feelings

Analyticals are less emotionally aware and less disclosing of their feelings than most people. You can get more in sync with Analyticals by being *less* emotionally disclosing. Be more reserved, without becoming cold or aloof.

1. *Limit your facial expressiveness.* Have your facial expression be a closer match to your co-worker's seriousness.

2. *Avoid touch.* Above-the-line people, like Analyticals, typically feel uneasy when someone touches them. Honor their preferences and avoid touch.

3. *Talk about what you think rather than about what you feel.* Think longer and harder about issues you're discussing with an Analytical. The words

you use are important, too. Saying "I *think* . . ." instead of "I feel . . ." can make a difference. Then follow up with factual statements. Analyticals appreciate the change in conversational ambience when you begin using phrases such as: "I've *analyzed* the situation . . . ," "My *objective* in doing this is . . . ," "My *plan* for the next quarter . . . ," or "A *logical conclusion*. . . ." Why not use words and phrases that are music to an Analytical's ears?

4. *Don't upset yourself over the Analytical's impersonal and unfeeling manner.* If the Analytical you are with seems distant or disengaged, don't take it personally unless you have reason to believe you've done something to offend. People of this style tend to be more impersonal than below-the-line styles. Accept that this is the way these people are and that it's OK for them to be this way. You make things far worse if you create judgmental labels about them in your mind, or start telling yourself how bad they are or how unpleasant they are to work with.

Be Systematic

Analyticals like to be systematic about most things they're associated with. Expressives prefer a much less regimented approach. This is often a point of tension between people of these styles. When you work with Analyticals, they find the relationship much more congenial when you are more systematic than usual.

1. *Set high standards.* Analyticals are the most quality-conscious of the styles. They like to base their systems on exceptionally high standards. Analyticals are partial to highly demanding standards like zero defects. So stretch as much as you can in setting standards for your work. Just be sure to deliver what you say you will. Analyticals get turned off sooner than most when someone makes a promise and doesn't deliver.

2. *Plan your work.* Analyticals are avid planners and like to work with people who develop detailed, step-by-step, written plans.

3. *Work your plan.* Many Analyticals think of a plan as a rational road to accomplishment—and something that should be strictly adhered to. Consider being more organized than usual, without necessarily being as rigorous as the Analytical might wish.

4. *Develop superior procedures.* One way Analyticals try to achieve outstanding quality is through superior procedures and processes. When it comes to ongoing activities, they like co-workers to discover the best way of doing a task and then create a step-by-step procedure which, when followed, consistently yields excellent results. Chances are, you can find some areas in which new procedures are needed. When you

develop them, you probably will enhance productivity while building stronger ties to the Analyticals with whom you work.

5. *Continuously improve procedures.* Even more than most people, Analyticals are concerned with continuous improvement. Support their quest for quality by improving some of the most important procedures in your area.

6. *Be more rigorous in following established procedures.* Make the effort to think of procedures that would produce better results if you followed them more consistently. Doing so will undoubtedly strengthen your relationship with the Analyticals in your work group.

Be Well Organized, Detailed, and Factual

Analyticals, the most perfectionistic of the styles, are particular about the way things are presented to them. They expect you to be well organized, detailed, and factual in your communication. Expressives, however, are often poorly organized, speak in generalities, and are less factual. That's a big communication chasm to bridge. In presenting ideas or making recommendations to Analyticals, your case will be stronger when you incorporate the following behaviors.

1. *Be prepared.* Analyticals expect you to make good use of their time. Don't wing it; think things through in advance. Dig up all the data you need. Anticipate questions you may be asked. Even for one-on-one meetings, it's often appropriate to create an agenda. Consider getting the agenda to the Analytical in advance; she may want to think about the topics beforehand. Most of the suggestions here are enhanced by using more than your customary preparation.

2. *Have a well-organized presentation.* Explain your thoughts systematically. It often helps to present your ideas as a series of points arranged in logical order; that's what Analyticals often do. You frequently hear them say, "In the first place . . . , in the second place . . . ," and so forth. When communicating with an Analytical, do likewise.

3. *Go into considerable detail.* When making a presentation to people of this style, don't just hit the high points. Analyticals want to delve into the particulars; they thrive on specifics. They want to make sure all the ground has been covered before they make a decision. You gain credibility with people of this style when they see that you've chased down every detail.

4. *Give a sound rationale for narrowing the options.* Analyticals want to consider all the alternatives. While this tendency often helps them make good decisions, it also increases their tendency to be inordinately inde-

cisive. You can help them weed out some of the weaker alternatives by giving them logical and factual reasons for doing so.

5. *Mention the problems and disadvantages of the proposal you put forth.* In addition to mentioning the pluses of the proposition you recommend, tell them about the downside, too. The Analytical respects you for doing so. Then, build your credibility further by recommending ways of dealing with the problems and disadvantages.

6. *Show why the approach you advocate is best.* For Analyticals, " best" is a combination of quality, economy, and low risk. You have to figure out the relative weight of each of these criteria for a particular Analytical in a particular set of circumstances. "Best" for this style includes *long-term benefits* as well as immediate advantages. Discuss the future in terms of probabilities: "Here's a projection of what's likely to happen. . . ." The Analytical is conservative when it comes to risk, so if possible, show why your approach is a fairly safe bet.

7. *Provide accurate factual evidence.* When talking with Analyticals, it's rarely advisable to use someone's opinion or recommendation as evidence. Hard facts persuade these folks. Since they like an objective presentation, avoid emotional appeals. People of this style are both precise and skeptical; they abhor a superficial gathering of information or careless reporting of it. Where others might settle for approximations, Analyticals want meticulously correct information. So be painstakingly accurate in what you report to people of this style.

8. *Stick to business.* Don't digress. As you discuss the business at hand and are reminded of things that are tangential to the discussion, don't pursue these side issues.

9. *Provide written support materials, and/or follow up in writing.* Analyticals tend to prefer the written word to the spoken. Even so, it's best to make an oral presentation. That way you can note reactions and answer the Analytical's questions. At the same time, cater to the Analytical's preference for written communication by preparing well-thought-out support materials and/or a follow-up report. If a decision was reached, you may want to include a step-by-step timetable for implementation.

10. *Be prepared to listen to far more detail than you want to know.* When Analyticals talk, they often present much more information than most people think is necessary. They explain their ideas or discuss progress on projects in what may feel like overwhelming detail. This much minutiae may be boring, especially for an Expressive, but be patient and try to stay tuned in. Analyticals appreciate your attentiveness. And there's probably information you need to know buried somewhere in all that detail.

In your initial efforts to flex to Analyticals, you'll probably find it helpful to review the portrait of the Analytical style found in Chapter 7, pages 58–62.

Be Careful in Relating to Other Expressives

When people of the same style work together, they may be too similar! They lack important differences that occur when people of two or more styles collaborate. Some of these style-based differences can be useful at times in developing productive work relationships. Thus when relating to another Expressive, you may sometimes find it advantageous to temporarily use behaviors that are more characteristic of one of the other styles. For example, Expressives are often entertaining. When a couple of Expressives are working together, they may be more productive if one becomes more serious. Also, Expressives typically focus on the big picture.

When two Expressives are collaborating, it's often helpful if one calls their attention to details. One of the two Expressives could help them both focus more on a systematic approach. Similarly, Expressives are so out-front and talkative that when they are engaged in a project they may become less productive over time, because neither of them puts in the effort required to listen and allow the other to shine, too. Or they may come up with a visionary recommendation that ultimately fails because they paid scant attention to the needs in the styles of the people who would have to implement the plan.

Therefore, in relating to another Expressive, make sure you don't overuse style-based tendencies or use them when it's inappropriate to do so. Also, look for times to add some of the strengths more characteristic of the other styles by temporarily modifying some of your behavior.

When two highly assertive Expressives work together, there's always a danger that they'll end up in a power struggle. This is the biggest threat to Expressive-Expressive relationships. If you find that you and another Expressive are beginning to butt heads, temporarily find ways of being less assertive. Listen more and listen better. Decrease your vocal intensity, phrase your ideas more provisionally, and be more negotiable.

For *Analyticals* Only: How to Flex to Each Style

The purpose of this appendix is to coach Analyticals on specific things they can do to create more productive relationships with people of each style.

Most of the recommendations are temporary behavioral changes that you can make for a few minutes, before resuming your more comfortable style-based ways. However, we also mention a few options, such as speaking up more often, that could become more of an ongoing part of your behavioral repertoire.

Since this appendix is a planning aid, don't try to read it straight through. Instead, find the section that applies to the style you want to flex to:

- Drivers, page 202
- Amiables, page 206
- Expressives, page 210
- Other Analyticals, page 217

Read that section and figure out what you can do to help people of that style work more effectively with you. Later, when you want to improve your relationship with someone of a different style, read the section dealing with that style. By working your way through the appendix on an as-needed basis, you'll soon read all sections and strengthen important relationships in the process.

FLEXING TO DRIVERS

As an Analytical, you have much in common with Drivers. You are similar on one of the two basic dimensions of style: Both of you are less responsive than most people. Consequently, Drivers tend to appreciate your focus on task and your objective approach to things.

In flexing to Drivers, your major challenge is to get in sync with some of their more-assertive behavior. You should be able to create a more-effective working relationship with a Driver by *temporarily* using some of the following six types of behavior, within each of which a number of specifics are mentioned. Do several, but not necessarily all, of the specifics within the types of behavior you plan to emphasize. You'll probably think of additional ways to work better with the specific Driver you have in mind.

Pick Up the Pace

Drivers tend to do everything at a fast pace. Analyticals move and speak slowly. You'll usually relate better to Drivers when you increase your pace considerably.

1. *Move more quickly than usual.* Walk at a faster pace. Do whatever you are doing as quickly as possible—on the double when you flex to a Driver.

2. *Speak more rapidly* than is normal for you. Also, pause less often.

3. *Use time efficiently.* When meeting with a Driver, don't exceed the allotted time. Do your business at a fast clip. Then leave quickly, yet graciously.

4. *Address problems quickly.* When problems arise, face them and dispose of them as soon as possible. From the Driver's point of view, there's no time like the present to resolve a troubled situation.

5. *Be prepared to decide quickly.* Knowing that the Driver makes decisions quickly, anticipate decisions he wants from you (or will want to make with you) and do whatever preparation you can to speed your decision making.

6. *Implement decisions as soon as possible.* Once a decision is made, try to put it into operation immediately. Drivers are do-it-now people. When you are action-oriented, they're less stressed.

7. *Complete projects on schedule.* More than any other style, Drivers value on-time completion. So don't miss deadlines. When you commit to a schedule, especially with a Driver, keep your commitment.

8. *Respond promptly to messages and requests.*

9. *When writing, keep it short.* Consider "bulleting" key points. Put supporting information in appendixes.

Demonstrate Higher Energy

Drivers are typically high-energy people. Analyticals, by contrast, display less energy than most people. When relating to Drivers, there are times when you'll need to put more energy into what you say and do.

1. *Lean into the conversation.* Keep your back straight and lean into the conversation. Keep your feet flat on the floor. Keep your head erect, not propped on your hands.

2. *Use gestures to show your involvement in the conversation.* Analyticals tend to gesture less than any of the other styles. Use more emphatic body English.

3. *Increase the frequency and intensity of your eye contact.*

4. *Increase your vocal intensity.* Speak a bit louder than you normally would. Show conviction through your voice. Let your vocal intensity communicate that you are taking the matter seriously.

5. *Move and speak more quickly.* The behaviors suggested under the heading "Pick Up the Pace" all help you interact more energetically.

Don't Get Bogged Down in Details or Theory

As an Analytical, you probably want a more detailed understanding of most things than people of the other styles do. Also, Analyticals have more of a theoretical bent than most people. When relating to a Driver, keep to a minimum any discussion of details or theory.

1. *Concentrate on high-priority issues.* Drivers seldom want to be briefed on as many topics as an Analytical may want to discuss.

2. *Present the main points and skip all but the most essential details.* The Driver will ask for more information if wanted. Assume that the Driver is interested in only a fraction of the information you might find interesting or important.

3. *Don't get sidetracked in theory or in recounting the history of the problem or the solution.* Drivers are not particularly interested in the theoretical and historical aspects of an issue. If it is truly necessary to touch on the history of a situation or the theory behind your approach, cover these matters quickly while showing their relevance to achieving the desired result. Then move quickly to more down-to-earth subject matter.

Say What You Think

Drivers tend to speak up and express themselves candidly and directly. Analyticals are apt to keep their thoughts to themselves and speak somewhat tentatively and indirectly. Here's how you can bridge that behavioral gap.

1. *Speak up more often.* Initiate conversations more frequently. In conversations and meetings, express yourself frequently enough so that there's a more balanced give-and-take. Drivers usually want to know where people stand. They would rather not have to try to interpret the meaning of your silence or have to pry thoughts out of you.

2. *Tell more; ask less.* Say, "Here's what I think . . . ," rather than, "Do you think it would make sense to . . . ?" Say, "Please do this," instead of, "Could you do this?"

3. *Make statements that are definite rather than tentative.* Avoid words like *try, perhaps, maybe, possibly,* etc. Be specific. Don't say you'll complete a project "as soon as possible." Say it will be done "by 12:00 noon next Tuesday."

4. *Eliminate gestures that suggest you lack confidence in the point you are making.* Don't shrug your shoulders, hold your palms up, or use facial expressions that undercut what you are saying, imply helplessness, or suggest the avoidance of responsibility.

5. *Voice your disagreements.* Drivers are more accustomed to conflict than Analyticals are. Face conflict more openly; state your opinion frankly but tactfully. At the same time, try to avoid situations where you and the Driver are battling from entrenched positions.

6. *Don't gloss over problems.* Beat bad news to the punch. Then give regular, brief, frank reports on your progress regarding the problem situation.

Speak in Practical, Results-Oriented Terms

There are important differences in what would be persuasive to a Driver and what would influence an Analytical. To get your point across to a Driver, emphasize what's convincing to her.

1. *Focus on the results of the action being discussed.* Very early in the discussion of a course of action, describe the outcomes that could be achieved by the approach you advocate. Then, factually demonstrate that the outcome you project is both desirable and achievable.

2. *Emphasize that it's a pragmatic approach.* Analyticals, in their quest for perfection, often seek the best solution even though something less costly or less time-consuming might do just fine. Drivers, in searching for a solution, often opt for something that is less than the best as long as it will do the job. Take a hard-headed approach when discussing solutions with a Driver.

Facilitate Self-Determination

Drivers are very self-directed. They want to do things their way. Although Analyticals are less assertive than half the population, they can be very precise about what they want done and the way they want it done. When Analyticals get highly specific about how things are to be done, Drivers often bridle at what seems to them like excessive control. Here are some ways Analyticals can constructively facilitate a Driver's sense of self-direction.

1. *Give Drivers as much freedom as possible in setting their own objectives.*

2. *As far as practicable, let the Driver determine how to do projects and achieve objectives.*

3. *When making recommendations, offer a couple of options for the Driver.* While an Analytical might want to consider additional alternatives, two options are usually enough to satisfy the Driver's desire to make a choice.

4. *When presenting options, provide a succinct factual summary* that helps the Driver assess the probable outcome of each alternative.

5. *Don't be a stickler for rules.* Drivers are prone to stretch or break rules in order to achieve results. When appropriate, be open to changing or bending the rules.

In your initial efforts to flex to Drivers, you'll probably find it helpful to review the portrait of the Driver style found in Chapter 6, pages 43–48.

FLEXING TO AMIABLES

As an Analytical, you have much in common with Amiables. You are similar on one of the two basic dimensions of style. Both of you are less assertive than most people. Amiables appreciate the similarity of your pacing and that you aren't as pushy as many of the more assertive people.

In flexing to Amiables, your prime challenge is to get in sync with some of their more-responsive behavior. You create a more effective working relationship with an Amiable by *temporarily* using some of the following types of behavior, within each of which a number of specifics are mentioned. Do several, but not necessarily all, of the specifics within the behavioral category you plan to emphasize. You'll probably think of additional ways to work better with the particular Amiable you have in mind.

Make Genuine Personal Contact

The Amiable wants to be treated as a human being and not as a function or a role only. The Analytical, who is more task-oriented than most people, may need to remember to show a sincere interest in the Amiable as a person.

1. *Don't seem aloof.* Without overdoing it, demonstrate more warmth in your words, your tone of voice, and your facial expression.

2. *When the situation permits, be more casual and informal* than usual. To Amiables, your tendency to be more formal than most other people may make you seem stiff and impersonal. Let your hair down a bit when with people of this style.

3. *At the outset, touch base personally.* When beginning a conversation, take a few minutes to build rapport. Show that you are interested in the Amiable as a person. Give Amiables an opening to talk about themselves.

4. *Disclose something about yourself.* The Amiable likes to invite you to talk about yourself. Don't brush it off with, "Oh, things are fine." Briefly, let her know something personal about yourself.

5. *Make the most of opportunities for conversations that are not task-related.* For example, when waiting for a meeting to begin, don't read a report; use that time to chat with Amiables and others who like more personal contact. When a meeting concludes, you can also create opportunities for social interchange. Find other occasions to be in touch with Amiables as people. The goal is to be appropriately though not excessively sociable.

Focus More on Feelings

Amiables are expressive of their emotions and sensitive to the feelings of others. You can get more in sync with Amiables by focusing more on feelings—both theirs and your own.

1. *Look at the person you are conversing with* so you can take in body-language cues. This is important because feelings are best discerned from nonverbals. This may take some effort on your part because, more than any other style, you tend to have less eye contact with the person you are talking to.

2. *Concentrate on the meaning of the person's body language.* Analyticals are apt to give excessive attention to the words that are spoken and overlook important nonverbal cues. Pay attention to the Amiable's nonverbal signals, and keep asking yourself, "What does this suggest about what this person may be feeling right now?"

3. *Note how the other person reacts.* Amiables dislike conflict and may not verbalize their disagreement or dissatisfaction. Changes in their body language can tip you off as to how they may be reacting to what is being said. Once you surmise that the other person has negative feelings about a proposal, you can invite his reaction: "Some people are leery of this part of the plan. I'm interested in your thoughts about it."

4. *Demonstrate more feelings yourself.* If you are pleased about something, say so. If you are disappointed, let that be known. Let your body language express your feelings more; put a bit more inflection into your voice. Smile more to demonstrate warmth toward the person you are with.

Be Supportive

Amiables are supportive of others, and they expect others to be supportive in turn. They feel that's the least that one human being should be able to expect from another.

1. *Listen empathically so the Amiable feels heard and understood.* To truly listen to another is one of the most supportive things we can do for a person.

2. *Express sincere appreciation for the Amiable's contributions.* Even more than most people, Amiables thrive on appreciation. Don't let your Analytical tendencies toward being perfectionistic and overly critical prevent you from seeing and acknowledging the good things the Amiable does. Also, decrease the number of critical and judgmental statements you make. When you do criticize, make sure it's constructive.

3. *Lend a helping hand.* Amiables are the most helpful of the people styles. They're apt to drop what they're doing to aid someone who's in a pinch. And they appreciate it when you spot an opportunity to give them a hand when they're under pressure.

Provide Structure

Amiables tend to be most comfortable and work best in stable, clearly structured situations. Do what you can to contribute to that stability and structure.

1. When it's within your area of responsibility, *make sure the Amiable's job is well defined and goals are clearly established.* Amiables work best when their roles are clarified and their goals are set.

2. *Help the Amiable plan difficult projects and design complex work processes.* Planning is not the Amiable's forte. When you help an Amiable develop a sound plan or design an effective work process, she usually takes it from there.

3. *Reduce uncertainty.* Amiables aren't likely to function well in highly ambiguous situations. Try not to put the Amiable in an unstable, rapidly fluctuating situation.

4. *Demonstrate loyalty.* In most cases, Amiables feel a greater-than-average loyalty to the people they work with and the organizations they work in. Consequently, they expect you to demonstrate your loyalty to them, their co-workers, and the organization. Amiables are turned off when they hear you take potshots at employees or the organization. Instead of voicing criticisms, make constructive suggestions for improvement and make them directly to the people involved.

Demonstrate Interest in the Human Side

Amiables tend to take a people-oriented approach whereas Analyticals are prone to be task-oriented. When working with an Amiable, give increased attention to the human side of things.

1. *Invite Amiables' input on matters that affect them.* Although they aren't as demanding as most people, they like to be consulted on matters pertaining to them.

2. *Discuss the effects of decisions on people and their morale.* Be alert to and speak about the effect on people of new policies, procedures, processes, and projects. For example, when discussing a new practice, in addition to pointing out its cost-cutting advantages, be sure to add statements like: "Most people will like the way it cuts down on the excessive overtime they've been complaining about."

3. When appropriate, *provide an opportunity for the Amiable to talk with others* before committing to a decision.

Don't Overdo Facts and Logic

Analyticals find facts and logic highly convincing. Amiables don't find facts and logic as persuasive as you do. Oftentimes, what seems like an appropriate amount of facts and logic to an Analytical is overkill to an Amiable.

1. *Edit out of your conversation any facts that aren't absolutely necessary to making your point.* You'll be surprised at how few are really needed.

2. *Don't overdo the appeal to logic.* It's not that Amiables are averse to logic, but they don't like it when someone piles reason upon reason to make a case. When Amiables feel that logic is being overused, they're likely to be bored or annoyed rather than persuaded.

3. *Don't be coercive in your use of facts and logic.* If you try to build an airtight case showing that the alternative you favor is the only way to go, the Amiable will probably think your amassing of facts is not convincing but is overly controlling.

4. *Show that other people support the idea you are advancing.* This people-oriented style is often influenced more by the experiences and opinions of others than by cold facts. Provide evidence from experts. Mention testimonies of others who have successfully used a similar approach. The opinions of trusted colleagues is especially convincing.

5. *Note factors that minimize the risk* of the course of action you are proposing. To the degree possible, provide assurance that there will be no glitches. If there are guarantees, highlight them.

In your initial efforts to flex to Amiables, you'll probably find it helpful to review the portrait of the Amiable style found in Chapter 7, pages 54–58.

FLEXING TO EXPRESSIVES

As an Analytical, you differ from the Expressive on both dimensions of style. The Expressive is both more assertive and more responsive than you. So you may experience more style-based differences with an Expressive than with either a Driver or an Amiable, each of whom has one of the basic dimensions of behavior in common with you. As a result, there are more types of behavior that you can modify when flexing to an Expressive than when flexing to any other style.

As you read the types of temporary adjustment of behavior that help you get in sync with Expressives, carefully select the one to four types you think will help you work best with the particular person you're relating to. It's not easy to change habitual behavior, even for a short time, so *be sure to select only one to four types of behavior to work on.* Within each type or category of behavior, a number of specifics are mentioned. Do several, but not necessarily all, of the specifics within the behavioral categories you plan to emphasize. You'll probably think of additional ways to work better with the particular Expressive you'll be flexing to.

Make Personal Contact

Expressives like to have personal contact with those they work with. It's important to them that they get to know you and that you get to know them personally. Analyticals, who tend to focus more on the task aspects of things, need to remind themselves to take the time and make the effort to establish personal contact with Expressives they work with.

1. *Don't seem aloof.* Without overdoing it, demonstrate more warmth in your words, your tone of voice, and your facial expression.

2. *Be more casual and informal* than usual. Expressives are inclined to informality. To them, the tendency of Analyticals to be more formal than most people may make them seem stiff and impersonal. Let your hair down a bit in this conversation.

3. *At the outset, touch base personally.* Take a few minutes to build rapport at the beginning of a conversation. Show Expressives that you are interested in them as people; give them an opening to talk about themselves. Perhaps you can inquire about their personal interests or their opinions on a topic that's being widely discussed.

4. *Disclose something about yourself.* Expressives are the most talkative of the styles, so you may have to look for an opening to get in a word about yourself. You don't have to go on at length, but do let them get to know you better.

5. *Talk about what's going on with other people, too.* The gregarious Expressive is interested in knowing the latest about people she knows.

6. *Look for opportunities for conversations that are not task-related.* When a meeting ends, there may be a few minutes for the two of you to catch up on one another's life. The goal is to be appropriately though not excessively sociable.

Pick Up the Pace

Expressives talk fast, move quickly, and decide quickly. When it comes to implementation, they want it done yesterday. Expressives find it easier to work with you when you pick up the pace somewhat.

1. *Move more quickly than usual.* Walk at a faster pace. Do things on the double when you flex to an Expressive.

2. *Speak more rapidly than is normal for you.* Also, pause less often. Expressives are fast-paced talkers and are quickly bored when pace slackens.

3. *Don't over explain.* Present the main points and skip the details. The Expressive will ask for more information if it's wanted.

4. *Address problems quickly.* When problems arise, face them and dispose of them as soon as possible.

5. *Be ready to decide quickly.* Knowing that Expressives make decisions quickly, anticipate decisions they expect you to make (or will want to make with you) and do whatever preparation you can to speed your decision making.

6. *Implement as soon as possible.* Once a decision is made, put it into operation immediately.

Demonstrate Higher Energy

Expressives are usually brimming with energy; Analyticals show less energy than most people. When relating to Expressives, you may find it helpful at times to put more energy into what you say and do.

1. *Lean into the conversation.* When you do, you will look much more alert and energetic than you do in the characteristic leaning-back mode of most Analyticals.

2. *Use more and bigger gestures.* Show your involvement in the conversation by using more body English. Gesture more frequently than is customary for you.

3. *Increase the frequency and intensity of your eye contact.* Expressives look you right in the eye when they talk to you. They expect you to do the same with them.

4. *Increase your vocal intensity.* Speak a bit louder than normal. Try putting more inflection in your voice; above all, don't speak in a monotone.

5. *Change your posture now and then.* Expressives always seem to be moving. Even when sitting, they don't sit still. They shift around in their chairs, tap a pencil, or fidget with a paper clip. So don't sit there like a bump on a log. Obviously, you want to avoid engaging in some of the Expressive's more distracting behavior, but you can change your posture now and then and gesture more.

Focus More on Feelings

Expressives are very in touch with and disclosing of their feelings. Whatever those feelings are, they influence and sometimes even dominate the Expressive's decisions, actions, and responses to others. Analyticals are seen as the least emotive of the styles, so relating well to Expressives' feelings is a key to working effectively with them.

1. *Be aware of what the Expressive is feeling.* It's not that an Expressive's emotional cues are apt to be subtle; they probably come across loud and clear. But everyone has selective perception, and the Analytical is likely to become engrossed in the *content* of the conversation and miss the emotional component even when it's quite obvious. Since the Expressive's emotions have a major impact on their decisions, actions, and reactions, it's crucial to stay in touch with what they're feeling.

2. *Acknowledge the Expressive's feelings.* When Expressives are "up" about something they're working on, acknowledge the feelings: "You're excited about the way project X is going." When they're down, reflect those feelings, too: "You're frustrated that just when you got Sandy trained, she was transferred to another department, and you'll have to start breaking in a new rep."

3. *Don't overreact to the Expressive's highs and lows.* Expressives have greater mood swings than any of the styles. When they're high, they are energetic and excited about what they're doing. When they're low, they feel discouraged and unappreciated. As an Analytical, you are probably very even-keeled in emotional terms. Don't read too much into the Expressive's extremes of feeling unless they persist over time. An Expressive's feeling states are more fleeting than most people's; she will probably be in a very different mood shortly.

4. *Show more feelings yourself.* If you are delighted about something, say so; if you are disappointed, let that be known. When you're annoyed, you can say something like, "I'm irritated that you missed this deadline." Let your body language convey more of your feelings, too. When expressing feelings, put more inflection in your voice and gesture a bit more.

5. *Demonstrate more enthusiasm.* Although Expressives get dispirited at times, they are the most enthusiastic of the styles. Analyticals are so matter-of-fact that when they feel enthusiastic, it may not be apparent to others. When working with an Expressive, it's important to let him see some of your enthusiasm. For example, when trying to sell an idea to an Expressive, your enthusiasm may be more persuasive than a logical presentation of the facts of the case. If you don't show excitement about the idea, the Expressive is apt to think you lack confidence in it. Also, when it's genuine, share your enthusiasm for the Expressive's projects and victories.

6. *Don't read too much into an Expressive's volatile verbal attacks.* Remember, under normal circumstances people of this style are very emotive and more given to exaggeration than any of the styles; when angry, both of these tendencies become more pronounced. What the Expressive says in anger often is an exaggeration. Try not to take the angry comments literally. Expressives have more temper to control than most people, so don't assume the derogatory things said in a fit of anger accurately communicate their thinking. However, if the verbal abuse becomes excessive, find a way to put an end to it.

Cooperate with the Expressive's Conversational Spontaneity

It's important to realize that when Expressives talk, they're often "thinking out loud." When discussing their own conversational style, Expressives commonly say, "I speak to find out what I'm thinking." The Analytical, by contrast, tends to think things through before speaking. If these differences in conversational style are not recognized and adapted to, communication snafus are probable.

1. *Allow enough time for the conversation.* Though Expressives' speech is fast-paced, their tendency to tell stories and skip from one topic to another can be quite time consuming, so don't impose tight time constraints on your meeting with an Expressive.

2. *Keep a balance between flowing with an Expressive's digressions and getting back on track.* With Expressives you can expect to have some long and meandering conversations. If you try to keep these highly assertive people from getting sidetracked onto other subjects, you're apt to end in an unproductive power struggle. However, after they've digressed for a while, you sometimes need to tactfully get the conversation refocused.

3. *Spend time in mutual exploration.* Once Expressives get enthusiastic about a solution, they may not want to explore other options. Similarly, you are apt to arrive at what you consider the best solution. But when the two of you argue from fixed positions, the result can be an unpro-

ductive "dialogue of the deaf." To avoid this, be sure to listen well and set up the conversation in such a way that there's a mutual discussion of the problem and possible solutions.

4. *Be patient with overstatements.* With their bias toward the dramatic, Expressives are likely to exaggerate to make a point. Unless a more accurate understanding of a particular matter is essential to the discussion, don't press for accuracy. Concentrate instead on the idea the Expressive is trying to get across, and let the conversation move on.

5. *Be tactful in responding to contradictions in what the Expressive says.* Since Expressives are thinking things through while they talk, they sometimes make contradictory statements in the same conversation without realizing it. If the conflicting thoughts are not germane to what's being discussed, just overlook the discrepancy. If it's central to what is being talked about, find a diplomatic way to get at the actual meaning of the Expressive's statements.

Be Open to the Expressive's Fun-Loving Side

Expressives are the most playful and fun loving of the styles. They like to mix pleasure with business. The Analytical, by contrast, is the most serious of the four styles. If you lighten up a little when working with an Expressive, you may be able to get more done than if you take a nose-to-the-grindstone approach.

1. *Don't get impatient if the Expressive indulges in a few jokes.* When you are ready to get down to business, an Expressive is apt to regale you with a few jokes. Instead of getting upset at what might seem like a waste of time, relax and enjoy the humor. There's no need for you to get into the act with jokes of your own, though. Analytical humor doesn't necessarily entertain an Expressive.

2. *Be relaxed about a certain amount of fooling around.* Even in the midst of serious business, an Expressive may engage in horseplay. Go with the flow for a while. It may be the release the Expressive needs before focusing again on the business at hand.

3. *Try to create a more pleasant atmosphere for your conversation.* Sitting behind a table in a sterile conference room or talking across a desk in someone's office is not the Expressive's cup of tea. So, if the weather and location permit, talk while taking a noontime stroll, or over breakfast or lunch at a favorite bistro. Put your mind to it, and you'll find some options.

Give the Expressive Recognition

Expressives, even more than most people, enjoy recognition.

1. *Show appreciation for the Expressive's contribution.* Expressives thrive on

sincere compliments. For the Expressive, it's even better if the appreciation is expressed publicly.

2. *Let the Expressive be in the spotlight.* By and large, people of this style find it easy to be the center of attention. Try to find ways for them to get the recognition they enjoy while making sure everyone on a project gets the credit they deserve.

Say What You Think

Expressives usually say what they are feeling and thinking. Their speech is direct; their statements are definite, and they are emphatic much of the time. Analyticals are apt to keep their thoughts to themselves and speak somewhat tentatively and indirectly. Here's how you can bridge that behavioral gap.

1. *Speak up more often.* Expressives, being the most verbal of the styles, enjoy having more than 50 percent of the air time. By contrast, they usually want to know where people stand and would rather not have to interpret the meaning of your silence or have to pry thoughts out of you. So initiate conversations more frequently. In conversations and meetings, express yourself more so that there's a somewhat balanced give-and-take.

2. *Tell more; ask less.* Say, "Here's what I think . . ." rather than, "Do you think it would make sense to . . . ?" Say, "Please do this," instead of, "Could you do this?"

3. *Make statements that are definite rather than tentative.* Avoid words like *try, perhaps, maybe, possibly,* etc. Be specific. Don't say you'll complete a project "as soon as possible." Say it will be done "by 12:00 noon next Tuesday."

4. *Eliminate gestures that suggest you lack confidence in what you are saying.* Don't shrug your shoulders, hold your palms up, or use facial expressions that undercut what you are saying, imply helplessness, or suggest the avoidance of responsibility.

5. *Voice your disagreements.* Expressives are more accustomed to conflict than Analyticals are. Face conflict more openly. State your opinion frankly. It's generally OK to let some of your temper show when you are in a conflict with Expressives. However, the highly competitive Expressive loves to win arguments. So don't let your disagreement degenerate into an argument. One option you have is to explore alternative solutions jointly, searching for one that meets both people's needs.

6. *Don't gloss over problems.* Beat bad news to the punch. Then give regular, frank reports on your progress regarding the problem situation.

Communicate on the Expressive's Wavelength

When speaking with an Expressive, realize that information you find convincing may carry little weight with the Expressive. Here are some ways to communicate on the Expressive's wavelength.

1. *Communicate face-to-face.* If you want your ideas to get a fair hearing with an Expressive, talk things over face-to-face. If that's not possible, try using the telephone. When you reach a definite conclusion in your face-to-face meeting or phone call, paraphrase it. Then, on important matters, follow up immediately with a *brief* written summary of what was decided.

2. *Try to support the Expressive's vision.* People of this style tend to be dreamers—in both the best and the worst senses of the word. They often have a vision of a better future for their department or organization. But their vision may be unrealistic or poorly aligned with the direction of the corporation. When you can, help Expressives inject realism into their proposed ventures. And on those occasions when you can't conscientiously support their visionary proposals, be respectful as well as clear in expressing your opposition.

3. *Focus on the big picture.* Analyticals are inclined to dig into the nitty-gritty of an issue; Expressives are mainly interested in the big picture. They have limited concern about specifics and they don't thrive on complexity. They go for the KIS formula: Keep It Simple. To the degree that the subject matter allows, when talking with an Expressive give an overview and skip the details. When Expressives want to know more, they'll ask.

4. *Don't overdo facts and logic.* What seems like a desirable amount of facts and logic to an Analytical seems like overkill to an Expressive. Edit out of your conversation any facts or logic that aren't absolutely essential to making your point; you'll be surprised at how little is really needed. Also, skip as much of the historical development and theoretical background as can be eliminated.

5. *Highlight recommendations of others*—especially recommendations of people the Expressive knows and respects. The testimony of people who have successfully used the same approach probably carries more weight than tables of statistics or other impersonal evidence.

6. *Demonstrate concern about the human side.* When possible, invite the Expressive's input before a decision is made. Discuss the effect on people of new policies, procedures, processes, and projects.

7. *Recommend a particular course of action.* Rather than present Expressives with options, it's often best to help them get enthused about what seems to be the best alternative.

8. *Provide incentives* when possible. Everybody likes an incentive, but few people are as motivated by them as Expressives.

Provide Considerable Freedom

Expressives are free spirits. When their improvisational spirit meets the Analytical's desire for precise systems and careful planning, there's a considerable gap to be bridged.

1. *Help Expressives put their personal stamp on what they do.* They want their work to be a form of self-expression. Regarding the things they are involved with, they want to be able to say, "I did it my way." However, Analyticals are often very precise about how they want things done. When possible, avoid pressuring the Expressive into doing things your way.

2. *Empower Expressives to do new things.* They hate doing the same old things in the same old ways. Look for ways to help them inject some novelty into their work. Also, try to find new approaches to the way the two of you work together.

3. *Don't be a stickler for rules.* More than most people, Expressives don't like rules. They hate red tape and are quick to stretch or break the rules, whether for their own convenience, to increase productivity, or to better serve a customer. So when you can, relax your own tendency to go by the book.

4. *Be willing to improvise when you can.* Although you probably want to plan your work and work your plan, for the Expressive, planning is a drag and following a plan feels like being put in a straitjacket. Be open to the possibility of winging it from time to time.

5. *Cater to their physical restlessness.* Expressives hate to sit still. So don't just sit and talk with an Expressive for long periods; create reasons to get up and move around a bit. Also, since Expressives don't like the confinement of a desk-type job, whenever it's in your power, help them find projects or roles that enable them to release some of their physical energy.

In your initial efforts to flex to Expressives, you'll probably find it helpful to review the portrait of the Expressive style found in Chapter 6, pages 48–53.

Relating to Other Analyticals

When people of the same style work together, they may be too similar! They lack important differences that occur when people of two or more styles collaborate. Some of these style-based differences can be useful at times in developing productive work relationships. Thus, when relating to another Analytical, you may sometimes find it advantageous to temporarily use behaviors that are more characteristic of one of the other styles. For example, Analyticals are often indecisive. When two Analyticals are working together, they may be more productive if one becomes more decisive. Also, Analyticals tend to be exceptionally focused on details. When two Analyticals are collaborating, it's often helpful if one challenges the need for so much detail. One of the two Analyticals could help them both focus more on the big picture. Similarly, Analyticals are so task-oriented that when two of them are engaged in a project, they may become less productive over time because neither of them puts in the effort required to maintain a good working relationship. Or they may come up with a sound recommendation that ultimately fails because they paid scant attention to the human side of the change they proposed.

Therefore, in relating to another Analytical, make sure you don't overuse style-based tendencies or use them when it's inappropriate to do so. Also, look for times to add some of the strengths more characteristic of the other styles by temporarily modifying some of your behavior.

More than most people, Analyticals have a need to be *right*. Unless this tendency is tempered, it makes them less open to other people's ideas and less negotiable than most people. So even though Analyticals are less assertive than most people, when two of them work together, it's not unusual for them to get locked in a power struggle about the way to proceed. If you find that you and an Analytical co-worker are getting deadlocked about issues, listen more and listen better. Phrase your ideas more provisionally and be more negotiable. Some tips on how to do these things are found in Appendix II. Although the tips in that appendix are written for Drivers, you'll be able to apply them to your situation.

BIBLIOGRAPHY

PART I

Ellison, Ralph, and Graham, Maryemma, and Singh, Amritjit. 1995. *Conversations with Ralph Ellison.* Jackson, MS: University Press of Mississippi, page 274.

CHAPTER 1

Bolton, Robert, and Dorothy Grover Bolton. 1984. *Social Style/Management Style.* New York: Amacom.

Hall, Edward T. with Colombo, Gary, ed. 2001. "Hidden Culture," in *Mind Readings: An Anthology for Writers.* New York: Macmillan, page 439.

Lam, David. "Marriage Markets and Assortative Mating with Household Public Goods: Theoretical Results and Empirical Implications." *The Journal of Human Resources,* vol. 23, no. 4, Autumn 1988, 462–487.

Mare, Robert. "Five Decades of Educational Assortative Mating." *American Sociological Review,* vol. 56, no. 1, 15–32.

Marston, William Moulton. 1928. *Emotions of Normal People.* New York: Harcourt, Brace and Company.

Merrill, David W. and Reid, Roger H. 1981. *Personal Styles and Effective Performance: Make Your Style Work for You.* Radnor, PA: Chilton Book Co.

Qian, Zhenchao. "Changes in Assortative Mating: The Impact of Age and Education, 1970–1990." *Demography,* vol. 35, no. 3, August 1998.

Suen, Wing and Lui, Hon-Kwong. "A Direct Test of the Efficient Marriage Market Hypothesis." *Economic Inquiry,* vol. 37, no. 1, January 1999, 29–46.

Tzeng, M. "The Effects of Socioeconomic Heterogamy and Changes on Marital Dissolution for First Marriages." *Journal of Marriage and the Family,* 1992 Aug; 54(3):609–19.

CHAPTER 2

Costa, Paul and McCrae, Robert. "Age Changes in Personality and Their Origins: Comment on Roberts, Walton, and Viechtbauer (2006)." *Psychological Bulletin* 2006, Vol. 132, No. 1, 26–28.

Costa, Paul and McCrae, Robert. "Age Differences in Personality Structure: A Cluster Analytic Approach." *Journal of Gerontology* 1976 Sep; 31(5):564–70.

Drucker, Peter F. 2007. *Management: Tasks, Responsibilities, Practices.* Piscataway, NJ: Transaction Publishers, page 424.

Hocking, William Ernest. 1918. *Human Nature and Its Remaking.* New Haven, CT: Yale University Press, page 10.

Jordan, Hamilton. 1982. *Crisis: The Last Year of the Carter Presidency.* New York: Putnam.

Judge Learned Hand. 1942. *Proceedings In Memory of Mr. Justice Brandeis,* 317 U.S. XI.

Mandell, Arnold J. "A psychiatric study of professional football." *Saturday Review,* 5 October 1974: 12–16.

Mehrabian, Albert. 1981. *Silent Messages: Implicit Communication of Emotions and Attitudes.* Belmont, CA: Wadsworth Publishing Company.

Thomas, Lewis. 1983. *Late Night Thoughts on Listening to Mahler's Ninth Symphony.* New York: Bantam Books, page 23.

Thurber, James and De Vries, Peter. *Lanterns and Lances*. 1963. New York: Time, Inc., page 63.

CHAPTER 3

Machiavelli, Niccolo and Marriott, William K. (translator). 1928. *The Prince*. London: J. M. Dent and Sons.

CHAPTER 4

Drucker, Peter F. 2007. *Management: Tasks, Responsibilities, Practices*. Piscataway, NJ: Transaction Publishers, page 616.

Merrill, David W. and Reid, Roger H. 1981. *Personal Styles and Effective Performance: Make Your Style Work for You*. Radnor, PA: Chilton Book Co.

CHAPTER 5

Franklin, Benjamin. 1750. *Poor Richard's Almanack*. White Plains, NY: Peter Pauper Press, page 26.

Noble, Andrew and Hogg, Scott, eds. 2001. *The Canongate Burns: The Complete Poems and Songs of Robert Burns*. Edinburgh, Scotland: Canongate, page 132.

CHAPTER 6

Carlyle, Thomas. 1899. *Critical and Miscellaneous Essays in Five Volumes*. Volume II. New York: Charles Scribner's Sons, page 56.

Thoreau, Henry D. and Cramer, Jeffrey S., ed. 2004. *Walden: A Fully Annotated Edition*. New Haven, CT: Yale University Press, page 315.

CHAPTER 7

Gordon, John Steele. 2004. *An Empire of Wealth: The Epic History of American Economic Power*. New York: HarperCollins, page 380.

Levinson, Harry. 1986. *Ready, Fire, Aim: Avoiding Management by Impulse*. Jaffrey, NH: The Levinson Institute.

Stein, Herbert. 1998. *What I Think: Essays on Economics, Politics, and Life*. Washington, D.C.: American Enterprise Institute, page 58.

Thoreau, Henry D. 1904. *Walden*. New York: E.P. Dutton & Co., page 120.

CHAPTER 8

Becker, Paula; Bledsoe, Larry; and Mok, Paul. 1977. *The Strategic Woman*. Dallas: London Enterprises, page 35.

Buckingham, Marcus and Clifton, Donald. 2001. *Now, Discover Your Strengths: How to Develop Your Talents and Those of the People You Manage*. New York: Simon and Schuster.

Buehler, Roger; Griffin, Dale; and Ross, Michael. "Exploring the 'planning fallacy': Why people underestimate their task completion times." *Journal of Personality and Social Psychology*, (1994) 67, 366–381.

Goldsmith, Marshall, and Goldsmith, Kelly. "Helping People Achieve Their Goals" *Leader to Leader*, 39 (Winter 2006): 24–29.

Levitin, Daniel J. 2006. *This Is Your Brain on Music: The Science of Human Obsession*. New York: Dutton, page 193.

Malone, Michael S. 2007. *Bill & Dave: How Hewlett and Packard Built the World's Greatest Company*. New York: Portfolio, page 68.

Peter, Laurence J. 1969. *The Peter Principle: Why Things Always Go Wrong*. New York: William Morrow & Co.

CHAPTER 9

Dryden, John and Saintsbury, George (ed.). 1884. "Absalom and Achitophel." *The Works of John Dryden*. Edinburgh, Scotland: William Paterson/T. and A. Constable.

Scott, Susan. 2004. *Fierce Conversations: Achieving Success at Work & in Life, One Conversation at a Time*. New York: Berkley Books, page 203.

Selye, Hans. 1956. *The Stress of Life*. New York: McGraw-Hill.

CHAPTER 10

Aurelius Antoninus, Marcus and Jackson, John (translator). 1906. *The Meditations of Marcus Aurelius Antoninus*. Oxford, England: Clarendon Press, page 60.

PART TWO

Beecher, Henry Ward. 1887. *Proverbs from Plymouth Pulpit*. New York: D. Appleton & Company.

CHAPTER 11

Branden, Nathaniel. 1999. *The Art of Living Consciously: The Power of Awareness to Transform Everyday Life*. New York: Simon and Schuster.

BusinessWeek. 1977. "Out at Simmons," *BusinessWeek*. September 5, 1977. Page 38.

Fromm, Erich. 1959. *Psychoanalysis and Religion*. New Haven, CT: Yale University Press, page 74.

http://www.thehenryford.org/exhibits/fmc/chrono.asp, accessed 1/30/09

Love, John F. 1995. *McDonald's: Behind the Arches*. New York: Bantam Books.

Notarius, Clifford and Markman, Howard. 1994. *We Can Work It Out: How to Solve Conflicts, Save Your Marriage, and Strengthen Your Love for Each Other*. New York: Perigree Books, page 20.

Pasternak, Boris. 1958. *Doctor Zhivago*. London: Collins and Harvill Press, page 483.

Perls, Frederick. 1972. *In and Out of the Garbage Pail*. New York: Bantam Books.

Sandburg, Carl. 2003. *The Complete Poems of Carl Sandburg*. New York: Houghton Mifflin Harcourt, page 478.

Saroyan, William and Tashijan, James H. 1983. *My Name Is Saroyan: A Collection*. New York: Coward, McCann & Geoghegan.

Shostrom, Everett. 1968. *Man, the Manipulator: The Inner Journey from Manipulation to Actualization*. New York: Bantam Books.

Thomas, Lewis. 1983. *Late Night Thoughts on Listening to Mahler's Ninth Symphony*. New York: Viking.

Twain, Mark. 1899. *Pudd'nhead Wilson and Those Extraordinary Twins*. New York: Harper & Brothers, page 145.

CHAPTER 12

Goffman, Erving. 1974. *Frame Analysis: An Essay on the Organization of Experience*. New York: Harper & Row.

Zunin, Leonard M. 1972. *Contact: The First Four Minutes*. Los Angeles: Nash Publishing.

CHAPTER 13

Doyle, Sir Arthur Conan. 1900. *The Adventures of Sherlock Holmes*. New York: Harper & Brothers Publishers, page 31.

CHAPTER 15

Bainton, Roland H. 2007. *The Travail of Religious Liberty—Nine Biographical Studies.* Warwickshire, England: Read Country Books, page 227.

Beverslius, Joel, ed. 2000. *Sourcebook of the World's Religions.* Novato, CA: New World Library, page 172.

Eliot, T. S. 1954. *The Confidential Clerk.* New York: Harcourt, Brace, and World, page 108.

Ephesians 4:15

Forker, Dom; Stewart, Wayne; and Pellowski, Michael. 2004. *Baffling Baseball Trivia.* New York: Sterling Publishing Company, page 245.

George Washington to Alexander Hamilton, 28 August 1788, in Evans, Lawrence B., ed., *Writings of George Washington.* New York: G. P. Putnam's Sons, 1908. Page 306.

http://www.worthingtonindustries.com/CorporateInformation/Philosophy.asp; accessed 2/3/09

Kohn, Steven D. and O'Connell, Vincent D. 2005. *6 Habits of Highly Effective Bosses.* Franklin Lakes, NJ: Career Press, page 117–118.

Mathews, Shailer and Smith, Gerald Birney. 1921. *A Dictionary of Religion and Ethics.* New York: The Macmillan Company, page 239.

Parker, Dorothy. 1970. *Constant Reader.* New York: Viking Press, page 42.

Rogers, F. G. "Buck." 1986. *The IBM Way: Insights into the World's Most Successful Marketing Organization.* New York: Harper & Row, page 11.

Schein, Edgar. 1987. *Process Consultation, Volume II, Lessons for Managers and Consultants.* Reading, MA: Addison-Wesley.

Sheridan, Thomas and Nichols, John, eds. 1812. *The Works of the Rev. Jonathan Swift, D.D.* New York: William Durell and Co., page 184.

Templeton, Sir John. 2002. *Wisdom from World Religions: Pathways Toward Heaven on Earth.* Philadelphia: Templeton Foundation Press, page 8.

CHAPTER 16

Camus, Albert. 1972. *A Happy Death.* New York: Knopf, page 116.

Chesterton, Gilbert K. and Perry, Michael W. 2002. *Chesterton Day by Day: The Wit and Wisdom of G. K. Chesterton.* Oxford, England: Inkling Books, page 23.

Dickens, Charles. 1908. *Martin Chuzzlewit.* New York: C. C. Brainard Publishing Co., page 197.

Freedman, Mervin B.; Leary, Timothy F.; Ossorio, Abel G.; and Coffey, Hubert S. "The Interpersonal Dimension of Personality." *Journal of Personality,* (20)1951: 143–161.

Fromm, Erich. 2000. *The Art of Loving.* New York: Continuum International Publishing Group.

Jung, Carl. 2006. *Contribution to Analytical Psychology.* Warwickshire, England: Read Country Books, page 193.

———. 1953. *Psychological Reflections.* ed. Jolande Jocobi. New York: Harper and Row, p. 269.

Kreider, Rose M. and Fields, Jason M. "Number, Timing, and Duration of Marriages and Divorces: 1996." U.S. Census Bureau, February 2002. Page 17. Available at: http://www.census.gov/prod/2002pubs/p70-80.pdf

Lindbergh, Anne Morrow. 1986. *Gift from the Sea.* New York: Pantheon Books, page 108.

Menninger, Karl. 1942. *Love Against Hate.* New York: Harcourt Brace and World, page 272.

Nash, Ogden. 1959. *Verses from 1929 on: From 1929 on.* New York: Modern Library, page 297.

Random House. 2005. *Random House Webster's Unabridged Dictionary.* New York: Random House.

Rilke, Rainer Maria and Mitchell, Stephen. 1989. *The Selected Poetry of Rainer Maria Rilke: Edited and Translated by Stephen Mitchell.* New York: Vintage Books, page 306.

Scarf, Maggie. 1987. *Intimate Partners: Patterns in Love and Marriage.* New York: Random House, page 27.

Shaw, George Bernard. 2008. *Getting Married.* Sioux Falls, SD: NuVision Publications, page 152.

Wile, Daniel. 1988. *After the Honeymoon: How Conflict Can Improve Your Relationship.* Hoboken, NJ: John Wiley & Sons, page 12–13.

CHAPTER 17

Ali, Lorraine. "Having Kids Makes You Happy." *Newsweek.* July 7–14, 2008, page 62. Available at http://www.newsweek.com/id/143792, accessed 2/5/09.

Eliot, T. S. 1954. *The Confidential Clerk.* New York: Harcourt, Brace and Company.

Gilbert, Daniel. 2005. *Stumbling on Happiness.* New York: Vintage.

Kopp, S. 1981. *An End to Innocence.* New York: Bantam, page 57.

Merrill, David W. and Roger H. Reid. 1981. *Personal Styles and Effective Performance: Make Your Style Work for You.* Radnor, PA: Chilton Book Co.

Myers Briggs, Isabel. 1991. *Gifts Differing.* Palo Alto. CA: Davies-Black, page 191.

Tournier, Paul. 1957. *Escape from Loneliness.* London: SCM Press, page 108.

APPENDIX I

Hayde, Michael J. and Morgan, Harry. 2001. *My Name's Friday: The Unauthorized but True Story of Dragnet and the Films of Jack Webb.* Nashville, TN: Cumberland House Publishing, page 73.

INDEX

acceptance, in adjustment phase of intimate relationships, 143
acquiescence, in backup mode, 77–78
adjustment phase, in intimate relationships, 142–145
Adkins, Stuart, on low flexibility in people, 93
aging, and behavior, 21–22
Amiables, 155–168
    and Analyticals, 155–160, 217–218
    in backup mode, 77–78
    characteristics of, 54–58
    communication by, 56–57
    decision making by, 58
    definition of, 36
    and Drivers, 163–168, 180–185
    and Expressives, 160–163, 201
    and other Amiables, 168
Analyticals, 202–218
    and Amiables, 155–160, 206–209
    in backup mode, 78–79
    characteristics of, 58–62
    communication by, 61
    decision making by, 60
    definition of, 35
    and Drivers, 175–180, 202–206
    and Expressives, 40, 194–201, 210–217
    and other Analyticals, 217–218
Ash, Mary Kay, 129
assertiveness, 21–22, 28–31
    and aggressiveness, 29
    and characteristic behaviors, 30–31
    continuum of, 29–30
    degree of, 109–110
    indicators of, 110
    on Self-Assessment Inventory, 38–40
    and submissiveness, 29
attack behavior, in backup mode, 76–77
attraction phase, in intimate relationships, 140–141

autocratic behavior, in backup mode, 77
avoidance, in backup mode, 78–79

backup behavior, 73–81, 82–87
    characteristics of, 73–76
    contagiousness of, 79–80
    dealing with others', 85–87
    identifying, 80–81
    managing your, 83–85
    reducing instances of, 82–83
    secondary, 80
    styles of, 76–79
basic flex, 93
Beecher, Henry Ward, on how to approach people, 89
behavior, 19
    adjusting your, 93–94
    clusters of, 20–21, 28–37
    extreme, inappropriate, and inflexible, 74–75
    habitual, 19–20, 141–142
    observation of, 108
    see also backup behavior
behavioral styles model, 12
    see also people styles model
Bill & Dave (Michael Malone), 71
body language
    of Amiables, 56
    of Analyticals, 61–62
    of Drivers, 45–46
    of Expressives, 51
    and style identification, 114
Brahmanism, 128
Branden, Nathaniel, on behavior and convictions, 97
Buckingham, Marcus, on human strengths and weaknesses, 69
Buddhism, 128
Burns, Robert, on how we are perceived by others, 41
BusinessWeek, 91

Camus, Albert, on deception in relationships, 143
Carlyle, Thomas, on the present moment, 46
Carter, Jimmy, 16
categorization, 14
Chesterton, G. K., on compatibility in marriage, 139
Chicago White Sox, 132
children
    accepting the basic nature of your, 150–151
    introducing people styles model to, 148–150
Christianity, 128
clusters of behavior, 20–21, 28–37
comfort zone, 20, 36
communication
    of Amiables, 56–57
    of Analyticals, 61
    of Drivers, 46
    of Expressives, 51–52
    opening in parallel during, 105, 122
complementary pairing, 71, 144–145
confidence, in relationships, 145
Confidential Clerk, The (T. S. Eliot), 130
conformity, flexibility vs., 97–98
Confucianism, 128
Conlan, Jock, 132
Contact: The First Four Minutes (Leonard Zunin), 105
content, of interaction, 98
continuum of assertiveness, 29–30
continuum of responsiveness, 32–33
co-parenting, 153
Costa, Paul, Jr., 21–22
Count of Monte Cristo, The (Alexandre Dumas), 66
couple relationships, long-term, 9–11, 137–139
critiquing, after style flex, 103–104
cultural norms, 130–131, 152

decision making
    of Amiables, 58
    of Analyticals, 60

in backup mode, 84–85
    of Drivers, 44–45
    of Expressives, 50
    predictions in, 17
devotion phase, in intimate relationships, 145–146
Dickens, Charles, 145
DiMaggio, Joe, 32
Doctor Zhivago (Boris Pasternak), 97
dominant style, 36
Drivers, 169–186
    and Amiables, 163–168, 180–185
    and Analyticals, 175–180, 202–206
    in backup mode, 77
    characteristics of, 43–48
    communication by, 46
    decision making by, 45–46
    definition of, 35
    and Expressives, 169–175, 191–194
    and other Drivers, 185–186
Drucker, Peter
    on behavior and top management, 19
    on personality and work, 19
Durant, Ariel and Will, on family and civilization, 135

Eliot, T. S., 130, 150
Ellison, Ralph, on learning to understand people, 5
emotions, of Expressives, 50
emotiveness, 21
    see also responsiveness
empathy
    in Amiables, 54–55
    toward others' backup behaviors, 86
End to Innocence, An (Sheldon Kopp), 151
Ephron, Nora, on people differences and falling in love, 9
evaluation, of style flex, 103–104
excessive stress, 75, 106
Expressives, 187–201
    and Amiables, 160–163, 187–191
    and Analyticals, 40, 194–201, 210–217
    in backup mode, 76–77
    characteristics of, 48–53
    communication by, 51–52

decision making by, 50
definition of, 36
and Drivers, 169–175, 191–194
and other Expressives, 201
extreme behavior, 74
extroversion, of Expressives, 50

fairness, 132
family styles grid, 148–149
Fierce Conversations (Susan Scott), 79–80
flexibility, 91–98
    conformity vs., 97–98
    interpersonal, 92–95
    manipulation vs., 96–97
    see also style flex
follow through, and Expressives, 49
Ford Motor Company, 92
Franklin, Benjamin, on knowing oneself, 39
Fromm, Erich
    on failure of relationships, 139
    on integrity and personality, 97
frustration phase, in intimate relationships, 141–142

Gallup Organization, 65, 69
General Motors, 92
gifts, developing your, 63–65
Gilbert, Daniel, 145
Goffman, Erving, 105
Goldsmith, Marshall, on overcoming weaknesses, 69–70
graciousness, 131–132
group members, and style flexing, 119–122
group tasks, and style flexing, 122–123
Gulliver's Travels (Jonathan Swift), 131

habitual behavior, 19–20, 141–142
Hall, Edward T., on possibility of understanding people, 11
Hewlett, Bill, 71
Hewlett-Packard Company, 71
Hillel, on treatment of others, 127–128
Hippocrates, 11
Hocking, William Ernest, on human nature, 21

home
    avoiding backup behavior at, 84
    people differences at, 9–11
Human Nature and Its Remaking (William Ernest Hocking), 21
Huxley, Aldous, on personal identification, 24

IBM, 129
implementation, of style flex, 103
inappropriate behavior, 74
individuality, 11
inferences, in style identification, 108
inflexible behavior, 75, 85
Internet, 61
interpersonal flexibility, 92–95
intimacy, in devotion phase of intimate relationships, 145
Intimate Partners (Maggie Scarf), 141
intimate relationships, 9–11, 139–146
    adjustment phase of, 142–145
    attraction phase of, 140–141
    devotion phase of, 145–146
    frustration phase of, 141–142
inventory, self-assessment, *see* People Styles Self-Assessment Inventory
Islam, 128

job compatibility, and strengths, 65–66
John, Tommy, 118–119
Jordan, Hamilton, on 1980 U.S. election, 16
Jung, Carl, 11
    on complementary relationships, 137
    on development in marriage, 141
"just-in-time flex," 105

Kaiser Foundation, 144
Kant, Immanuel, 132
Kauffman, Ewing, on Golden Rule, 128–129
Kopp, Sheldon, on not being accepted as a child, 151
Kroc, Ray, 94

"language of action," 47
Learned Hand, on strands of a man's life, 20

Lindbergh, Anne Morrow, on fluctuations of love, 145
long-term couple relationships, 9–11, 137–139
Love, John, 94

Machiavelli, Nicolo, on leadership and knowledge of self, 24
Malone, Michael, 71
Man, the Manipulator (Everett Shostrom), 96
managers
    style flexing by, 118–119
    style flexing with, 117–118
Mandell, Arnold, 16–17, 20
manipulation, flexibility vs., 96–97
manners, 130–131
Marcus Aurelius, on expectations of people, 85
Marion Laboratories, 128
Markham, Howard, on leading changes in relationships, 95
McCrae, Robert, 21–22
McDonald's, 94
Mehrabian, Albert, on composites of behavior, 20–21
Menninger, Karl, on relationships and human nature, 137
Merrill, David, 12, 36
misapplication, of strengths, 66–68
models, functions of, 18
monitoring, during conversation, 103–104
Morgan, J. P., 32
Myers Briggs, Isabel, on understanding and accepting a child's type, 150

National Football League, 17
National Institute on Aging, 21–22
Nettles, Graig, on New York Yankees pitcher Tommy John, 118–119
New York Yankees, 118–119
Nixon, Richard, 80–81
Notorius, Clifford, on leading changes in relationships, 95

observation, in style identification, 108–109

opinion polls, 17
opportunities, people differences as, 14–15
out-of-the-box behavior, 74
overuse, of strengths, 66–68

Packard, Dave, on business partnership with Bill Hewlett, 71
pairing, complementary, 71, 144–145
parenting, *see* style-based parenting
Parker, Dorothy, on etiquette, 131
Pasternak, Boris, on health and saying what you feel, 97
Penney, J. C., on Golden Rule, 128
people differences
    emotional cost of, 7
    at home, 9–11
    as opportunities, 14–15
people problems, 7–9
people style(s), 34–36
    definition of, 18–19
    determining your, 38–39
    names for, 39, 115
    and others' perceptions, 39–42
    potential strengths of each, 64
people styles grid, 34–36
    Amiable style quadrant in, 54–55
    Analytical style quadrant in, 58–59
    backup styles demonstrated in, 74
    Driver style quadrant in, 43–44
    Expressive style quadrant in, 48
    for tentative style identification, 112
people styles model, 2, 18–22
    with foreign cultures, 22
    origins of, 12
    style grid in, 34–36
People Styles Self-Assessment Inventory, 24–27, 38–42, 100
Perls, Fritz, on manipulation and neuroses, 96
personality, definition of, 19
Peter Principle, 65
Peterson, Donald, 92
phases of intimate relationships, 139–146
planning, for style flex, 102–103
planning fallacy, 70
polls, opinion, 17

Poor Richard's Almanack (Benjamin Franklin), 39
predictability, 16–18
probabilities, 22–23
process
    of interaction, 98
    of style flex, 101–104
Proverbs from Plymouth Pulpit (Henry Ward Beecher), 89
put-downs, communicating without, 130

Red Poling, 92
reframing, 86
Reid, Roger, on behavior and success in workplace, 36
relationships, 127–134
    fairness in, 132
    and Golden Rule, 127–129
    honesty in, 133–134
    respect in, 129–132
religion, and treatment of others, 128
rescheduling, 83
respect, 129–133
responsiveness, 21–22, 31–34
    and characteristic behaviors, 32–34
    degree of, 110–111
    on Self-Assessment Inventory, 38–40
Rilke, Rainer Maria, on challenges of love, 146

St. Louis Browns, 132
Sandburg, Carl, on excessive adaptability, 95
Saroyan, William, 93
Scarf, Maggie, on partner qualities in marriage, 141
Schein, Edgar, on cultural rules for communication, 131
Scott, Susan, on dysfunctional communication, 79–80
secondary backup behavior, 80
Self-Assessment Inventory, *see* People Styles Self-Assessment Inventory
Selye, Hans, 75
Shaw, George Bernard, on passion and commitment, 141

Sherlock Holmes, 107
Shostrom, Everett, on manipulation, 96
Simmons, Grant G., Jr., 91
Simmons Company, 91
Simon, Robin, on emotional well-being and parenting, 148
Snyder, Ross, 146
special situations, flexing in, 117–120
stereotyping, 12–14
strengths
    developing your gifts into, 63–65
    and job compatibility, 65–66
    overreliance on, 66–69
stress
    backup behavior in response to, 73
    excessive, 75
    management of, 82–83
style-based parenting, 147–154
    and accepting your child, 150–151
    and cultural stereotypes, 152
    introducing your child to, 148–150
    mapping your family with, 148
    synchronizing with your partner in, 152–154
style flex (style flexing), 2, 99–106, 117–126
    at beginning of conversation, 105
    with group members, 119–122
    by managers, 118–119
    with people of unidentified styles, 123–125
    with people of your style, 125–126
    as process, 101–104
    when to use, 104–106
style identification, 101–102, 107–116
    assertiveness and responsiveness in, 109–111
    determining subquadrants in, 111–113
    improving your, 113–116
    observation vs. inference in, 108
styles grid, *see* people styles grid
submissiveness, and assertiveness, 29
subquadrants in style identification, 111–113
Swift, Jonathan, on manners and communication, 131

Taoism, 128
team meetings, 119–122
Thomas, Lewis
    on behavior toward others, 16
    on biology and truth, 97
Thoreau, Henry David
    on following through, 49
    on spending time alone, 61
Thurber, James, on probability, 23
time management
    by Amiables, 56
    by Analyticals, 60
    by Drivers, 45
    by Expressives, 50
"time outs," 83
Tournier, Paul, on conflicting parenting
    styles, 153
treatment of others, and religion, 128
Truman, Harry, on indecisiveness of advis-
    ers, 61
Turner, Fred, 94

Twain, Mark, on changing people's habits,
    93
Tyler, Robert P., Jr., 91
types approach, 11–12
    see also people styles model

uniqueness, relating to others', 11

Washington, George, on the virtue of hon-
    esty, 133
Watson, Thomas, Jr., on respect and profit,
    129
weaknesses, dealing with your, 69–71
Wile, Daniel, on working out negative side
    effects in relationships, 144
Williams, Roger, 133
win–win approaches, 132
Wolf, Warner, 32
Worthington Industries, 128

Zoroastrianism, 128
Zunin, Leonard, on enhancing relation-
    ships, 105